D1116764

THE STATE HOUSE (INDEPENDENCE HALL), IN 1750.

Pennsylvania Politics

AND THE

Growth of Democracy

1740 - 1776

By THEODORE THAYER

COMMONWEALTH OF PENNSYLVANIA

PENNSYLVANIA

HISTORICAL AND MUSEUM COMMISSION

HARRISBURG, 1953

PENNSYLVANIA HISTORICAL AND MUSEUM COMMISSION

CHARLES J. BIDDLE, *Chairman*

LAMBERT CADWALADER
LEROY E. CHAPMAN*
FRANCES DORRANCE
JOHN R. HAUDENSHIELD*
A. ATWATER KENT, JR.
THOMAS MURPHY

JOHN W. OLIVER
JAMES B. STEVENSON
ISRAEL STIEFEL*
CHARLES G. WEBB
RICHARD NORRIS WILLIAMS, 2D
NORMAN WOOD*

FRANCIS B. HAAS, *ex officio*
Superintendent of Public Instruction

DONALD A. CADZOW
Executive Director

SYLVESTER K. STEVENS
State Historian

TRUSTEES—EX OFFICIO

JOHN S. FINE
Governor of the Commonwealth

CHARLES R. BARBER
Auditor General

WELDON B. HEYBURN
State Treasurer

---

* Members representing the General Assembly.

ii

PREFACE

BY ROYAL CHARTER William Penn became the governor and proprietor of Pennsylvania. William Penn, in turn, gave the people of Pennsylvania their Charter of Liberties by which, in 1701, a unicameral legislature was established with powers greater than were found in any Royal or proprietary colony in America.

William Penn, however, soon discovered that his generosity was quite unappreciated. Pennsylvania Quakers looked upon his concessions as no more than their natural rights as freeborn Englishmen. Still more surprising was the fact that many of them saw fit to criticize him for not relinquishing more of his governing powers to the colony. Thus the stage was set at an early date for Pennsylvania's struggle to undermine the Proprietors and to throw all the powers of government into the hands of the legislative Assembly.

Although the struggle for political power in England between the Crown and the dominant groups in the House of Commons had already been won by the latter, similar contests at the dawn of the Eighteenth Century in the American colonies were in but their initial stages. The contests in America, however, were as inevitable as the one that had shaken England. There the landowners, nobility and gentry, had clashed with the absolutist, divine right tendencies of the monarchy, and had triumphed. In America, the struggle took the character of a union of town merchant and freehold farmer or planter pitted against proprietors or Crown governors and their satellites.

The controversy between the legislative Assembly and the Proprietors in Pennsylvania moved into high gear after 1740, when Thomas Penn, a grasping, stubborn and determined man, became the principal proprietor. The long struggle which ensued was made exceptionally intense by the fact that Thomas Penn, unlike the Crown, was free to devote his undivided attention to the problem of governing a single colony. Obsessed by the fear that any concession to the province might jeopardize the proprietary interests, he laid his deputy governors under the strictest instructions, thus allowing the Assembly no choice but to bow to his will or forego legislation of the greatest importance. But in the final stages of the struggle the determination of Thomas Penn to be the master of his colony was more than matched by the resourcefulness of Benjamin Franklin, who as leader of the Quaker or Popular party had, by 1764, completely broken the power of the Penns.

iii

ALMA COLLEGE
MONTEITH LIBRARY
ALMA, MICHIGAN

Popular as was the Quaker campaign against the Proprietors, it did not prevent a rising tide of criticism of the Quaker party which was controlled by a junto of politicians. The frontier, for example, in 1764, bitterly complained that the Assembly had never adequately provided for the defense of the West and had refused the western counties representation in the legislature proportional to population. But there was nothing at all sectional in the widespread criticism of the Quaker party which appeared with the advent of the great controversy with the mother country. The Quaker party, its enemies charged, was in fact Tory. Although the party lost followers by not taking a firm stand against the Stamp Act and the Townshend Acts, there were enough people in the province who approved of a policy of moderation for the party to maintain control of the Assembly right down to 1776. But the Quaker party after 1765, it was plain, no longer represented the democratic interest in the province. Many of its leaders, of whom Joseph Galloway was the principal, feared the pretensions of Great Britain much less than the rising power of the people in Pennsylvania. This fear, therefore, was one of the main reasons why the Assembly tried vainly to keep the dispute with Great Britain from becoming a popular movement.

After 1775 the advent of war afforded the democratic interest in the province an opportunity to advance its cause. The independence movement in 1776 demanded that Pennsylvania set aside its colonial charter and adopt a new constitution emanating from the people. By this time the radical revolutionary party, led by Benjamin Franklin, Thomas Paine, James Cannon, Timothy Matlack, David Rittenhouse, George Bryan and others, and backed by the powerful Scots Irish element, had obtained the upper hand in Pennsylvania. Liberal and democratic, the party was strongly supported by middle class yeoman farmers and city artisans and by almost all of the poorer element in the state. By dominating the military associations, the triumph of the Radicals was assured. After blocking all Conservative opposition to Pennsylvania's casting its vote for independence, they made themselves masters of the constitutional convention. In this way Pennsylvania came to have the most liberal and democratic constitution adopted in America during the Revolutionary period.

ACKNOWLEDGMENTS

A S THE GREAT MASS of manuscript material which has been used in writing this book is housed at the Historical Society of Pennsylvania, I am indebted to Catherine H. Miller and J. Harcourt Givens of the Manuscript Division for their very kind and untiring assistance.

In like manner I am indebted to members of the staffs of the Cornell University Library, the University of Pennsylvania Library, Friends Library in Philadelphia, Ridgway Library, the New York Historical Society, and Yale University Library. My very frequent visits to the Library of the American Philosophical Society, the Public Records Division at Harrisburg, and the New York Public Library make me especially indebted to Ruth Duncan, Henry Howard Eddy, Colonel Henry Shoemaker, Lewis M. Stark, Percy E. Clapp, and Sylvester Vigilante.

For favors I am owing to Professor Paul W. Gates of Cornell University, Professor Richard H. Shryock of Johns Hopkins University, and Dr. Edward Riley, Historian of Independence National Park, Dr. Paul A. W. Wallace, Editor of *Pennsylvania History,* and Professors Edward Fuhlbruegge and Hubert G. Schmidt of Rutgers University.

For grants in aid for conducting my research I wish to thank the Social Science Research Council and the Research Council of Rutgers University.

I am deeply grateful for the enouragement and help given by Professor Roy F. Nichols of the University of Pennsylvania and by Dr. Sylvester K. Stevens, Pennsylvania State Historian. I wish also to thank Doctor Stevens, Donald H. Kent, Associate Historian, and the staff of the Pennsylvania Historical and Museum Commission under whose guidance this book has been published.

THEODORE THAYER

CONTENTS

PAGE

Preface iii

Acknowledgments v

Illustrations ix

    I   The Frame of Government 1

   II Politics—Pacifism—War. 1739-1748 9

  III Governor Hamilton. 1748-1754 25

  IV Governor Morris vs. Franklin. 1755 35

   V Franklin the Tribune. 1756-1757 49

  VI Party Politics and Defense. 1758-1760 67

 VII The Western Problem. 1760-1764 77

VIII Movement for a Royal Government. 1764 89

  IX The Stamp Act. 1765-1766 111

   X Economic and Domestic Issues. 1760-1775 127

  XI The Townshend Acts. 1767-1770 139

 XII Outbreak of the Revolution. 1774-1775 153

XIII Triumph of the Radicals. 1776 175

Bibliography 199

Appendix I: The Charter of Privileges 205

Appendix II: The Constitution of Pennsylvania. 1776 211

Index 229

ILLUSTRATIONS

The State House (Independence Hall), in 1750
—The Historical Society of Pennsylvania . . . . *frontispiece*

facing pages

Benjamin Franklin
—Print in The Historical Society of Pennsylvania   x

Thomas Penn
—Painting in The Historical Society of Pennsylvania   1

James Hamilton
—Painting in The Historical Society of Pennsylvania   44

William Denny
—Sketch by Guy Colt based on copy in The Historical Society
of Pennsylvania from original in Dilettante Club, London . .   44

John Penn
Richard Penn
—Prints in The Historical Society of Pennsylvania   44

William Allen
Isaac Norris
William Smith
John Dickinson
—Paintings in The Historical Society of Pennsylvania   45

Quaker Party Politics, 1764, as Pictured by Their Opponents . .   88
Cartoon Depicting the Defence of Philadelphia Against the
Paxton Boys
Cartoon Representing Franklin and the Quaker Party as the
Source of Pennsylvania's Woes
—Cartoons in The Historical Society of Pennsylvania   89

Cartoon on the Repeal of the Stamp Act
Cartoon Representing American Views in the Tea Episode, 1774
—Cartoons in The Historical Society of Pennsylvania 152

ILLUSTRATIONS—Continued

A Map of the Province of Pensilvania, By T. Kitchin, 1756
—Library of Congress 153

Joseph Reed
George Bryan
—Paintings in The Historical Society of Pennsylvania 190

Timothy Matlack
—Painting in National Gallery of Art, Mellon Collection 190

David Rittenhouse
—Painting in the American Philosophical Society 190

Thomas Mifflin
—Painting in Independence Hall Collection 191

Thomas McKean
—Painting in Fogg Museum of Art, Harvard University 191

Charles Thomson
—Painting in Independence Hall Collection 191

George Clymer
—Painting in Pennsylvania Academy of Fine Arts 191

BENJAMIN FRANKLIN

Thomas Penn

I

THE FRAME OF GOVERNMENT

THE GROWTH AND DEVELOPMENT of Pennsylvania, first settled by the Quakers in 1682, was more rapid than that of any other English colony. By the middle of the Eighteenth Century (regardless of the fact that it had been next to the last colony founded by the English) it had surpassed in population all but Virginia and Massachusetts. At that time Pennsylvania had a population of about two hundred thousand. Twenty-five years later, on the eve of the Revolution, it had nearly doubled in population and was almost as populous as Virginia and Massachusetts.[1]

The growth of Philadelphia, the only city of any size in Pennsylvania before the Revolution, was no less rapid than the province. By 1750, with a population of nearly eighteen thousand, it could boast of being the largest city in the English colonies. A quarter century later, it had more than doubled in population, and ranked with the larger cities of the British Isles, with the exception of the metropolis of London.

The rapid increases in population in Pennsylvania resulted from a high birth rate and a great influx of German and Scots Irish immigrants in the Eighteenth Century. During the first quarter of the century nearly forty-five thousand Germans entered the province; in the next quarter the numbers were even greater. The Scots Irish immigration was nearly as heavy as the German: in the year 1729 alone over six thousand of these sturdy pioneers from northern Ireland entered the colony. By 1765, with a population of approximately three hundred thousand (excluding the Indians), Pennsylvania contained approximately equal proportions of English, Germans, and Scots Irish. These three groups represented about four-fifths of the population. Smaller numbers of Welsh, Scotch, French Huguenots, Swedes, Dutch, and Negroes made up most of the rest.

The remarkable growth of Pennsylvania was due in large part to the natural advantages of the province. A temperate climate, ample rainfall, and wide reaches of fertile land made it the principal grain colony in America. A natural outlet to the sea was provided by the Delaware River. Besides the soil, the province was rich in timber, iron ore, furs, and other natural resources which could be readily utilized. With surprising rapidity, the settlers converted the vast

---

[1] Evarts B. Greene, *American Population before the Federal Census of 1790*, 115-116; Struthers Burt, *Philadelphia, Holy Experiment*, 143.

1

stretches of forest into fertile farms and bustling villages, and erected a large city to care for their commerce.

Some measure of the size and importance of Philadelphia's commerce can be grasped by the fact that the Reverend Israel Acrelius, the Swedish missionary, in 1754 counted in a single day one hundred and seventeen large ships at anchor in the Delaware. Indeed, the city, with its rich hinterland, had a trade which stretched from the West Indies to the Mediterranean and to the ports of northern Europe and the British Isles. Its principal exports were wheat, corn, flour, bread, bacon, beef, barrel staves and headings, lumber, pig iron, flaxseed, furs and deerskins. Its shipyards were already constructing many of the largest and finest vessels of the day. Between 1772 and 1774, alone, over forty-two ships were built and launched at Philadelphia.

Cultural attainments kept pace with the growth of the province. By 1765, Philadelphia, the center of social activity in the colony, was second to none among the English colonies in the pursuit of better living. The city had a liberal arts college, a medical school, and a number of private institutions devoted mainly to vocational instruction. Among the subjects favored in the latter schools were navigation and accounting. Private instruction could also be had in French, dancing, fencing, and other subjects of special interest. As in all the colonies outside of New England, elementary education was cared for in parochial and private schools. Several library companies had been established in Philadelphia since the early part of the century and one was even to be found in frontier Lancaster. Wealthy men prided themselves upon their private collections and had standing orders in England for the latest works by European and British writers.

As one walked along the streets of Philadelphia attention was attracted to the several large churches and to the handsome State House[2] surmounted by a belfry which housed a large iron bell. Markers on the brick buildings which lined the streets indicated membership in one of the volunteer fire companies of the city. One company, too, had offered new service in the form of fire insurance on a mutual basis. There were in the city numerous societies from the fraternal and professional to those dedicated to the pursuit of philosophy and science. Music, painting, literature and the theatre were patronized by the large liberal portion of the population and quite a number of gifted persons had achieved recognition for their creations in one field or another. In the arts and crafts, the German element distinguished itself for its skilled workers in metal, glass, and textiles. Among the physicians, John Morgan, Thomas and Phineas Bond, William Shippen, and Benjamin Rush were men of eminence who had fostered the

---

[2] Later, Independence Hall.

founding of the medical school in 1765. Finally, the city could boast
of Benjamin Franklin, known throughout the world for his electrical
experiments, and could name as its own John Bartram, David Rittenhouse, and other citizens of acknowledged scientific achievements.

Of inestimable importance to the development of Pennsylvania was
the liberal and advanced form of government which William Penn
granted the people of the province. Settlers from nearly every country
of northern Europe were attracted to the colony by the guarantees of
religious freedom, the absence of specific military obligations, and the
general spirit of freedom emanating from the charter privileges granted
Pennsylvania by William Penn. In his first message to the scattered
settlers already in his province, Penn had promised, "You shall be
governed by laws of your own making, and live a free, and, if you will,
a sober and industrious people."[3]

William Penn received Pennsylvania from the Crown at a time when
proprietary colonies were no longer favored by the ministers of state.
However, in spite of this policy, Penn obtained his grant with fewer
reservations than might be expected. As proprietor, Penn became the
governor of the province with the power to appoint a lieutenant governor and such judges and magistrates as the province required.[4] The
governor with the "Advice, Assent, and Approbation" of the freemen
of the province could make all laws necessary for the governing of the
colony providing only that they were "consonant to Reason, and not
repugnant to the Laws and Statutes and Rights of this Our Kingdom
of England." All laws thus enacted were to be submitted to the Privy
Council within five years, after which the Council was given but six
months to decide upon their legality. The King also retained the right
to hear, determine, and reverse any and all judgments rendered by
courts of law in Pennsylvania. As for taxation, the King promised that
he would not tax the province "unless the same be with the Consent
of the Proprietary, or chief Governor, or Assembly, or by Act of Parliament in England."[5]

Liberal as were the provisions of William Penn's charter, the several
important checks placed upon the government of Pennsylvania clearly
indicated the temper of the Crown's new colonial policy. This was
especially apparent in the clauses pertaining to the enforcement of the
Navigation Laws. If the Proprietor allowed "any wilful Default or

---

[3] Letter to the Inhabitants of Pennsylvania, April 8, 1681, *Memoirs, HSP,* III,
Part 2, 205-206; also in *Remember William Penn,* 76.

[4] *Votes and Proceedings of the House of Representatives of the Province of Pennsylvania (Pennsylvania Archives,* Eighth Series, 1931), I, xxx. This reference will
be hereafter cited as *Votes.* The Proprietors could not veto a law signed by a
Deputy-Governor. *Pa. Mag.,* X, 286.

[5] *Ibid.,* I, xxxix.

Neglect"' in the execution of these laws, he would be liable for the losses suffered by the Crown. If Penn did not pay for all damages sustained from nonenforcement of these laws within a year, the colony could be seized and held by the Crown until satisfaction was given.[6]

Acting within the charter conferred upon him by the King, William Penn in 1682 gave the people of Pennsylvania a frame of government and charter of liberties. In a long preface setting forth his philosophy of government, Penn declared that "Any Government is free to the People under it (whatever be the Frame) where the Laws rule, and the people are a Party to those Laws, and more than this is Tyranny, Oligarchy, or Confusion."[7] A second frame of government, aimed at correcting deficiencies in the first, came in 1683 and remained the constitution for Pennsylvania until it was superseded by Penn's third frame of government in 1701. This one was destined to endure until the end of the colonial period in 1776.

The principal change in Penn's second frame of government was that of greatly reducing the number of representatives in the Council and the Assembly. The Council was reduced from seventy-two to eighteen and the Assembly from two hundred to thirty-six. The basic system remained the same, however. The Governor and the Council were to initiate legislation which would be submitted to the Assembly for approval or rejection.[8]

As might be expected, the popular and more democratic Assembly but awaited a favorable opportunity to challenge the leadership of the Governor and the Council. Such an occasion appeared in 1692 when William Penn lost his governing rights and Pennsylvania became for two years a Royal colony under Governor Benjamin Fletcher of New York. As a military measure, rule of all the colonies from Maryland to Massachusetts had been united in his hands. Whether from good will or practical considerations, he allowed the Assembly to assume a more prominent role in legislative affairs. In 1694, David Lloyd, as Speaker of the Assembly, by means of his ability and leadership, brought the prestige and power of the lower chamber to new heights.[9]

Upon the restitution of Pennsylvania to William Penn, the Assembly insisted upon its traditional right to pass upon any new frame of government proposed by the Proprietor. After much discussion this new frame called the Charter of Privileges was worked out by William Penn

---

[6] *Ibid.,* I, xxxvi. See also Andrews, *The Colonial Period of American History,* III, 283-284; Winfred T. Root, *The Relations of Pennsylvania with the British Government, 1696-1765,* 40-41.

[7] *Votes,* I, xlviii.

[8] *Ibid.,* I, xlix-lvi, 334-340.

[9] Andrews, III, 313-319; *Votes,* I, 154ff.

and the Assembly. The final draft was approved by the Assembly in 1701 before the Charter went into effect. Here was a major victory for the people of Pennsylvania, one which signified that they were determined to exercise as much control as possible over all questions of vital importance to the province.

The privileges conferred upon the Assembly by the Charter of 1701 were greater than those found in any but the corporate colonies of Connecticut and Rhode Island. In the first place, the Assembly became the sole legislative chamber, the Council being shorn of this power and relegated to a purely advisory capacity to the Governor. Chief credit for this startling innovation apparently belongs to David Lloyd. Of Welsh extraction, Lloyd was a prominent lawyer who became the first popular leader in Pennsylvania. In David Lloyd, it might be said, the spirit of Roger Williams, the Rhode Island democrat, was carried over into the Eighteenth Century.

The Charter of Privileges conferred upon the Assembly the power to "choose a Speaker and other theire Officers and . . . be Judges of the Qualifications and Elections of theire owne Members, sitt upon theire owne Adjournments Appoint Committees prepare Bills in or[der] to pass into Laws Impeach Criminalls and Redress Greivances and . . . all other Powers and Priviledges of an Assembly according to the Rights of the ffreeborne Subjects of England, and as is usuall in any of the Kings Plantations in America."[10] These extraordinary powers were subject to broad construction in favor of republican government, and the Assembly during the course of the next seventy-five years made the most of them.

Occasion for expanding its powers by liberal interpretations of the Charter emerged at once in the course of conducting the affairs of government. In a manner characteristic of seventeenth and eighteenth-century legislative bodies, the Pennsylvania Assembly experienced no qualms in claiming to itself powers not at all warranted by legislative history. As early as 1707, Governor John Evans related no secret when he declared that the Assembly led by Speaker Lloyd aimed "to reverse the method of Gvmt. according to our English Constitution, and Establish one more nearly resembling a republic in its stead."[11] That same year, Robert Quary informed the Board of Trade that the Assembly "Resolved to have all the Government and powers into their own hands, they insist to have the sole regulation of all Courts, and the nomination of all officers."[12] Thus the stage was set for the bitter and prolonged

---

[10] Appendix I; Votes, I, 389; Andrews, III, 319. Sitting upon their own adjournments was an extraordinary power not even possessed by the House of Commons. See Lewis Evans, A Brief Account of Pennsylvania, 1753, HSP.

[11] Andrews, III, 320.

[12] Root, 41.

struggle between the legislative and executive branches of the government which came to a climax during the third quarter of the century when Thomas Penn became pitted against Benjamin Franklin, the popular leader of the Assembly.

Quite as important as the powers vested in the Assembly by the Charter were the qualifications for voting and holding office in Pennsylvania. The Charter prescribed that the rules governing this should be in accordance with laws passed in Newcastle in 1700.[13] This law provided that any male twenty-one years of age, who professed a belief in Christ as the Savior of the World, and had resided two years in the province, could vote and hold office provided he owned fifty acres of land (of which twelve were cleared) or owned fifty pounds in other property.

With the exception of the fifty pounds ruling which disqualified many city dwellers, the standard for voting and holding office in Pennsylvania was very liberal considering the age in which it was made.[14] Most of the people of Pennsylvania were farmers who owned at least fifty acres of land and could otherwise qualify under the act.[15] In 1766 fifty acres on the Pennsylvania frontier cost only two or three pounds of sterling. The cost of clearing twelve acres was about double the cost of the land.[16] Most men, of course, would save this money by clearing the land themselves. Anyhow, few inspectors of the elections, it seems, ever troubled themselves to inquire if this requirement had been met. The property qualification for the suffrage on the Pennsylvania frontier was therefore not hard to meet.

The raw frontier condition did not last long in any one locality. An original five pound investment for one hundred acres of new land was soon converted into a farm with buildings, cleared land, fences, and live-stock. It seems reasonable to suppose, therefore, that a large proportion of the voters in rural Pennsylvania owned property in excess of fifty pounds. This would tend to put them on the same basis as the voters of Philadelphia who must own property worth fifty pounds. The framers of the suffrage law may have had something like this in mind when they created the dual property qualifications for voting in Pennsylvania.

---

[13] *Votes,* I, 389.

[14] See Albert E. McKinley, *The Suffrage Franchise in the Thirteen Colonies in America,* 281-285, for a different interpretation.

[15] As might be expected, many freeholders often did not trouble themselves to vote. In 1774 a citizen of Chester County complained that the freeholders too often allowed the choice of their public officers to be made by a small number of men. Wayne MSS., I, 8.

[16] In 1772 a man paid six pounds sterling or ten pounds Pennsylvania currency for having fifty acres cleared. *Pa. Mag.,* VIII, 318.

The Pennsylvania charter provided that the members of the Assembly should be elected annually. The three existing counties in 1701—Philadelphia, Chester, and Bucks—were each alloted eight representatives.[17] The city of Philadelphia was given two seats in the Assembly. The counties created thereafter were given a smaller number of representatives, but representation of the western counties was reasonably adequate until after the Seven Years' War when population growth in the newer counties made the original apportionment insufficient.

Except for the judicial offices, county government was controlled by the freeholders. According to the Charter, the Governor had the right to appoint a sheriff and coroner for each county from the two candidates with the highest number of votes for each office. If the Governor did not see fit to make the appointments within three days after receiving the presentments, the candidates with the highest vote became the winners. This became the practice and to all intents and purposes the rule in electing sheriffs and coroners. Throughout the colonial period the election of local officers—sheriffs, coroners, assessors, and commissioners for the counties, burgesses for Lancaster and aldermen for Philadelphia—often excited more interest and were more highly contested than the seats in the provincial assembly.[18] The latter entailed being away from home several months of the year, and occasioned more often than not considerable sacrifice to one's business interests. The local offices, besides not having this drawback, generally yielded a sizable income from fees and other emoluments. The justices of the peace, as in the case of all judicial officers in the province, were appointed outright by the Governor. Naturally, around this department of government centered Proprietary politics in the counties.

In a country enjoying so much liberty as Pennsylvania it was inevitable that a conflict would develop from opposing interests of the Proprietors and the people. It was principally from this cause that two political parties emerged in the very early days of the colony and continued until broken by the upheavals of the Revolution. Beside the political issues which divided men into parties stood the ever-present rivalry for public office or favor. Outside of political motives men were attracted to one another by bonds of religion, national origins, social background, and friendship. But notwithstanding the existence of cohesive forces, political parties in colonial Pennsylvania were but loosely knit entities. They tended to assume the character of so many

---

[17] *Votes*, I, 392. Elections were held on October 1. The new Assembly convened on October 14. Members were paid five shillings per diem. They also received pay for serving on special committees such as the Committee on Accounts.

[18] *Ibid.*, I, 389-390. See John Smith to Elizabeth Hudson, Oct. 10, 1750, Correspondence of John Smith, 1740-1770. HSP; Shippen Papers, VI, 71, 201, 213, 215, VII, 17, 19, 69. HSP.

county parties, whose leaders when acting collectively formed a provincial party.

America no doubt owes much to colonial politics for its traditional two-party system. In Pennsylvania, the Popular or Quaker party became the defender of the Frame of Government which bestowed upon the Assembly such great power.[19] In the early days it was composed mainly of members of the Society of Friends. In later years, however, it became an amorphous body, as persons of all descriptions were attracted to it. Its rival, the Proprietary party (sometimes alluded to as the Governor's party, the Gentlemen's party, or the Court party) was of a more select composition being made up primarily of persons of the gentleman class who from interest or inclination supported the Penns. They were inclined to favor constitutional changes calculated to emasculate the powers of the popular Assembly and center political control in the hands of the Governor and Council.

But the Pennsylvania conservatives never won their objective, thanks to the vigilance of the Quaker party in defending the liberties of the province. Blessed with a liberal frame of government, a powerful legislative Assembly, liberal suffrage laws adapted to make voters of the great majority of frontiersmen and farmers, it was inevitable that Pennsylvania should lead America on the road to political democracy. When the Quaker party, grown conservative and unpopular, gave way to the Radicals in 1776, the latter retained the unicameral system of government, believing it best suited to preserve the liberties of the people. In general, the framers of the constitution of 1776 simply added several innovations to the old charter system with the thought that these would further strengthen the democratic character of the constitution.

---

[19] The Quaker party's espousal of a Royal government in 1764 was ostensibly for the purpose of increasing the powers of the Assembly by removing the Proprietors. See Chapter VIII.

II

POLITICS—PACIFISM—WAR. 1739-1748

THE POLITICAL HISTORY of colonial Pennsylvania stems in large part from issues which arose from the problems of war and defense. This was especially true for the years between 1740 and 1763 when the struggle between Great Britain and France for supremacy in North America reached its final stages. The question of defense, however, first confronted Pennsylvania in 1689, only eight years after its founding. A war in Europe between England and France and their allies, known as the War of the League of Augsburg, spread to America where it was called King William's War.

Under orders from the Crown, Deputy-Governor John Blackwell commanded the Quaker Assembly to contribute to the war, the brunt of which was being borne by New York and New England.[1] The Assembly, as would be expected of a body composed almost entirely of pacifists, steadfastly refused to comply with the repeated orders from the Governor. Pennsylvania, the Quakers argued, was, in recognition of the fact that it was founded as an asylum for all people principled against war, exempt from military obligations.

The Assembly's answer should not be taken to mean that, but for the presence of Quakerism, the colony would have readily supported the war. All the colonies were in fact narrowly provincial and shamelessly parsimonious, reluctant at all times to contribute anything to imperial defense unless actually threatened with invasion. Everywhere there existed a deep-seated feeling that Britain should defend the relatively poor and undeveloped colonies, from which England realized great wealth through trade and commerce.

The failure of Pennsylvania to contribute to the defense of the Empire was one of the chief reasons for the conversion of the colony into a Royal province in 1692. Shortly afterwards, the new Governor, Benjamin Fletcher, reported to his superiors in England that the change had not materially improved the situation in Pennsylvania. He was convinced that no military aid could be expected from Pennsylvania so long as Quakers remained in control of the legislature.[2] Proposals were presently heard both in England and America for excluding Quakers by act of Parliament from holding office during war. But no action was taken by the British government, burdened as it

---

[1] Andrews, III, 312.
[2] Root, 226, 263; Andrews, III, 314-315.

was with problems of much greater importance than the shortcomings of a small colony.

In 1701, during Queen Anne's War (the War of the Spanish Succession in Europe), the question of Pennsylvania's contribution to the defense of the Empire reappeared. William Penn (reinstated as Governor of his colony in 1694) was given strict orders that Pennsylvania must help the northern colonies against the French. The first response of the Assembly was to excuse itself by stating that Pennsylvania, burdened by the expense of maintaining friendly relations with the Indians, could not afford any further outlays. The legislatures of Maryland and Virginia likewise evaded meeting requests for military aid by one excuse or another.

But Andrew Hamilton, William Penn's Deputy-Governor, soon found means to circumvent Quaker pacifism and provincial localism. On his own authority he commissioned a number of officers and gave them orders to enlist men for the defense of the province. Although many of the Quakers tried to reason otherwise, the Governor had ample authority to take the matter of defense into his own hands. The Charter granted to William Penn by the King gave the Governor of Pennsylvania power to "Levy, Muster and Traine all Sorts of Men, of what condition soever, or wheresoever born, in the said Province of *Pennsylvania* for the Time being, and to make War, and to pursue the Enemies and Robbers aforesaid, as well by Sea as by Land, even without the Limits of the said Province."[3]

Most of the Quakers seemed, in reality, quite pleased to have the Governor undertake to carry out the order of the Crown and thus free the Quakers from an embarrassing dilemma. Beset with fear that the King might again seize the colony, the Assembly soon voted money for arming and fitting out the men being raised. The Quakers absolved themselves from any responsibility for the way in which the funds were used by appropriating it to the Queen's use. "We did not see it inconsistent with our principles," the Quakers declared, "to give the Queen money, not withstanding the use she might put it to, *that* being not our part, but hers."[4] Their contribution, the Quakers felt assured, fully demonstrated Pennsylvania's loyalty and desire to help the mother country in every way consistent with the religious principles of the people.

With the peace of Utrecht in 1713, the American colonies experienced twenty-seven years of peace, years during which they developed with surprising rapidity. By 1740, the year in which Great Britain became embroiled in a war with Spain, Pennsylvania had grown from a tiny

---

[3] *Votes,* I, xxxvii.
[4] Root, 278.

colony fringing the Delaware to a province of nearly two hundred thousand souls. The Quakers were now no longer the majority, since thousands of immigrants, chiefly Germans and Scots Irish, had been attracted to the country by its unusual advantages.[5]

In 1740, the Proprietors of Pennsylvania were the three sons of William Penn by his second marriage: John, Richard, and Thomas. None of them had acquired either the religious fervor of the father or his splendid benevolence and rare idealism. Richard and Thomas joined the Church of England, and only John remained a Quaker. Thomas began attending the Church of England in 1751 upon his marriage to the daughter of the Earl of Pomfret, but at first out of regard for the feelings of the Quakers he refrained from taking communion. John, a bachelor and the eldest, inherited one-half of the proprietary interest in Pennsylvania. Upon his death in 1746, he bequeathed his share to Thomas, who thereby became the principal proprietor with three-quarters interest in the province.[6] This made him, according to Franklin, the largest landholder of his time.

These sons of William Penn, aspiring to no virtue other than honesty and respectability, were cast in the usual mold of conservative Eighteenth Century English gentlemen. Seldom, indeed, could Thomas Penn rise above personal and pecuniary considerations in governing Pennsylvania. Having experienced the hardships of family poverty because of his father's philanthropy, Thomas customarily thought of Pennsylvania purely in terms of the profits to be derived therefrom. In a letter to the Reverend Richard Peters, Proprietary Secretary in Pennsylvania, he revealed that which was always closest to his heart: "People imagine, because we are at the head of a large Province, we must be rich but I tell you that for fifteen years from 1732 to 1747, I laid by only about 100£ a year."[7] This situation had greatly changed by 1760, when Isaac Norris declared that the Penns were deriving immense sums from their holdings and creditors in Pennsylvania.

True it is that on occasion Thomas Penn made gifts to public institutions and enterprises in Pennsylvania. But these were invariably made, it would seem, from the prompting of policy rather than from a true spirit of benevolence. "I shall ever think myself obliged to serve the public both with my person and pocket," he wrote in 1737, but cautiously added, "I never desire to have views so noble, extensive, and benevolent as my father, unless he had left a much larger fortune, because these views, though good in themselves, yet by possessing him so much, lead [sic] him into inconveniences which I hope to avoid."[8]

---

[5] See *Pa. Arch.*, 1st. Ser., III, 440.
[6] Arthur Pound, *The Penns of Pennsylvania and England*, 276-277.
[7] J. B. Nolan, *The Foundation of the Town of Reading in Pennsylvania*, 30-31.
[8] Pound, 282.

The rather narrow limits of Thomas Penn's mind also made it hard for him to see the true value of cultural and civic improvements. He once said that the Pennsylvania Assembly "misapplied" money: that the "hospital, steeple, bells, unnecessary library with several other things, are reasons why they should not have the appropriations to themselves."[9]

Thomas Penn visited Pennsylvania twice during his life, once in 1732 at the age of thirty and again in 1740-1741. After that, although he often thought of living in Philadelphia and governing the province in person, he continued the practice of placing the province under lieutenant-governors, bound by rigid instructions calculated to safeguard the proprietary interests.

The year before Thomas Penn paid his second visit to the province, he appointed George Thomas, a wealthy planter of Antigua, to be Deputy-Governor of Pennsylvania. A man of military experience, possessing a combination of courage, good judgment, and tact, Thomas seemed an ideal choice. His possession of a fortune, the Penns hoped, would place him above the temptation of bowing to every demand of the Assembly. The venerable James Logan, Secretary for the Proprietors, was confident that George Thomas would be a suitable governor.[10]

With the outbreak of war between England and Spain in 1740, Governor Thomas informed the Quaker Assembly that he had instructions from the home government for Pennsylvania to provide provisions and transports for troops to be sent to the West Indies. Although not at all alarmed for fear the war would reach Pennsylvania, the Assembly, to ward off criticism and in view of the precedent set in Queen Anne's War, prepared a bill providing £3000 for the King's use.

In the meantime, the Governor, again following ministerial instructions, began recruiting men for service in the West Indies. Thomas not only ordered his officers to enlist any freemen who would volunteer, but also rather encouraged them to enlist "all the servants they could get in the midst of harvest."[11] In doing this the Governor maintained that he was obliged to seek recruits wherever found because of the scarcity of volunteers. This would not have been necessary, he declared, had the Assembly passed a draft act with exemptions for conscientious objectors. The Quakers, however, would not consent to a law which forced others to fight, especially in foreign lands, although they were willing to have the Governor raise an army of volunteers from among the freemen of the colony.[12]

[9] Peters MSS., IV, 4. HSP.
[10] Herbert L. Osgood, *The American Colonies in the Eighteenth Century*, IV, 46-47.
[11] Pemberton Papers, III, 34. HSP.
[12] Franklin Papers, X, 2. U. of Pa.; Osgood, IV, 54-58.

By August over two hundred and fifty white servants had deserted their masters in the midst of the summer work for service in the King's army. The reaction to the Governor's policy was immediate and almost universally unfavorable throughout the province. Samuel Blunston, an Assemblyman from Lancaster County, wrote from his home that people in the West were as exasperated by the enlistment of servants as were those living in the eastern counties.[13]

The Quaker Assembly, only too happy to have a people's cause to defend, soon resolved not to furnish the £3000 voted the King until the servants were released and returned to their masters. It was further resolved to withhold the Governor's salary until such time as he showed a disposition to do right by the colony. The next thing done was to hire Joseph Murray and William Smith, New York attorneys, to come to Philadelphia to prosecute the captains who had enlisted the servants.[14] John Kinsey, the Attorney-General of Pennsylvania and Speaker of the House, argued that the enlistment of servants without the consent of their masters was positively illegal. In modern terminology, it constituted in the minds of people a deprivation of property "without due process of law." The furor stirred up by the enlistment was indeed amazing. Everywhere, Richard Peters declared, one could hear insolent and rude talk against all in authority, "the King not excepted." Especially outspoken were the "young fry of Quakers" such as Israel Pemberton who did not appear to Peters so meek and pacific as they professed to be.[15]

Supporting Governor Thomas was the small group of gentlemen and Proprietary officeholders which had long constituted the chief political opposition to the Quakers. Formerly they had consisted largely of Anglicans, but by 1740 there were about as many Presbyterians among them. They were now led by the young and able William Allen, a Presbyterian whose great wealth and affluence placed him at the head of the Pennsylvania aristocracy.

Born in Philadelphia in 1704 of Scots Irish parents, William Allen grew to maturity with every advantage that wealth and social position could bestow. In 1720 he went to England and entered the Middle Temple, after which he became a pensioner at Clare Hall, Cambridge. He rounded out his European education by touring the Continent in 1725. Upon the death of his father in that year, he returned to Philadelphia with the hope of practicing law, but the demands upon his time from his land holdings and mercantile pursuits pushed law into the background. Besides his inheritance, Allen made a fortune in trade,

---

[13] Lancaster Co., Miscel. Papers, 1724-1772, 65. HSP.
[14] Peters to Proprietors, July 31, 1740, Peters Letter Book, 1737-1750. HSP.
[15] *Ibid.*, Peters to John Penn, August 30, 1740.

much of which was derived from illegal trading with the French during King George's War.[16]

William Allen, called "the Giant" by his contemporaries, was an unusually tall man with a huge well-proportioned frame and great physical powers. He was, indeed, a handsome man with blue eyes and a pleasant countenance. Gentle in manners, sparkling with wit and pleasantries, he was as charming a gentleman as could be found in the colonies. At the age of fifty he was as portly, as heavily bewigged, and as richly dressed as any aristocrat in London or Paris. Allen certainly had the appearance of a leader: he might have left a much greater name in history had he gone along with the independence movement when the Revolution came.

As cultivated in his tastes as he was urbane in manners, Allen had in his home at Mt. Airy, a fine collection of paintings from the great masters. He gave encouragement to the theater by frequenting the performances offered in Philadelphia. Among his friends he included nearly all the men of letters in the colonies. Indeed, his circle of friends extended to England where he numbered among them such men of distinction as Shelburne, Bute, and Barré. Like most Eighteenth Century gentlemen, Allen derived one of his greatest pleasures in overseeing his gardens at Mt. Airy and planning out the work on his plantations.

Allen married Margaret Hamilton, daughter of Andrew Hamilton, the famous lawyer who defended John Peter Zenger in the libel suit. The match made him the brother-in-law of James Hamilton, twice Deputy-Governor of Pennsylvania. His children were well-disciplined and taught to value the simple things of life: Calvinistic lessons in frugality and thrift were never neglected in the Allen home. One of his daughters, Ann, married John Penn, grandson of William Penn, in 1766. His four sons were rapidly rising in Pennsylvania life and politics when their careers were blighted by their espousal of the Tory cause after the colonies declared their independence.

Perhaps the greatest American philanthropist of his day, Allen surpassed the Quakers, whose acts of public charity have often been exaggerated by historians. He advanced money for the erection of the State House (Independence Hall), money which was not repaid for thirty years. He gave more for the establishment and development of the Pennsylvania Hospital and the College of Philadelphia than any other contributor. Likewise he gave freely to the German Charity Schools, The Newark Academy in Delaware, and other educational enterprises. He was the patron of many promising young men of talent, helping to finance the education in England of such persons as Dr. John Redman, Dr. John Morgan, and the painters, Benjamin West and

---

[16] Theodore Thayer, *Israel Pemberton: King of the Quakers*, 17. See *Pa. Mag.*, I, 202-211; *Pa. Hist.*, I, No. 3 (July, 1934), 169-171.

Charles Willson Peale. It was through his efforts that the Rev. Francis
Alison came to Philadelphia and became a noted professor at the College of Philadelphia. Benjamin Franklin, too, owed him a debt of grati-
tude since Allen was principally responsible for his appointment as
Deputy-Postmaster-General in 1753. When an Arctic expedition was
launched in 1753 to seek a northwest passage, Allen was one of its foremost sponsors. Science fascinated him as much as art pleased him.

With all his varied interests, Allen found time to devote much attention to politics. In 1727 at the age of twenty-three he became a member
of the Governor's Council. Four years later he was elected to the
Assembly, in which body he served with few interruptions until the
Revolution. He was elected Mayor of Philadelphia in 1735 and held
the office of Recorder from 1741 to 1750. In 1751, on the death of John
Kinsey, he was appointed Chief Justice of Pennsylvania, an office which
he held until his resignation in 1774.

For over thirty years William Allen was in many respects the most
influential figure in Pennsylvania politics. Scores of young men found
in him the means of securing political preferment by way of Proprietary
appointment to public office. In fact, after about 1740 almost all appointments made by the Proprietors were at the suggestion of William
Allen.

Whether William Allen's choice in supporting the Proprietary cause
proceeded from principle or from self-interest is debatable. Be that
as it may, when the constitutional dispute with England developed in
the 1760's, Allen became one of the most outspoken critics of the British
policy of taxation: a stand which presumably proceeded from the principles involved. Like James Otis and other legal minds, he maintained
that there was a clear and definite constitutional law binding upon
England as well as upon America, and that the British taxation claims
violated American rights. Skeptics, however, may see in Allen's be-
havior no more than a deep resentment against the British government
for its recent iron and trade laws which had all but ruined his extensive
iron business in Pennsylvania and New Jersey.

In 1740, with the British Empire at war, William Allen and his friends
thought that the time had come for them to gain control of the Assembly. The case of the servants, they knew, was not helpful in winning
votes for their side, but the war might well put the Quakers on the
defensive in both England and America. It was not improbable that
the servant case might prompt Parliament to place a prohibition on the
Quakers holding office during times of war.

It was with keen interest that Thomas Penn, on his visit to America,
watched the political maneuvers preceding the annual election that
year. The Allen party, he observed, relied mainly on picturing the
calamity which would befall the colony unless a non-pacifist Assembly

were elected. The Quakers, with much more effect, told the people that the Quaker party was the only thing that stood between them and onerous military duties, burdensome taxation, and the arbitrary rule of a few. The Governor's action in ordering the enlistment of servants, they declared, was an example of what lay ahead if the Quakers were not re-elected. Confident of success, the Quakers held their usual caucus at their yearly religious meeting at Burlington and decided "who should be chosen members of the Assembly" in the coming election.[17]

As customary and in spite of all that the Allen party could do or say, the Quakers won a sweeping victory. There still was some hope among the gentlemen, however, that Parliament would step in and bar the Quakers from the offices they had won. Governor Thomas, whose fighting spirit was thoroughly aroused by the tactics of the Quakers, sent a long letter to the Board of Trade in which he strongly censured the Assembly for sabotaging his military program. The British ministry, he advised, would do well to seek Parliamentary action to strengthen the Governor's hand in Pennsylvania.[18]

The Assembly, however, convinced that the British government would recognize the justice of its claims, went right ahead and petitioned the Crown for compensation for all losses sustained by the enlistment of the servants. It was not long after that Richard Partridge, the Pennsylvania agent in London, reported that sentiment in England was much against Pennsylvania. Compensation, he told Kinsey, was out of the question, as most of the ministers considered the account already balanced by the fact that the Assembly had withheld from the Governor the £3000 voted for the King's use.[19]

In this manner Crown officials soon dismissed the case of the servants by advising Pennsylvania to satisfy the claims of the masters from the money withheld by the Assembly. This was done and £2600 was subsequently paid to the claimants. The Assembly, it would seem, had completely won its case. The Crown, aware of the dilemma presented by it, had cautiously avoided making a decision between the claims of the King upon all persons for military service, and the rights of property under the law.

Any disciplinary measure against the Quakers on the part of the British government was warded off by the Assembly in 1741 when £3000 was again voted for the King's use.[20] This sum, unsolicited by

[17] Franklin Papers, X, 2. U. of Pa.

[18] Osgood, IV, 57-60.

[19] Pemberton Papers, III, 38. Richard Partridge (1681-1759) was born in New Hampshire of Quaker parents. He went to England at the age of twenty-one and never returned to his native country. He was the agent for several colonies other than Pennsylvania, among them being Rhode Island, which he served for forty-four years. He was a man with wide acquaintances and great influence.

[20] Osgood, IV, 62.

the Governor, together with the £2600 paid the masters for the enlisted servants, fulfilled Pennsylvania's quota assigned by the Crown. It was, in fact, more than any other colony not threatened by invasion had provided.[21]

Disagreement among the Quakers as to the extent to which their pacific principles should be observed, especially in respect to the colony's imperial obligations, manifested itself from the earliest days of the Society of Friends. By 1740 the number of those favoring more concessions in way of defense was considerable. Convinced that the strict Quakers were carrying their pacific ideals too far, the moderates, supported by such influential persons as James Logan, made a bid in 1741 to win over the Yearly Meeting. They failed in this, as well as in their appeal for all Quakers who could not support a militia law to decline standing for election to the Assembly.[22]

Despite the defeat of the moderate Quakers, the Allen party believed that their political prospects looked brighter in 1741. The division among the Quakers, William Allen thought, might make it possible for his party to win the crucial German vote, which was enough to swing the elections. The election, in any event, was to be hotly contested by both sides. At Philadelphia, when no less a person than the Reverend Richard Peters was accused of casting two ballots, some one struck him in the course of the wrangling. Upon seeing the commotion, the officious Quaker, Israel Pemberton, moved to separate the men. For his pains he was in turn hit by James Hamilton, the Proprietary gentleman, who threatened to give him a thorough going over if he did not get out of the way. Pemberton brought the scene to a close by taking it "very easy" and replying that he had no fear of Hamilton.[23] Gentlemen in the Eighteenth Century, it seems, took their politics seriously.

In spite of the division among the Quakers and the great effort put forth by the Allen party to win votes, the Quakers carried the election by a wide margin. Their failure caused the Proprietary interest to appeal once more to England for a law to curb the Quakers. Their appeal this time was spear-headed by a petition signed by two hundred and sixty-five prominent persons in Pennsylvania, charging the Assembly with failure to pass a militia law and otherwise provide for the defense of the colony.[24]

---

[21] Norris Letter Book, 1719-1756, 11. HSP. *Votes,* III, 2677; Osgood put the account at £2354. See Osgood, IV, 60.

[22] Pemberton Papers, III, 48; Isaac Sharpless, *Political Leaders of Provincial Pennsylvania,* 148.

[23] Samuel Noble to John Smith, 3rd. 8th mo., 1741, Corresp. of John Smith, 1740-1770. HSP.

[24] Root, 284.

Partridge countered this move in England by insisting that the Assembly had not refused to contribute to the King's use, and was opposed in Pennsylvania only by those who wished to deprive the legislature of its powers and to replace it with the arbitrary rule of a few. He attempted to convince the ministry that the petitioners were alarmists, in view of Pennsylvania's sheltered position and the presence of friendly Indians on its borders. Furthermore, he made known that the Assembly was of the opinion that if expensive defenses were to be maintained, the Proprietors should be made to bear a fair share of the cost.[25] The intercessions of Partridge may have had some influence, but the best protection to the colony was the constant presence before the ministry of more pressing business. Be that as it may, any action by the British government was postponed indefinitely.

Having failed to arouse the British government to take action against the Quaker Assembly, the Proprietary party was compelled to resume its labors in the American vineyard. Each year regardless of previous defeats, the leaders revived their hopes that they could get control of the Assembly by securing the non-Quaker vote.

When the day dawned for the election of 1742, there was more excitement than usual in the air. Election days, with the county seats crowded and noisy, had the reputation of being "the most turbulent days in the whole year."[26] On this occasion the Quaker leaders were forewarned that the Allen party would try something unusual. Israel Pemberton, on the alert at seven in the morning, had his suspicions confirmed when a large body of sailors appeared on the streets. When the polls opened at nine, a great throng of electors, estimated at one thousand, had collected for the Quakers while William Allen stood quite deserted with only about fifty gentlemen around him.

Just then the band of sailors, who had been instructed that a "plain coat and broad hat" would identify their victims, made their appearance and launched an attack upon the crowd collected on the Court House yard. They "fell at a barbarous rate on the Magistrates, constables, and gentlemen that were near them, knocking down all before them without regard to party." Presently they withdrew but only to return again. This time they "dispers'd 500 Dutch and others, knock'd all down that were upon ye stairs and laid ab't 'em in ye most shocking manner eye ever beheld."[27] But victory did not rest long with the sailors. The Germans rallied and made a furious charge

---

[25] Pemberton Papers, III, 51. The Assembly maintained that William Penn had intended that all or part of the quitrents should go into the provincial treasury.

[26] The Journals of Henry Melchior Muhlenberg, II, 517.

[27] Peters to Proprietors, Nov. 17, 1742, Peters Letter Book, 1737-1750; Pa. Mag., XXVIII, 40.

which completely routed the sailors. Many of them were caught and carried off to the city jail.

Following the election, which was another sweeping victory for the Quakers, politicians on each side endeavored to fasten the blame for the riot on the other party. The evidence looked bad for the gentlemen, and William Allen, in what would seem unrighteous indignation, sued Israel Pemberton for openly charging that he had plotted with the sailors. The Assembly presently undertook an investigation of the whole affair, partly to vindicate Pemberton and partly to put the gentlemen in as bad a light as possible. In England, the agents of the Assembly played up the scandal for all it was worth, to the detriment of the Proprietary party.[28]

Before the excitement died down, the Governor and the Assembly fell into an argument as to how the sailors should be tried. The Governor wanted them tried in the city court, while the Assembly contended that the county court had jurisdiction.[29] Who won or what happened to the victims of party politics is not known.

After 1742, Pennsylvania politics assumed a quieter tone, partly because Governor Thomas had finally decided that the Quakers could not be intimidated or driven from power and partly because John Kinsey, the Speaker, who disliked wrangling and discord, did what he could to promote harmony. Richard Peters thought all along that if only Thomas and Kinsey could be brought together to talk matters over, an understanding could be reached. Peters' efforts to bring this about were finally rewarded in May, 1744. The Governor agreed to pass certain bills much desired by the Assembly and not to press the Quakers too hard on matters affecting their religious principles. Kinsey on his part promised that the Governor would be paid his arrears in salary and that the Assembly would "let no expense be wanting proper to put ye country into a posture of defence in such manner as their known principles wou'd admit of."[30]

The improved relations between the Governor and the Assembly were threatened in October when Israel Pemberton attempted to have elected an Assembly with stronger pacific opinions.[31] John Kinsey, however, kept the party in line and nearly all the old members were returned. James Pemberton, who did not always hold with his brother's ideas, was confident that the Governor and Assembly would continue on good terms.

---

[28] Thayer, 49; *Votes,* IV, 2957ff.
[29] Osgood, IV, 64.
[30] Peters to Proprietors, May 24, 1744, Peters Letter Book, 1737-1750.
[31] *Ibid.,* Oct. 3, 1744.

The improved relations between the Governor and the Assembly, however, seemed headed for the rocks after France, in June, 1744, entered the war on the side of Spain. To the Governor's new demands for military measures to safeguard the colony, John Kinsey replied that the Assembly would consider carefully all proposals but not to expect too much in that Pennsylvania was protected by friendly Indians on the frontier and by the British Navy on the seas.[32] A little later when the Governor requested aid for New York and New England, in the expedition against Louisburg, the Assembly replied that since Pennsylvania had not been consulted in planning the campaign, it was under no obligation to extend aid. The next year, however, after the fort was taken, the Pennsylvania Assembly came around and voted £4000 toward provisioning the English garrison at Louisburg.[33] A year later, with a complete absence of enthusiasm, it appropriated £5000 for raising five companies which were presently used in an abortive expedition launched from New York against Canada.

Meanwhile, good news for the Quakers came from England. The Crown attorneys, in answer to the Privy Council's request for an opinion regarding Pennsylvania's responsibility toward defense, replied that although the Assembly was obliged to provide for the defense of the colony, it remained the only immediate judge as to what measures, if any, were needed to safeguard the province. If it were thought that the Assembly was not meeting its responsibility, recourse could be found only in Parliamentary action.[34] This expedient, however, as was commonly known, would be recommended by the Crown only as a last resort, for the ministry no more relished the thought of Parliamentary intervention than did the colonies.

In 1747, his health impaired, Governor Thomas returned to England leaving the administration in the hands of Anthony Palmer, President of the Council. Political friends and foes alike realized that Pennsylvania had lost an admirable chief executive. Palmer was not considered a very forceful leader, but inasmuch as James Logan declined serving as President, no change was made. Before leaving, however, Thomas strengthened the Council, which for many years had played a very minor role in provincial affairs, by appointing three new members. A year later, the Reverend Richard Peters, a man of energy and insight, was added to the Council.

During the final stages of King George's war, French privateers appeared off the coast of British America. In July, 1747, a French vessel ventured into the broad bay of the Delaware, where it did some damage

---

[32] *Ibid.*, Aug. 2, 1744; Pemberton Papers, III, 62; Osgood, IV, 64.

[33] Osgood, IV, 66; *Col. Rec.* V, 46.

[34] Pemberton Papers, III, 141; Osgood, IV, 66; Root, 285; Mabel P. Wolff, *The Colonial Agency of Pennsylvania, 1712-1757,* 107.

to shipping and even sent a raiding party ashore near Newcastle. Upon
receiving this news, Philadelphia became greatly alarmed and a clamor
arose for forts at strategic positions along the Delaware. Pennsylvania
in truth was utterly defenseless; not only did it have no batteries to
guard the approaches to Philadelphia, but it had no militia or military
organizations to call up in case of need.[35] Reports were soon circulating
that the French had obtained knowledge of the navigation of the river,
of the complete absence of defenses, and of the great and easily secured
plunder to be had. Rumor arose that the French in the West Indies
were preparing to attack the city with six privateers early the next
spring.[36]

In spite of the alarm, the Quaker Assembly refused to take the situa-
tion very seriously, refusing even to make an appropriation for fitting
out a ship to defend the city. Finding that nothing could budge the
Assembly, a group of merchants raised a sum for fitting out a privateer.
When ready, the ship was christened the *Warren,* after Admiral Peter
Warren of the Royal Navy.[37]

To provide further for the defense of the province, Benjamin Franklin advanced a plan which sought the support of all moderate people
in the province, whom he believed constituted the majority. Aware that
most of the people were opposed to strict and harsh militia regulations,
Franklin wisely devised a plan which met with their approval. Peters
accurately reported that the plan fell "fowl of the Quakers & their
opposers equally, as people from whom no good cou'd be expected, and
by this artifice to animate all the middling persons to undertake their
own defense in opposition to the Quakers & the Gentlemen."[38]

Steps were immediately taken to put the plan into execution. To
win over the moderate Quakers, Franklin published a pamphlet entitled
Plain Truth or Serious Considerations, in which he placed some extracts
from the writings of well-known Quaker preachers which ostensibly
sanctioned self-defense. Then he called a meeting for forming an
association to implement his plans for defense. A petition for financial
aid from the Assembly was quickly prepared and signed by two hundred and fifty prominent citizens, of whom at least sixty were Quakers.
But the Assembly did nothing.[39] Recourse was then sought in a lottery
for £20,000, which was expected to yield £3000 for the Association.
So successful was the lottery that another and slightly larger one was
undertaken. With money thus raised, the Association purchased cannon and erected batteries at strategic positions on the Delaware.

[35] Thomas Lawrence Letter Book, 1746-1754, 54. HSP.
[36] Peters to Proprietors, Nov. 29, 1747, Peters Letter Book, 1737-1750.
[37] Osgood, IV, 74.
[38] Peters to Proprietors, Nov. 29, 1747, Peters Letter Book, 1737-1750.
[39] *Ibid.;* Wolff, 114.

But the unique feature of Franklin's plan was the creation of the Association itself which consisted of volunteer companies to take the place of a militia. The volunteers from among themselves elected their officers below the rank of colonel. The colonels in turn were chosen by the officers. Both men and officers met annually and by ballot elected four deputies from each county, who formed a general military council with powers to make rules and regulations for the Associators. The deputies were prohibited from making members subject to fines or punishments, as the organization existed purely upon a voluntary basis and in a spirit of good will.[40] The whole program proved a great success from the start. Soon Philadelphia could boast of ten companies, and the counties upwards of ninety more. Peters estimated in May, 1748, that there would soon be ten thousand volunteers in the organization.[41]

It was soon apparent that the Association, as fashioned by Benjamin Franklin, was not at all pleasing to William Allen and his political henchmen. Richard Peters, happy to see something being done to protect the colony, was altogether disgusted with the pettiness of the gentlemen. Even Thomas Penn agreed that "Such want of Spirit in people that have been finding fault with the Friends, is really surprizing & I am sure it would not have been believed had a prophet foretold it."[42]

William Allen's refusal to cooperate with Franklin in launching the Association proceeded purely from political considerations and personal jealousy. Franklin and Allen were then friends and fellow Masons, but the latter perceived in Franklin a dangerous political rival. Franklin, in fact, was fast becoming a power in Pennsylvania politics, and Allen could see that the Association was gaining him great prestige throughout the province. Franklin and other popular leaders, and not the gentlemen, were being chosen to officer the Association. The whole plan, the Allen party now declared, was illegal. The organization of a militia and the appointment of officers, they insisted, belonged to the Governor alone.

The reaction among the Quakers to the Association was mixed, a large number having the courage to support it, if not actually joining. The more liberal members of the Society of Friends were by this time exasperated by the conduct of the Pembertons and other "stiff-necked" Quakers. The latter had initiated an "inquisition" into the names of all Quakers who had contributed to the "manning out the *Warren* privateer for a cruise—in order to drive away the French and Spanish

---

[40] Broadsides, Box 2, Folder E. HSP.
[41] Peters to Proprietors, May 11, 1748, Peters Letter Book, 1737-1750.
[42] Wolff, 114-115.

privateers." Those exposed were threatened with excommunication by the Meeting if they did not recant and withdraw from all militaristic undertakings.[43]

Although Thomas Penn was at first rather amazed at William Allen's attitude toward the Association, it was not long before he came to agree that the experiment was a dangerous innovation. Like Allen, Penn perceived in Franklin a natural leader of the democratic masses in the province, who, if not checked, would trample under foot well-nigh every vestige of proprietary authority. In a letter to Peters, Penn declared: "Mr. Franklin's doctrine that obedience to Governors is no more due them than protection to the people, is not fit to be in the heads of the unthinking multitude. He is a dangerous man and I should be glad if he inhabited any other country, as I believe him of a very uneasy spirit. However, as he is a sort of tribune of the people, he must be treated with regard."[44]

By June, 1748, Peters' early enthusiasm for the Association had likewise cooled. He now admitted that William Allen had reason enough to suspect that Franklin would use the Association politically in the October election.[45] As it turned out, although apparently giving the matter some thought, Franklin did not attempt to use the Association in this way. If the war had continued, it is possible that he might have done so in order to get an Assembly controlled by the moderates. But with the termination of the war in 1748 and the disappearance of the conditions which gave rise to the Association, he apparently considered it unwise to risk alienating the now reunited and powerful Quaker faction.

In November, 1748, James Hamilton returned from a trip to England to become Lieutenant-Governor of Pennsylvania. The war was over, and Hamilton, who was a Pennsylvanian by birth, looked forward to a quiet administration. The leaders of the Quaker party were cordial in receiving him. "John Kinsey in particular," Peters noted, "stay'd all afternoon, talk'd affectionately & drank heartily, & very frankly offer'd his services to the Governor." In the afternoon, too, Israel Pemberton called with his father, and "behav'd with much courtesy." Such evidence was sufficient to convince Peters that everyone would aspire "to render Mr. Hamilton easy in his administration."[46]

The events of the war with Spain and France, it has been shown, did not in the least shake the people's faith in the Quaker party, despite the fact that the great majority of the inhabitants no longer were either

[43] Peters to Proprietors, Nov. 29, 1747, Peters Letter Book, 1737-1750.
[44] William R. Shepherd, *History of Proprietary Government in Pennsylvania*, 222n.
[45] Peters to Proprietors, June 16, 1748, Peters Letter Book, 1737-1750.
[46] *Ibid.*, Nov. 25, 1748.

Quakers or pacifists. Quaker government in the eyes of the people was synonymous with good government, freedom, and low taxes. When, in the later stages of the war, fear arose for the safety of the province, the people saved the Quaker Assembly embarrassment by adopting Franklin's extra-legal military association. The war ended, the popularity of the Quaker party reached new heights by its spirited crusade for more paper money. With this issue in store for him, James Hamilton would not be "rendered easy" for very long.

III

GOVERNOR HAMILTON. 1748-1754

CONTRARY TO EXPECTATION, James Hamilton did not experience a pleasant and placid life as Governor of Pennsylvania. In fact, after six years, he gave up the office, a disappointed and disillusioned man. Hamilton was the son of a more famous father, Andrew Hamilton, who had given memorable services to the province as a lawyer of distinction and Speaker of the Assembly. The Hamiltons were Scotch and members of the Episcopalian Church. Although a man of ability, James had a conservative frame of mind which kept him narrowly loyal to the Penns and quite unappreciative of the desires as well as the capabilities of the average citizen of Pennsylvania.

Prior to becoming Lieutenant-Governor in 1748, Hamilton had been prothonotary of the Supreme Court of Pennsylvania, a member of the Assembly for five years, Mayor of Philadelphia, and a member of the Governor's Council. Thus, when he became the Penns' Deputy-Governor at the age of thirty-eight, he was a man of maturity with a good background of political experience.

The question which caused James Hamilton ceaseless trouble and embarrassment during his term of office, and finally prompted him to resign, was that of paper money. The history of paper money or bills of credit, as they were called, goes back to 1723 in Pennsylvania. That year the Assembly authorized the emission of £45,000, in bills of credit, to provide a circulating medium in an economy where gold and silver were almost non-existent, as a result of unfavorable balance of trade with Great Britain and the attraction which that money market offered for specie.

During times of war, bills of credit went directly into circulation as the money was laid out for military uses. At other times they were put into circulation through loans from a government agency in the form of mortgages on real estate and other property.[1] The fact that the currency appeared to stimulate business convinced the people that paper money was a blessing to a country starved by a lack of specie. The law made the bills legal tender for all debts equal to sterling. Naturally this provision was disliked by the Proprietors, whose collections in Pennsylvania were depreciated because paper money never attained a par with sterling. British merchants, many of whom had sustained losses through the excessive issues of bills of credit in New England

---

[1] Root, 189. See *Statutes*, III, 389ff.

and South Carolina, added their weight to the opposition. In 1726, the Board of Trade therefore advised the Governor of Pennsylvania not to allow any further issues of paper money.[2]

Despite this admonition of the Board of Trade, Governor Patrick Gordon in 1729, after experiencing no end of pressure and "turbulent noise," was persuaded to allow an additional sum of £30,000 in bills of credit.[3] Supplementary acts during the next decade were made in order to reinstate currency due by law to be retired. By this means the amount of currency in 1739 stood at £68,000. That year it was increased to £80,000. Proprietary opposition was alleviated at this time by a provision compensating the Penns for their losses by awarding them a sum of £1200 plus an annual stipend of £130.[4] Likewise criticism of the Pennsylvania currency by the British merchants had been greatly lessened. Perceiving no injury to themselves from the rather modest issues of bills of credit in Pennsylvania and having been tutored by the Philadelphia merchants on the necessity of paper money in the province, the British merchants had reversed their stand and informed the Board of Trade that "they rather thought them (bills of credit) absolutely necessary for carrying on of commerce."[5]

Viewing the American scene as a whole, however, the British government was not at all convinced that the colonies would generally act with moderation in issuing paper money. Currency inflation in New England, especially in Rhode Island, threatened creditors everywhere. In 1740, therefore, the Privy Council, at the suggestion of the House of Commons, gave orders to colonial governors not to allow any more paper money legislation without a suspending clause whereby the money could not be released until the measure was approved by the Crown.[6] This order in effect prevented any further issues of paper money in Pennsylvania (with the exception of £5000 for defense allowed by Governor Thomas in 1746) until the demands for war after 1754 opened the gates and forced the Governors to accept paper money legislation without suspending clauses.

When James Hamilton became governor in 1748, the House of Commons again had the currency question before it. At this time, opinion

---

[2] *Ibid.*, 190-192; *Votes*, III, 1791-92. Local fear of paper money seemed to have disappeared for the most part when it was discovered that the currency did not fluctuate very much.

[3] *Votes*, III, 1963-64.

[4] *Votes*, III, 2521-22; *Pa. Gazette*, Jan. 25, 1738/39; Beverly W. Bond, *The Quit Rent System in the American Colonies*, 144-145.

[5] Root, 195; *Votes*, III, 2668-70.

[6] *Votes*, IV, 3575-76; Root, 195-196; Osgood, IV, 66. Royal governors were instructed to demand suspending clauses on paper money acts as early as 1720. Leonard W. Labaree, *Royal Instructions to British Colonial Governors, 1670-1776*, I, 218-219.

seemed to be less hostile to paper money than on some former occasions. There were extremists, however, who advocated outlawing the use of bills of credit altogether in the colonies. But more members appeared satisfied with the customary requirement of having payments to England made in sterling or the rate of exchange. Nevertheless, it was generally felt that the amount of paper money should be restricted as a necessary precaution against inflation. Lord Halifax, in a spirit of complete detachment from British commercial interests, suggested that the colonies might compensate for this restriction by encouraging their domestic manufactures, in order to curtail their purchases from England. By this means, he said, a balance might be struck in the gold supply of the empire.[7]

Fully realizing the danger confronting paper money in the colonies, Thomas Penn assured the Board of Trade and the leaders in the House of Commons that no further issues would be made in Pennsylvania until Parliament had thoroughly considered the question and arrived at a decision.[8] But the Pennsylvania Assembly paid no heed to his promises and before long framed a bill for the emission of £20,000. Opinion in the colony was that Pennsylvania would soon be in urgent need of more money, considering the rapid decrease of specie and the growing demands of business.[9] Governor Hamilton, in obedience to his instructions, refused to sign the bill. Not the least annoying to him was the exclusion of the executive from any part in the making of appointments to the Loan Office (the agency in charge of loaning out the money) or in the disposal of the profits arising from interest of the loans.[10] He rested his case in the main, however, upon the assumption that it would be unwise to pass a paper money act at a time when the system was under attack in Parliament.[11]

After a long study of the paper money problem, Parliament, in 1751, passed a law forbidding legal-tender bills of credit in New England but making no reference to the other colonies. Petitions from British and Pennsylvania merchants, in conjunction with the solicitations of Thomas Penn, Richard Partridge and others, had convinced Parliament, for the time being at least, that the moderate use of paper money in the middle and southern colonies should not be prohibited.[12]

Henceforth Proprietary instructions regarding bills of credit were very positive in warning the Governor against allowing any sizable

[7] Thomas Penn to James Hamilton, June 6, 1749, Penn-Hamilton Correspondence, HSP; *Votes*, IV, 3277-78.
[8] *Ibid.*
[9] Peters to Proprietors, April 29, 1749, Peters Letter Book, 1737-1750; *Votes*, IV, 3249, 3284.
[10] *Votes*, IV, 3249, 4284.
[11] *Ibid.*, 3277.
[12] *Wolff*, 155-156.

issues without first sounding out the ministry. Thomas Penn believed that a limited supply of paper money was beneficial to the colony (provided his personal interests were safeguarded), but he had little confidence in the self-restraint of the Pennsylvania Assembly. If the prohibition against paper money should be extended to Pennsylvania, he thought that it not only would hurt the economy of the country, but also, by establishing another precedent for Parliamentary intervention, endanger the very existence of Proprietary government.

But regardless of the dangers involved, Hamilton was thoroughly convinced that the people of Pennsylvania would not rest until they had secured a greater quantity of paper currency. The Assembly, he told Thomas Penn, would introduce a money bill at every session and use every means at its command to force its passage.[13] Privately, he felt that Thomas Penn's instructions were much too rigid, affording him—as it were—too little room in the use of discretion in dealing with the Assembly.

After being compelled to refuse one paper money bill after another and to endure weeks of wrangling over the question, Hamilton's patience with both the Proprietors and the Assembly ebbed fast. Obedience to his instructions containing any manner of provisions as to the life, control of interest money, funding, and other details of the paper money system, he realized, was making him odious throughout the province. Indeed, Hamilton had by this time become so exasperated with his instructions that he had a mind to show them to the Assembly, come what may. One glimpse of them by the Assembly, he knew, would "create such a Flame in the province as would not be quench'd in many years."[14]

Thomas Penn was not left in the dark as to how everyone in Pennsylvania felt about his instructions. Protests came not only from Hamilton but from William Allen and other friends of the Proprietors. Their criticism, indeed, became so persistent that Penn felt obliged to make a few concessions. These, however, were too minor to do any good.[15]

Hoping perhaps to rid himself of the paper money problem once and for all, Hamilton, in 1753, refused a bill because it did not have a suspending clause. When this became known, the wrath of the people was intense. Having this requirement in their instructions was proof enough, it was declared, that the Proprietors had no real intention of allowing a paper money act on any terms whatever. Suspending clauses, as invoked by the Royal Order of 1740, they argued, were not

---

[13] Penn MSS., Off. Corresp., V, 227. See Pemberton Papers, X, 75.

[14] *Ibid.*, Add. Miscel. Letters, I, 79; *Votes*, IV, 3500-04.

[15] *Ibid.;* Peters MSS., III, 68.

required in Pennsylvania by virtue of the terms of its Charter. The allowance by the Privy Council of the emission of £5000 in bills of credit in the administration of Governor Thomas they cited as proof of their assertion.[16] It was difficult to conceive, wrote Peters, how much the whole idea that Pennsylvania was bound by the Royal Order was ridiculed by everyone.[17]

Even Hamilton's friends criticized him for invoking the Royal Order. William Allen, for instance, told him that he should have signed the bill and thus avoided the "wrath of the people."[18] The British government could then, if it chose, veto the measure. Hamilton's patience by now was all but exhausted. "I think there is little probability," he told Thomas Penn, "of my ever doing any further Business with these People in the legislative way, as they seem determined to proceed upon no other, until they have their beloved paper money."[19]

In this frame of mind Hamilton had already informed Penn that he wished to be relieved of his office within about a year.[20] In reply, Thomas Penn pleaded with Hamilton not to leave the service at a time of impending war and of grave danger to the province. He assured Hamilton that he was endeavoring to put his affairs in shape so that he could come over and assume the governing of the colony himself.[21] Hamilton answered that he would give Penn time to get another governor or to take the office himself, but that he wanted to be relieved at the earliest possible time.

In 1754 with the French already invading the Ohio Valley and the imminence of war felt by all, Hamilton offered to forego a suspending clause in order to raise £15,000 to assist Virginia in fortifying the West. But disagreement arose over the length of life of the bills and over an excise for sinking them. Acting as usual upon his instructions, Hamilton refused to approve the measure as written by the House. The Assembly would not capitulate and the net result could be measured only in more hard feelings. Penn's comment over the dispute was that Hamilton had put a stop to the bill "in the best manner he could without showing his instructions."[22] This was Hamilton's last brush

[16] Votes, IV, 3576, 3579ff; Root, 200-201.

[17] Penn MSS., Off. Corresp., VI, 99, 103. Governor George Thomas in 1740 was instructed by the Privy Council not to allow any paper money act without a suspending clause. Votes, IV, 3575-76.

[18] Peters MSS., III, 68.

[19] Penn MSS., Off. Corresp., VI, 99, 103.

[20] Ibid., Add. Miscel. Letters, I, 82.

[21] Thomas Penn to James Hamilton, Jan. 29, 1754, Penn-Hamilton Corresp. HSP.

[22] Peters MSS., II, 107; Root, 200. The bill would create £35,000 in bills of credit, £15,000 of which would be appropriated for the King's use. Votes, V, 3705, 3726-31. An earlier version of the bill was for £30,000 of which £10,000 was earmarked for the King's use.

with the Assembly over paper money during his first administration. His successor, Robert Hunter Morris, who took office in October, 1754, found the issue awaiting him, intensified and further complicated by the impending war with the French and Indians.

Realizing the almost negligible value of having representative government if no laws could be passed but those authorized by the Proprietors or by the Crown from a distance of three thousand miles, the Assembly resolved that no Governor could "be laid under instructions, either from the Crown or from the Proprietor, for that, the King having delegated his powers to you [Proprietors], by the Charter, has nothing further to do with us, and that the Proprietors having delegated theirs by a commission to their Governor are not thereafter, capable of restricting him, in any point of Government whatever."[23] It took another decade, however, before the Assembly could finally bring Thomas Penn to change his governing policies.

Fully as important, if not so vexing as the paper money question, were the Western and Indian problems which continually worried Hamilton's administration. Reports had been rife during King George's War that the French were planning to move into the Ohio Valley, where as yet Pennsylvania and other English fur traders remained unmolested in the pursuit of their gains. In 1747, the Pennsylvania Assembly had set aside General William Shirley's advice to send presents to the western Indians to keep them loyal to the English. But in the next year it had taken a more favorable attitude and had appropriated funds to send Conrad Weiser with presents to the Ohio.[24]

In the period immediately following the peace of Aix-la-Chapelle in 1748, the rivalry between England and France for the Ohio Valley was accelerated. At a treaty with the Ohio Indians, at Logstown, in 1748, Conrad Weiser learned directly from Joncaire de Chabert, an agent of the French government, that France intended to compel the Indians to drive the English from the Ohio.[25] During the next year the French planted a series of leaden plates in the Ohio Valley to signify their rights to the territory. Meanwhile, the English, most of whom were Virginians, formed a land company with rights to about five hundred thousand acres west of the Alleghenies and prepared to settle their claims.[26]

With the French preparing to drive into the Ohio Valley in earnest, it was evident that if the English were to hold the country and retain

---

[23] Penn MSS., Off. Corresp., VI, 99; *Votes*, V, 3713-17.

[24] Peters to Proprietors, May 11, 1748, Peters Letter Book, 17737-1750; Osgood, IV, 69.

[25] Osgood, IV, 297.

[26] Kenneth P. Bailey, *The Ohio Company of Virginia and the Westward Movement of 1748-1792;* Peters to Proprietors, July 5, 1749, Peters Letter Book, 1737-1750.

the loyalty of the Indians, they must build a fort on the Ohio without delay. Fully alive to the gravity of the situation, Thomas Penn advised James Hamilton to request the Assembly to vote a sum for fortifying the West out of regard for the large Pennsylvania fur interests and the Proprietary claims to trans-Allegheny territory. As early as February, 1749, Penn offered to contribute £400 plus £100 annually toward building and maintaining a fort, provided the Assembly would bear the remainder of the cost. The initial cost of a fort, he estimated, would be not more than £800.[27]

Unfortunately for the English, Thomas Penn's offer was turned down because of the determined opposition of the Quakers led by Israel Pemberton, the intransigent pacifist. Having failed in this move, Penn expressed his hope that the Ohio Company of Virginia would be successful in fortifying the West so long as Proprietary rights in western Pennsylvania were not infringed. [28] The Ohio Company, however, was slow in moving to protect its claims, a slowness due perhaps to the influence of the wealthy London Quaker, John Hanbury, a stockholder whose pacifism and fear of offending the Indians caused him to oppose fortifying the country.[29]

Although refusing to contribute toward fortifying the West, the Quaker Assembly did not hold back funds for retaining the good will of the Indians. Between 1748 and 1751, it laid out over £5000 for this purpose. Even Richard Peters felt compelled to acknowledge that the Assembly had "behaved well in Indian affairs."[30]

As was almost sure to happen, the Proprietary question crept into that of Indian expenses. The Assembly insisted that the Proprietors were obligated to maintain peaceful relations with the natives for which purpose William Penn, it was said, had appropriated the proceeds of the Proprietary quitrents.[31] In answer to this attack upon his purse, Thomas Penn declared that there was no foundation for such an assumption. Anyhow, he argued, the Proprietors had freely assumed a fair share of the Indian expenditures. For example, he pointed out, the Proprietors bought the land from the Indians, paid Conrad Weiser his salary as Indian interpreter, and other expenses incident to Indian affairs.[32] Naturally his arguments were not convincing to the people of Pennsylvania, who thought of these expenditures as being prompted by the purely personal interests of the Proprietors. The Assembly's demands for greater proprietary aid for the support of the government

---

[27] Thomas Penn to James Hamilton, Feb. 12, 1749, Penn-Hamilton Corresp. HSP.
[28] *Ibid.*, July 13, 1752; Thayer, 57-61.
[29] Osgood, IV, 79.
[30] Peters to Proprietors, July 27, 1748, Peters Letter Book, 1737-1750.
[31] Osgood., IV, 297-298.
[32] *Ibid.*

at this time was only a harbinger of the intense controversy soon to develop over the taxation of Proprietary estates in Pennsylvania.

In 1753, with the French actually moving toward the Ohio from their base at Niagara, the condition of Indian relations in the Middle Colonies became alarming. Many of the Indians, who had been on friendly terms with the English fur traders and who feared reprisals at the hands of the French, appealed to Virginia and Pennsylvania for help. The Pennsylvania Assembly, acting for once with unusual speed, placed £800 in Governor Hamilton's hands for presents to the Indians.[33] Hamilton thereupon appointed Richard Peters, Isaac Norris, Benjamin Franklin and Conrad Weiser to be commissioners in charge of treating with the Indians.

The commissioners met representatives of the Western tribes at Carlisle, Pennsylvania, in 1753, where promises of peace and friendship were exchanged and the Indians given a large quantity of presents. But the commissioners left with a feeling of foreboding; no one knew better than they how slender was the loyalty of the Indians to the English.[34]

At Carlisle the Indians signified their willingness to have the English build a fort on the Ohio.[35] In March, 1754, therefore, Governor Dinwiddie of Virginia announced that his province had raised £10,000 for sending six companies into the Ohio country to build a fort. Upon hearing this, James Hamilton called upon the Assembly to make a contribution to the King's service for the defense of the West.[36]

By this time the Assembly was much divided on the question of defense. The strict Quakers, who were losing their grip on the Assembly, after exhausing all their powers of persuasion succeeded in mustering only a minority in opposition to Hamilton's proposal. Of these not a few appeared to be motivated more by jealousy of the Ohio Company than by conscientious objections. The minority, led by the Speaker, Isaac Norris, voted to raise £15,000 for the King's use only to have their measure run afoul of Proprietary instructions as already related.[37] As yet the threat of war was not serious enough for either side to make concessions for the sake of defense.

The other colonies, with the exception of North Carolina, apathetically allowed Governor Dinwiddie's call for aid to go unanswered. Even

---

[33] Penn MSS., Add. Miscel. Letters, I, 82.

[34] Paul A. W. Wallace, *Conrad Weiser, 1696-1760: Friend of Colonist and Mohawk*, 344-349; Penn MSS., Off, Corresp., VI, 133; *Votes*, IV, 3553, V, 3637.

[35] Norris Letter Book, 1719-1756, 68.

[36] *Johnson Papers*, IX, 131-132; *Votes*, V, 3686-87.

[37] *Votes*, V, 3690 ff; Norris Letter Book, 1719-1756, 49. Some historians have unrealistically believed that the root of Pennsylvania's failure to meet defense needs during the period between 1754-1764, lay in Quaker pacifism. However, Charles Stillé, Herbert Osgood, and Winfred Root have rightly credited it to differences over taxation, paper money, and politics. *Pa. Mag.*, X, 286; Root, 306; Osgood, IV, 48, 297-298, 337.

the House of Burgesses in Virginia viewed the Ohio Company, of which Dinwiddie was a stockholder, with the greatest suspicion; funds for fortifying the West were voted by the Virginia Burgesses with nothing more than the most obvious reluctance.

The Virginia forces sent out to secure the Ohio country were unequal to the task in point of numbers. At Great Meadows on July 4, 1754, the commanding officer, George Washington, was compelled to surrender his fortified camp (Fort Necessity) and to abandon the country to the enemy.[38] In November, Thomas Penn informed Hamilton that the defeat of Washington had "alarmed everybody" who were now convinced "of the absolute necessity of sending assistance from hence."[39] But the burden of governing Pennsylvania was now no longer on Hamilton's shoulders. In October, with no regrets, James Hamilton handed over the government of Pennsylvania to Robert Hunter Morris, the former Chief Justice of New Jersey, and retired from office.

Throughout the six years of Hamilton's incumbency, the Quaker party had experienced no difficulty in maintaining its popularity. Nothing, in fact, could better recommend it to all classes and sections of the province than its championship of paper money. So great was the desire for more paper money that it became inseparably bound to the French and Indian question and the whole problem of defense. The obstruction of paper money legislation by the Proprietors, their Governors, and the Crown, had the effect of greatly widening the breach between the people and the executive branch of the government. The controversy was a fitting one to open the ensuing quarter-century struggle for popular government in Pennsylvania.

[38] Lawrence H. Gipson, *The Great War for the Empire, 1754-1757*, 35-43.
[39] Thomas Penn to James Hamilton, Nov. 17, 1754, Penn-Hamilton Corresp. HSP.

IV

GOVERNOR MORRIS vs. FRANKLIN. 1755

A T THE TIME of his appointment, Robert Hunter Morris was in England where he had gone in the interest of New Jersey Proprietors. Previous to this he had held the office of Chief Justice of New Jersey under his father, Governor Lewis Morris. Robert Hunter Morris was fifty-four years of age when he became Lieutenant-Governor of Pennsylvania. Having gained the reputation in New Jersey for thinking in terms of prerogative first, and the interest of the colonists last, he was about as ill-qualified for the Pennsylvania post as anyone could be. It is no wonder that his governorship was as stormy as it was brief.

For some years before Robert Hunter Morris became Governor of Pennsylvania, the question of the desirability of limiting German immigration had been under serious consideration. The Germans, more frugal than the Irish who "lived high and fell into debt," had been preferred to the latter.[1] Of late, however, such great swarms of Germans had flocked to the colony that grave fear had arisen that they might Germanize the country by the very weight of numbers.

Benjamin Franklin, who was as concerned as anyone over the rapid increase of the Germans, proposed in 1752 that all non-English speaking people should be barred from holding civil or military office. In addition, he held that a prohibition should be placed on the importation of German books, and that all German publications should be obliged to carry an English translation on each page, while deeds, bonds, and other legal documents should be in English only. Intermarriage, he thought, should be encouraged to break down the clannishness of the Germans, and a limitation or quota should be placed on German immigration. Futhermore, he recommended that English schools be established among the Germans to Anglicize the younger generation.[2]

The Reverend William Smith, who shared Franklin's views, warned the English in 1755 that the Germans "give out that they are a Majority, and strong [enough] to make the Country their own, and indeed, as they are poured in upon us in such Numbers (upwards to 5000 being imported this year), I know nothing that will hinder them, either from soon being able to give us Law and Language, or else by joining with the French, to eject all the English Inhabitants."[3] Smith reckoned that

---

[1] Penn MSS., Off. Corresp., V, 217.
[2] Franklin Papers, LXIX, 65. APS.
[3] William Smith, *Brief State of the Province of Pennsylvania, etc.* (1756 ed.), 30-31.

the German population in the colony in 1755 was already nearly one hundred thousand in a total population of two hundred and twenty thousand.[4]

Although Franklin's program for curtailing the numbers and influence of the Germans was never adopted, a society for establishing English schools for them was presently founded. Among the trustees were James Hamilton, William Allen, Richard Peters, Conrad Weiser, William Smith and Benjamin Franklin. Subscriptions for the support of the schools were made. Thomas Penn gave £20 toward a school at York and a like sum for one at Carlisle.[5]

From the start the response among the Germans was not at all cordial to the English schools. Christopher Sauer, editor of the German newspaper published at Germantown, threw his great weight against the project. Notwithstanding this opposition, at one time the schools had over four hundred students enrolled. But the enterprise failed rapidly after 1759 and five years later, for want of students, the schools were closed. The net result of it all was to cause the Germans to retreat more within themselves, to found schools of their own, and by other means to resist assimilation.

Believing that they saw a political motive in the English schools, the Quakers generally remained aloof or outwardly opposed the project. When it became known by the election of 1754 that the schools had been instrumental in changing a few German votes, the Quakers were convinced of the truth of their suspicions. A letter of Thomas Penn reveals that it was the intention of the Proprietary party to use the schools politically, thus confirming this belief among the Quakers. He told Richard Peters not to be impatient or expect to change the votes of the Germans at once. "Very prudent, soft and cautious measures," Penn assured him, were "necessary to bring them over, which may be effected in time by the management of the Trustees for the school."[6] Similarly, the Reverend William Smith felt confident that if the Germans were properly instructed, "so as to be capable of using their own judgment in matters of Government, they would no more be misled by Acts of a Quaker preacher, than a lurking French priest."[7]

The German Moravians, who were settled on the frontier of Northampton County, were singled out by Smith and others as suspicious elements. They were suspected of being a peculiar branch of the

---

[4] *Ibid.*, 6.

[5] Thomas Penn to James Hamilton, Jan. 9, 1753, Penn-Hamilton Corresp. H.S.P. In 1760 it was reported that the Germans had plenty of schools and schoolmasters for them. Instruction in these schools was entirely in German. *Pa. Mag.*, IV, 69.

[6] Peters MSS., IV, 4.

[7] Arthur D. Graeff, *The Relations Between the Pennsylvania Germans and the British Authorities (1750-1776)*, 62-63.

Roman Catholic Church and therefore sympathetic to France.[8] Speaking of this highly imaginary danger, William Smith exclaimed, "Many are also Moravians, who, as they conceal their Principles, are suspected to be a dangerous People, more especially as they hold some tenets and Customs, as far as we have any Opportunity of judging of them much a-kin to those of the Roman Catholic."[9]

As to Germans who were known Catholics, the Reverend William Smith and others stirred up what threatened when war came to become a witch hunt against these unoffending immigrants. For security reasons, in 1757, a count was taken of all Catholics in Pennsylvania. The investigation revealed only thirteen hundred sixty-five, of which four hundred sixteen were Irish and the rest Germans. All were found to be quite evenly distributed over the province. Soon orders were issued placing them under the care and surveillance of citizens responsible for their conduct.[10]

In 1754 with war imminent, the leaders of the Proprietary party again surveyed the political scene in Pennsylvania with a measure of confidence. Some, it has been shown, already expected the English schools among the Germans to yield political dividends. However, they were again disappointed. Under the leadership of Christopher Sauer the Germans turned out in mass to vote for the Quakers and swept all the old members back into office. Completely disillusioned, the Proprietary leaders appealed to Parliament to disfranchise the Germans for the sake of the security of the province.[11]

In picking up the reins of government so willingly handed him by James Hamilton, Robert Hunter Morris at once found himself confronted by the ubiquitous paper money question. In December, 1754, the Assembly offered him a bill for raising £20,000 in bills of credit for aiding General Braddock's expedition against Fort Duquesne. Morris vetoed the bill, quoting Sir Dudley Ryder to the effect that it was not in order to accept paper money legislation without a suspending clause in compliance to the Royal Order of 1740. As before, the Assembly argued that this was not the case as the bill was exactly like the one, except for the amount, signed by Governor Thomas in 1746 and confirmed by the Crown.[12] Morris also objected to a life of twelve years for the bills. He based his objection upon the Paper Money Act of 1751 which limited the New England colonies to emergency issues for a term of five years. The Assembly answered that this law applied only to New England colonies. On this point Morris admitted that he

---

[8] Osgood, IV, 77.
[9] *Brief State,* 38.
[10] *Pa. Arch.,* (1st Ser.) III, 144-145.
[11] Graeff, 55-56, 63.
[12] Norris Letter Book, 1719-1756, 74; *Votes,* V, 3771-72, 3789.

was in error, but he steadfastly maintained that the Royal Order applied to all the colonies.   After this there followed weeks of bitter wrangling over the Royal Order and the Proprietary instructions.[13]

Like the bill submitted to Governor Hamilton a few months earlier, the money bill had in addition to the £20,000 for the King's use, a further sum of £20,000 to supplement the volume of currency in the province.   It is clear that the Assembly was using the emergency as a means to acquire a sizable increase in the volume of Pennsylvania currency.[14]

In view of the urgency of getting supplies to General Braddock, the Assembly on January 3 commissioned members of the House to borrow £5000 from the Loan Office for aiding the expedition.[15]   This was done, without doubt, with one eye on the effect the appropriation would have in England.   Full well did the Assembly know that the Proprietary party would not be slow in presenting the dispute with the Governor in the most unfavorable light to the ministry.

Upon receiving an application from Governor Shirley of Massachusetts for funds to aid the Northern colonies to capture Crown Point, the Assembly in March framed a defense bill for £25,000 in terms similar to the last one refused by the Governor.   His veto followed.[16]   Realizing the uselessness of arguing further with the Governor and desiring to meet Shirley's request, the Assembly appropriated £10,000 from funds in the Loan Office for purchasing provisions for the New England troops.[17]

During the course of the long dispute with the Governor, the Assembly took the precaution to prepare and send off to England a defense of its position.   As was usual, this had little good effect there.   The Board of Trade, after receiving a report from Governor Morris, sharply criticized the conduct of the Assembly.[18]   This however, made little impression on the Assembly which under Franklin's tutelage pictured the contest as a struggle to maintain the "Liberty and Rights" of the people.[19]

When the £5000 was voted in January for the Braddock expedition, the Assembly chose a committee, headed by Franklin, to supervise the spending of the money.   The commissioners acted with commendable

---

[13] *Votes,* V, 3771, 3795ff.

[14] *Ibid.,* V, 3768.

[15] *Ibid.,* V, 3841.

[16] *Votes,* V, 3874, 3894; Root, 200-201; In his message Morris gives the Royal Order as his reason for not allowing the bill. Morris said that he also objected violently to having the appropriation placed in the hands of Commissioners chosen by the House as called for in the bill. Morris Letter Book, 1719-1756, 74.

[17] *Ibid.,* V, 3877.

[18] Wolff, 168.

[19] Norris Letter Book, 1719-1756, 72-73.

speed in procuring provisions for Braddock's army, but when it came to building a road through the Pennsylvania back country to Fort Cumberland, they were accused of gross negligence and procrastination. Sir John St. Clair, Braddock's Quartermaster General, flew into a rage when he found in April that work on the road was not yet started. It should have been begun in January, he declared, on receipt of the first letter from the General. Troops must start moving toward the Ohio on May 1, and delay might well wreck the whole expedition and cost the lives of many men. If Pennsylvania did not act at once, he threatened to take the matter into his own hands and to impress men, horses, fodder, wagons, and provisions. He would then build the road and deliver the supplies to General Braddock.[20]

After another month, and not without some more irritating delay, the road was at last completed by the Pennsylvania authorities. Supplies reached Braddock at Fort Cumberland in June, after Franklin had persuaded Pennsylvania farmers to loan their teams and wagons for the service.[21] The latter was an accomplishment of no mean sort, as other commanders in America were to find. Although they received compensation at a fixed rate, the farmers apparently would about as soon part with their wives as with their horses and wagons. General Braddock, who had been led by St. Clair into thinking that Pennsylvania would do little toward helping the expedition, now was warm in his praise of the province he had so recently condemned.[22] In contrast to Pennsylvania, the much lauded colonies of Virginia and Maryland had grossly defaulted on their commitments to the Army.

Early in the year there was published a political pamphlet by the Reverend William Smith which provided an endless amount of controversy. Smith was an Anglican clergyman of Scotch descent who had but recently come to America. Recognizing his abilities, Franklin and others had him appointed Provost of the newly founded College of Philadelphia. It was soon apparent to everyone that Smith possessed a definite bias in favor of the Proprietors and the Crown. Not the kind to hide his light under a bushel, Smith in February, 1755, published his pamphlet entitled *A Brief State of the Province of Pennsylvania*. Fiercely attacking the Assembly and the Quakers, Smith declared that the province would not be safe so long as the Quaker party

---

[20] Shippen Papers, I, 177, HSP; *Col. Rec.*, VI, 365-369; Graeff, 81.

[21] Peters MSS., IV, 16.

[22] Norris Letter Book, 1719-1756, 78. While the preparations for Braddock's expedition were progressing, Philadelphia and New York merchants sold provisions to the French who were thereby able to supply their forces on the Ohio. No less than forty ships from the English colonies, it was reported, were at Louisburg during the summer of 1754. However reprehensible this may appear, it was entirely legal, as the two nations were still at peace and the trade in no way violated the Navigation Laws. Root, 76-77; *Col. Rec.*, VI, 323; The Official *Records of Robert Dinwiddie*, I, 473, 476.

controlled the legislature. The Assembly, Smith said, not only was factious and disrespectful to authority, but even had the temerity to exhibit an air of independence toward the mother country.[23]

Smith acknowledged that political considerations rather than pacifism motivated the Assembly. In regard to this, he wrote:

> Our Assemblies apprehend that as soon as they agree to give sufficient Sums for the regular Defense of the Country, it would strike at the Root of all their Power, as Quakers, by making a Militia-Law needful, in Time of Danger. Such a Law, they presume, would alter the whole Face of Affairs, by creating a vast Number of new Relations, Dependencies, and Subordinations in Government. The Militia, they suppose, would all vote for Members of the Assembly, and being dependent on their Officers, would probably be influenced by them. The officers, again as they imagine, would be influenced by the Government, and thus the Quakers fear they would soon be out-voted in most Places.[24]

This was true enough if it is understood that the strict pacifist Quakers were then in a minority in the Assembly and that the Quaker party, as now led by Franklin, was for defending the province as well as safeguarding the rights and interests of the people. Smith also recognized the popular nature of the Assembly and had much to say of the bad consequences of the growth of republican government in Pennsylvania.

Underestimating the effect which Smith's pamphlet would have, the Assembly at first paid little heed to it.[25] Fearing that the Assembly was assuming too much, Franklin advised making a response to it without delay. It was not long, therefore, before an answer was published. It has been generally thought that a man named Cross, a resident of London, was the author, who, after going into debt with the printer, was rescued by Dr. John Fothergill, the prominent Quaker physician.[26] According to William Franklin, however, the real author was Joseph Galloway, a rising young Philadelphia lawyer.[27] Certain it is that someone in Pennsylvania must have had a hand in writing it, as no Englishman was familiar enough with the intricacies of Pennsylvania politics to write a pamphlet on the subject.

The attack upon the Assembly and the Quakers, the *Answer* said, was motivated solely by political considerations. To gain their end, the complete command of government in Pennsylvania, the Governor

---

[23] After giving the *Brief State* careful reading, Thomas Penn reported that he did not consider the work one of high performance and rather feared that it would do more harm than good to the Proprietary interest. Wolff, 172-173.

[24] *Brief State*, 17-18.

[25] Norris Letter Book, 1719-1756, 71.

[26] Wolff, 175.

[27] Norris Letter Book, 1756-1766, 115.

and his party had blocked all measures for defense, and then cast the blame for this state of affairs upon the Quakers and the Assembly. Realizing that they could not achieve their political ambitions without first subverting the rights and privileges of the people, the Proprietary party was conspiring to destroy the liberties of the colony. The *Answer* charged, among other things, that they would bar the Quakers from holding political office and deprive the Germans of the franchise. Against such an attack upon the liberties of the people the author of the *Answer* spoke with the convictions of a Locke or a Milton. "But as I am a zealous advocate for liberty," he wrote, "and think it cannot be supported but on general principles, I should be for excluding no people from liberty of conscience in their civil rights, who should formally disclaim and renounce all such tenets as seemed inconsistent with the safety of government or good of society."[28]

The object in writing *Brief State* had been to foment sufficient resentment in England against the Quakers and Germans to cause Parliament to deprive them of their political rights. An article such as this could not in ordinary times hope to achieve such extreme action, but now with the war overtaking the Empire, it constituted a dangerous indictment of government and politics in Pennsylvania. Consequently the colonial agents, as well as prominent London Quakers and other friends of the Assembly, labored hard to remove the impressions created by it. By July, 1755, the *Pennsylvania Journal* could note that British anger against the colony was subsiding and that many people were beginning to blame Governor Morris for not approving the supply bills.[29]

Although the frontier of Pennsylvania lay exposed after Braddock's defeat in July, 1755, the peace of the province remained undisturbed until after the annual election in October.[30] Of little avail were the warnings by the Proprietary party that the security of the province was in danger. The Germans as usual gave their votes to the Quaker party: everywhere the old leaders were returned to the Assembly.

In describing the results of the election, Norris declared that it was almost absurd to call the opposition a party. "It is remarkable," Norris wrote, "that the Frontier county of Lancaster, composed of all sorts of Germans, & some Church of England Electors, have chosen all their Representatives out of ye Quakers, tho' there are scarcely one hundred of that Profession in the whole county, and they have made the Return

---

[28] *An Answer to an Invidious Pamphlet, Intitled, A Brief State of the Province of Pennsylvania* (London, 1755). Quotation from page 30.

[29] *Pa. Journal*, July 25, Sept. 25, 1755; Pemberton Papers, IX, 10, X, 137.

[30] When word of Braddock's defeat reached Philadelphia, it received but one small paragraph on the inner page, while news of Madrid, London, Boston, Halifax, Brest, Frankford, and Brussels, occupied the first page. *Pa. Journal*, July 24, 1755.

without the least solicitation on the part of the Present members."[31]
In Chester County, he noted, where the Presbyterians had begun "to
look upon themselves of considerable importance" the Quakers likewise won an easy victory.[32]

After Braddock's defeat the question of defense appropriations
assumed new importance. In July, immediately following this disaster,
the Assembly voted to raise for defense £50,000 in bills of credit to
be funded by a tax on all property including the Proprietary estates.[33]
The taxation of the property of the Penns was a subject upon which
political leaders in Pennsylvania had long speculated. In recent years,
in view of the mounting provincial expenses as well as the immense
profits of the Proprietors, agitation for the taxation of the Proprietary
increased noticeably.

The Proprietors were not caught unprepared when confronted with
a bill to tax their property. Acting upon instructions already in his
hands, Governor Morris refused to allow the measure without a clause
exempting the Proprietary estates. Thus was touched off a dispute
which for the next decade would be the cause of more bitterness and
contention than any other political issue of the day. In the Assembly,
Benjamin Franklin became the great champion of the people in their
struggle to get all property in the province taxed on an even basis.[34]

Upon receiving the Governor's objections to its tax bill, the Assembly
resolved that it was but "equitable and just" that the principal landowners of the province should bear their share of the cost of defense.
Morris replied that the Proprietors by the nature of their office could
not be taxed. "All Governors," he declared, "whether hereditary or
otherwise, are, from the Nature of their office, exempt from the Payment of Taxes; on the Contrary, Revenues are generally given to them
to support the Honour and Dignity of Government, and to enable them
to do the Duties of their Station."[35] This was, indeed, an extraordinary
interpretation of the rights of a governor. Isaac Norris thought the

---

[31] Norris Letter Book, 1719-1756, 70, 83; Pemberton Papers, XI, 9-10. It should
not be supposed that because religious groups tended to act together politically,
that there existed a great deal of ill-feeling between the members of different
denominations. Norris explained that: "We live in great charity for one another,
inter-mix in Conversation, in Trafick & all ye other affairs of Life, with great
friendship—when Jennings, or any other Silly Parson Preaches against ye Quakers,
or other Societies, they are only Condemned for it, by the far Greater Part of
their Congregations. To do them Justice, this is but Seldom done, after they
have made a Tryal or two." Norris Letter Book, 1719-1756, 70.

[32] Pemberton Papers, XI, 9½.

[33] *Votes*, V, 3932. There was no land tax in Pennsylvania before 1755. Thereafter
the cost of defense made the excise and the tavern taxes insufficient. *Pa. Mag.*
X, 285.

[34] Penn MSS. Off. Corresp., VII, 129.

[35] *Votes*, V, 3937-39.

pretensions of the Proprietors were fantastic, claiming privileges possessed only by the King of England.[36] Besides the unreasonableness of the claims of the Proprietors, their secret and countless instructions to their governors had the effect of constantly baiting the Assembly into acts of defiance.

From July to late September the Governor and the Assembly were deadlocked over the tax question. Upon adjourning, the Assembly cryptically addressed the Governor as follows: "We are now to take our Leave of the Governor, and indeed, since he hopes no Good from us, nor us from him 'tis Time we should be parted. If our Constituents disapprove our Conduct, a few Days will give them an Opportunity of changing us by a new Election; and could the Governor be as soon and as easily changed, Pennsylvania would, we apprehend, deserve much less the Character he gives it, of *an unfortunate Country.*"[37]

But the Assembly did not adjourn without raising some money for frontier defense. The Loan Office was able to scrape together another £1,000 with which arms were purchased and sent to western towns. Furthermore, Isaac Norris initiated a subscription for £10,000 for aiding Colonel Johnson in his attack on Crown Point. Norris, who was a Quaker, gave £700 which, he thought, was proof enough that the dispute with the Governor was founded entirely upon the principles of law and equity and was not merely a pacifist device to hamstring defense as the Proprietary partisans maintained.[38]

In October, with nearly all the same members back in their seats after the election, a debate arose in the Assembly whether or not there existed any real danger to the Pennsylvania frontier. While the Assembly discussed the question, Governor Morris, sensing an opportunity of embarrassing the legislature should war descend upon the province, held back alarming reports he had received from the frontier. This was going too far for Richard Peters, the Governor's secretary, who angrily wrote that "the lives of people were not to be plaid with nor thrown away because the two parts of the legislature differ." At least, he concluded, "I am determined not to be accessory to such a step."[39]

Peters apparently warned Norris that the Governor was holding back important information on the state of affairs among the Indians. Anyhow, the Assembly, which was on the point of adjourning until December, sent the Governor a special message asking if he had any further business to put before the House. Morris caustically replied

[36] Norris Letter Book, 1719-1756, 80.

[37] *Votes,* V, 4039.

[38] *Ibid.,* V, 4041, 4072-80; Norris Letter Book, 1719-1756, 84; Peters Letter Book, 1755-1757, 19.

[39] Weiser Corresp., I, 57. HSP.

"that if he had any Business to lay before the House, he should have done it before now" and that he could see no good reason why the Assembly should not adjourn."[40]

The Assembly had hardly taken its leave when Pennsylvania was thrown into an Indian war by an attack by the natives upon the isolated Penn's Creek settlement. A few days later the Indians struck the Great Cove in Cumberland County, burning and killing as they went.[41]

On receipt of the news the Assembly was at once recalled. Without delay the members resolved to strike £60,000 in bills of credit for defense. Like the former bill, the measure provided for the funding of the money by a tax on all property including the Proprietary estates.[42]

While the Assembly was preparing their supply, there was much speculation among the members as to why the Indians had chosen to attack Pennsylvania. The Quakers, especially, could not believe that the Indians had attacked the province without a cause. The Indians, they said, must be nursing some grievances against the colony. With this thought in mind, the Assembly, prodded by the pacifists, undertook a hasty investigation of Pennsylvania's Indian relations.

Reports were soon current in Philadelphia that the Indians were dissatisfied with land purchases, presumably the Albany purchase of 1754. Attention, too, was drawn to the fact that some of the Indians had suffered much at the hands of unscrupulous traders. The Assembly, therefore, prepared to write a bill for correcting these abuses. Peters was disgusted. How could anyone imagine that these Indians who had been scalping in Virginia all summer had turned against Pennsylvania because of wrongs committed?[43]

Governor Morris received the message relating to Indian grievances and the supply bill on the same day. On reading them, the Governor was seized with great rage. "You have been now sitting six Days," he told the Assembly, "and instead of strengthening my Hands, and providing for the Safety and Defense of the People and Province,— you have sent me a message wherein you talk of regaining the affections of the Indians now employed in laying waste the Country, and butchering the Inhabitants, and of enquiring what Injustice they have received." Furthermore, he said, it was madness for the Assembly to send him a money bill like the one he had refused to sign all through August and September. If the Assembly did not intend to do anything for the defense of the province, Morris declared, he would act alone. He was leaving for the West, he told the Assembly, "and if you shall

---

[40] Votes, V, 4091-92.
[41] Pa. Journal, Oct. 30, 1755.
[42] Votes, V. 4101-03.
[43] Peters Letter Book, 1755-1757, 8.

James Hamilton   William Denny
John Penn   Richard Penn

WILLIAM ALLEN   ISAAC NORRIS
WILLIAM SMITH   JOHN DICKINSON

have any Bills to propose that are consistent with the Duties of my Station, and the Rights of Government, I shall readily give my Assent to them."[44]

By November 10, the state of affairs on the frontier was approaching disastrous proportions, with mass hysteria and fright overspreading the countryside as whole sections were abandoned.[45] Still the Assembly, led by Franklin, refused to frame a bill exempting the Proprietary estates from taxation.[46] Morris finally offered to sign a bill taxing the Proprietors if the rates were set by commissioners appointed by the Governor with the advice and consent of the Assembly and not by assessors elected by the people as contained in the bill. The measure must also have a suspending clause relative to the provision for taxing the Proprietary estates whereby it could not be enforced until approved by the Crown. The Assembly, however, categorically resolved to "adhere to the said Bill."[47]

While the Governor and the Assembly fought doggedly over the tax question, remonstrances were poured upon the Assembly pleading that the dispute be terminated in view of the calamity overtaking the province.[48] Again the Proprietary leaders sent off to England petitions for restrictions against the Quakers and Germans.[49] But the Assembly would not budge from its position until word was received from the Proprietors that they were giving £5000 toward defending the colony.[50] The presence of several hundred enraged and threatening men from the frontier who had come to Philadelphia to protest the inaction of the government, was also a factor in causing the Assembly to forego taxing the Proprietors for the time being.[51] The Assembly made it plain, however, that this action in no way repudiated the right of the

---

[44] *Ibid.*, V, 4106; Penn MSS., Off. Corresp., VII, 151; Peters Letter Book, 1755-1757, 12.

[45] *Pa. Journal*, Nov. 6, 1755.

[46] The Assembly revised its original bill by a provision for a judgment from the King on the right of taxing the Proprietors.

[47] *Ibid.*, V, 4121; Norris Letter Book, 1719-1756, 89.

[48] *Votes*, V, 4151-53; *Pa. Journal*, Oct. 30, Nov. 6, 20, 1755. Peters wrote: "The Assembly rose in their demands as our distress increased." Peters Letter Book, 1755-1757, 18.

[49] Lewis B. Walker, *The Burd Papers: Extracts from Chief Justice William Allen's Letter Book*, 24-25. This is hereafter cited as *William Allen's Letter Book*.

[50] The gift of £5000 was estimated to be ten times as large as their tax would have been under the act. *Pa. Mag.* III, 24-25. However, the money had to be collected from arrears in quitrents, fees very hard to collect. A notice in the *Pa. Journal*, Feb. 12, 1756 asked the people to pay their back quitrents so that the Receiver-General could turn the money over to the province. As the £5000 was needed at once, Hamilton, Norris, Mifflin, Franklin, Fox, Morgan, and Hughes agreed to advance the money until the province could repay it. Peters Letter Book, 1755-1757, 18.

[51] Penn MSS. Off. Corresp., VII, 173. Peters said that the Westerners came to Philadelphia to make both sides agree. Peters Letter Book, 1755-1757, 18.

province to tax the Proprietors. "The Right of granting Supplies to
the Crown in this Province," it declared, "is alone in the Representatives of the Freemen met in Assembly, (this being essential to an
English Constitution)."[52] The Governor accepted the amended bill
which appropriated £60,000 for the King's use of which £55,000 would
be struck off in bills of credit. Richard Peters now admitted that
though the majority of the Assembly "have been stiff in opposition
against Propr. & Gov.—they are for defense."[53]

While the contest over the taxation of the Proprietary estates was
in progress, Franklin found time to prepare a "militia" bill for the
province.[54] Remembering the success of the Association in 1748, he
fashioned the measure along similar lines. Enlistment was voluntary,
the officers were chosen by the men, trial by jury was allowed offenders,
and guarantees were made that the men would not be used beyond the
inhabited parts of the province without their consent. This was the
only kind of law, he believed, that would work in a land where individ-
ualism and frontier democracy ran rampant.[55] The militia bill was
sent to the Governor after only four staunch Quakers voted against it.[56]

Although forced by the state of affairs to accept the militia law,
Governor Morris and his supporters only awaited the time when they
could replace it with a regular law. As Morris explained it, he had no
choice but to sign the bill or face the "Mob" which was moving upon
the city from the frontier.[57] Peters admitted that the people in general
were adverse to a regular militia and overwhelmingly in favor of Franklin's law.[58]

With the enactment of the supply and militia bills the political tension lessened considerably. Peters reported to Penn that the passage
of the laws had acted like a charm and attention could now be turned to
defending the colony.[59] But meanwhile morale in the West was fast
deteriorating. A committee at Reading addressed the following to the
Governor:

> We are all in an uproar, all in Disorder, all willing to do but
> have little in our power. We have no Authority, no Commis-
> sions, no Officers practiced in War, and without the Commis-
> eration of our Friends in Philadelphia, who think themselves
> vastly safer than they are. If we are not *immediately* sup-

[52] *Ibid.; Votes,* V, 4150, 4159.
[53] Peters Letter Book, 1755-1757, 18.
[54] *Votes,* V, 4130; *Pa. Journal,* Nov. 20, 1755.
[55] Smyth, III, 9-11.
[56] *Votes,* V, 4130; *Statutes,* V, 197-201.
[57] *Col. Rec.,* VI, 729-741; *Votes,* V, 4143; *William Allen's Letter Book,* 32.
[58] Peters Letter Book, 1755-1757, 10.
[59] *Ibid.,* 24.

ported, we must not be sacrificed and therefore, all determined to go down with those that will follow us to Philadelphia and quarter ourselves on its Inhabitants, and wait our Fate with them.[60]

William Allen believed that there were four thousand families living beyond the Susquehanna, most of whom were Scots Irish. If they were driven back across the river among the Germans and others, he declared, "there will be next to a Civil War among them."[61] At best, the prospect of thousands of settlers being driven from their homes by the Indians was not a pleasant one to contemplate. Fortunately, the situation improved in a few weeks as help arrived and the people regained assurance.

The year 1755 was most significant in the political history of Pennsylvania. That year the old pacifist power crumbled before the rising tide of French expansion in the Ohio Valley. At the same time the Quaker party came under the spell of Benjamin Franklin who projected a popular program for Pennsylvania which was to direct the course of Pennsylvania politics for the next ten years. Eventually Pennsylvania democracy broke the power of the Proprietors. In the following decade it went on to achieve independence and to provide for the State a democratic constitution.

---

[60] Horsefield Papers, I, 31, APS; Peters Letter Book, 1755-1757, 19; *Pa. Journal,* Dec. 18, 25, 1755, Jan. 1, 8, 1756.

[61] *William Allen's Letter Book,* 25.

V

FRANKLIN THE TRIBUNE. 1756-1757

THERE MAY BE some significance in the fact that the first Indian raid on Pennsylvania occurred against the Penn Creek settlement. This region was part of the land purchased from the Six Nations in 1754 without consulting the Delawares and Shawnees who occupied it. The Pennsylvania authorities did not feel obliged to treat with the occupants of the land who were tributaries to the Six Nations.

Pennsylvania started the practice of conducting business with the Pennsylvania Indians through the councils of the Six Nations early in the Eighteenth Century. When the Delaware lands on the Lehigh were taken over by the "Walking Purchase" in 1737, the Six Nations were called upon to officiate at the meeting held in 1742 with the Indians. As the Delawares showed a reluctance to leave their homes, the Mohawks ordered them to move to the Wyoming Valley. The Delawares had no recourse but to obey. In 1749 the Penns purchased directly from the Six Nations a great tract of land east of the Susquehanna. Five years later the Proprietors bought from them an immense tract to the west of the river.

The last purchase was occasioned by the fact that there was comparatively little good land in the purchase of 1749, the area which included the Poconos and adjacent mountain regions. The line of march of the settlers was generally west and not north as settlers pushed into the Juniata Valley and westward toward the Allegheny and Ohio. In 1749 Peters reported to the Proprietors:

> Now there is peace numbers are going over the hills to settle in the lands at Juniata, & all along the road to Allegheny, & tho' the sheriff & four of the most prudent & intrepid magistrates will be sent to remove them, yet I cannot promise that it will be in the power of the government to prevent these mutinous spirits from settling those lands.[1]

Three years later, with hundreds of settlers moving to Virginia and the Carolinas for want of available land in Pennsylvania, Peters declared that "a new Purchase is absolutely necessary."[2]

An opportunity for making a new purchase from the Six Nations presented itself in 1754 when the Board of Trade called a meeting with these Indians at Albany for the purpose of reaffirming the friend-

---

[1] Peters to Proprietors, April 29, 1749, Peters Letter Book, 1737-1750.
[2] Penn MSS., Off. Corresp., V, 219.

ship with them. At this meeting the Pennsylvania agents, Richard Peters and John Penn, purchased most of western Pennsylvania for two thousand pieces of eight. This was done with the approval of William Johnson, the Mohawk Valley squire. The sale did not include the Wyoming Valley, which the Indians promised would not be sold to anyone but Pennsylvania.[3]

This purchase was as fairly made as was customary in business transactions with the Indians. Nevertheless, many of the Six Nation Indians, especially those not present at the meeting, soon voiced their displeasure. They complained that the purchase had not been consummated in full council at Onondaga, or by delegated chiefs, as was required by tribal custom. But it was by the Ohio Indians, who were experiencing the pressure of the onward march of the frontier, that the sale was most resented.

Pennsylvania officials first became aware of the displeasure of the Ohio Indians (Delawares, Shawnees, Wyandots, and emigrant Six Nations Indians) when Conrad Weiser met some of them in August, 1754, at Aughwick, George Croghan's headquarters on the Pennsylvania frontier.[4] In February, 1755, Thomas Penn told Peters that he was sorry to hear that the Ohio Indians had disputed the sale of the Six Nations. Without taking into consideration the delicate nature of Indian relations at this time, Penn contemptuously brushed aside the complaint of the Ohio Indians. "If they are any way troublesome," he advised Peters, "complain to the Six Nations of them, who will make them quiet as they formerly did the Delawares."[5]

George Croghan, Peter Wraxall, William Johnson, Edward Shippen, and many others corroborated Weiser's report that the Indians on the Ohio were exasperated by the Albany purchase.[6] Robert Hunter Morris, relying upon reports from the frontier, in November, 1755, made the following statement regarding the cause of the Indian war.

> It seems clear from the different accounts I have received that the French have gained to their Interest the Delawares and Shawanese Indians under the ensnaring pretense of restoring them to their Country, their intimate knowledge of which will make them dangerous Enemies of the Colonys in general, and to this in particular.[7]

---

[3] Weiser to Peters, Feb. 7, 1754, Miscel. MSS., Berks & Montgomery counties. HSP. The same year, 1754, unmindful of the promise to Pennsylvania, a party of Mohawks and others of the Six Nations sold the Wyoming Valley to a Connecticut land company.

[4] Graeff, 99.

[5] Peters MSS., IV, 4.

[6] *Documents Relative to the Colonial History of the State of New York*, VII, 18, 130, 169-170, 276, 323, 329-333; Shippen Papers, IV, 211. HSP; Bailey, 116.

[7] *Col. Rec.*, VI, 670-672; Penn MSS., Off. Corresp., IX, 51.

At a treaty with the Six Nations in July, 1755, the Indians served notice on William Johnson that they wished to recall that part of the Albany purchase for which payment had not been received.[8] Johnson obligingly transmitted their request to the Board of Trade. The purchase, he said, was regular enough but it would seem best for the Proprietors to release the land in view of the critical state of Indian affairs. The Board of Trade, acting upon Johnson's advice, eventually obtained Thomas Penn's consent to have the land restored to the Indians.[9]

After the Ohio Indians had begun their attacks upon the Pennsylvania frontier, a few natives who had attached themselves to the English outposts came to Philadelphia and offered to help fight the enemy. Scarroyady, the faithful Oneida, who served as a sort of superintendent for the Six Nations over the Pennsylvania and Ohio Indians, said that there were still about three hundred warriors living along the Susquehanna Valley who would join the English if given arms and proper encouragement. The chief even offered to have the Indian wives and children placed with the English as hostages if there was any doubt of their sincerity.[10]

Governor Morris and the Council desired to accept Scarroyady's offer. But with no funds at their disposal and with the Governor still deadlocked with the Assembly over the terms of the £60,000 appropriation, they were compelled to decline his offer.[11] The Assembly was unwilling to offer assistance, partly out of consideration for the pacifist minority that persisted in the hope that the Susquehanna Delawares would not make war on Pennsylvania and partly because of the belief that the proximity of the Six Nations would keep these Indians in check. In any event, here was a serious act of omission on the part of all concerned, the gravity of which was learned a few weeks later when the Delawares, led by Teedyuscung, launched the fiercest attacks of the whole war against settlements along the northern frontier of Pennsylvania.

During the winter of 1755-1756, Pennsylvania built a line of forts on the frontier studding the Blue Mountains from Fort Hamilton near the Delaware Water Gap to the Maryland border. But the Indian raids continued in spite of all precautions, and sentiment was rapidly devel-

---

[8] *Johnson Papers*, IX, 199-200.

[9] Julian P. Boyd, ed., *Indian Treaties Printed by Benjamin Franklin, 1736-1762*, LXXXIV; *Documents Relative to the Colonial History of the State of New York*, VII, 329, 388-389; Thayer, 169.

[10] Penn MSS., Indian Affairs, 1757-1772, 66; *Votes*, V, 4107-09; Peters Letter Book, 1755-1757, 12.

[11] Weiser Corresp., I, 59.

oping in favor of direct attacks upon the Indian villages.[12] Finally, early in the spring, with the menace of the savages daily increasing, Governor Morris promulgated a declaration of war against the Delaware Indians, placed a bounty on their scalps, and made plans for building a fort at Shamokin (now Sunbury) at the forks of the Susquehanna, from which expeditions could be launched against the enemy.[13]

The announcement of this hard-fisted program brought forth a vigorous protest from a group of Quaker idealists who were convinced that the Indians would make peace if only their grievances were satisfied. Their leader, Israel Pemberton, soon found an occasion to propose a message of peace to the Susquehanna Delawares. Believing that nothing would come of it, Governor Morris signified his willingness to have the Quakers send their message of peace. Then he abruptly changed his mind upon learning that Johnson, working through the Six Nations, was expecting to bring the Delawares to terms. Morris now decided to send a message in his own name and thus reap for himself the credit for restoring peace.

Not at all sure but that an appeal from the Quakers would inspire confidence among the Indians, Morris consented to have it mentioned to the Delawares that the descendants of the first settlers who came over with William Penn would willingly act as mediators. When the messengers returned, they brought word that the Delawares would cease fighting and make peace.[14]

In all probability the Delawares were constrained to accept the Pennsylvania offer on hearing that otherwise the Governor planned to invade the Indian country in force and destroy them. There was also the possibility that the Mohawks who had ordered them to make peace would come against them from the north. Perhaps, however, fear was less a factor than want as the Delawares were now quite destitute of both food and clothing by being cut off from their customary sources of supply.[15]

It was not until July that it was reported in Philadelphia that Teedyuscung and his band of warriors were waiting for the Governor near Easton. After some procrastination as was his way, Morris met the Indians. A truce was declared and plans were made for Teedyuscung to bring in the principal men of all the neighboring tribes to make a general peace with the natives. More than a score of Quakers, led by Israel Pemberton, were active at the meeting and ever watchful

---

[12] Thayer, 95-96.

[13] Norris Letter Book, 1719-1756, 97; *Votes*, V, 4225.

[14] *Ibid.*, 98-105.

[15] *Pa. Journal*, June 15, 1756. The Delawares could not hunt as they were out of powder and lead and none could be procured from Canada, where military stores were very low owing to the watchfulness of the British Navy.

that the rights of the Indians were observed. Presents from both the Government and the Quakers climaxed the affair which was apparently a success.[16]

Yet it may be doubted if many of Teedyuscung's warriors went away with any serious intention of keeping the peace. During the summer it was reported that some of these Indians were again terrorizing the frontier. But the Indian bravado was given a severe clipping in September when Colonel John Armstrong successfully attacked a Delaware stronghold at Kittanning on the Allegheny and inflicted great losses. This blow may well be the main reason why Teedyuscung kept his promise and reappeared at Easton in October.

As at the previous meeting, a great number of Quakers attended fully prepared to take an important part in the proceedings. Under the leadership of Israel Pemberton they had formed an association dedicated to restoring peace with the Indians. The Quakers were now fully convinced that the Indians had gone to war because of wrongs committed by the Proprietors and their agents. It was also clear to them that if this could be confirmed by the Indians, the Quakers would be cleared of the charge of having brought on the war by leaving the province unprepared and defenseless in an extremely critical time.

There can be little doubt but that Teedyuscung had at times heard the Minisink Delawares complain of the way the Lehigh Valley had been taken from them by the Proprietors. But the fact is that he had not mentioned or even hinted at the previous meeting that grievances against the English had caused the Indians to take up the hatchet. Rather he had merely blamed the French for inciting them to make war for the sake of plunder and scalps. This time, however, from the start, Teedyuscung was full of talk of serious offenses committed by the Proprietors.

Richard Peters was certain that the Quakers were the authors of Teedyuscung's charges. They had come to Easton, declared Peters, with this purpose in mind. Peters vainly tried to have the Quakers muzzled but it was useless. Israel Pemberton and Teedyuscung were seen earnestly talking together on many occasions, and the latter was a frequent visitor to Israel's lodging house.

Governor William Denny, who had succeeded Robert Hunter Morris in August, insisted that Teedyuscung be given an opportunity to freely speak his mind. Thereupon, Teedyuscung in full council charged the Proprietors with defrauding the Delawares in the Walking Purchase. This grievance, long nursed by the Indians, had made the blow fall harder, he said, when the Delawares decided to attack the English. He truthfully added that none of his band, consisting mostly of remnants of

---

[16] Thayer, 97-112.

the New Jersey Delawares, had any claim upon the land in question. In order, therefore, to make a firm peace it would be necessary, he said, to bring in the Minisinks to treat with the Governor.[17]

Nine months went by before Teedyuscung returned to Easton to ratify the peace with Pennsylvania. This time instead of bringing the Minisink Delawares with him, he brought along a band of Senecas. The Minisinks, it would seem, preferred to remain at war with the English and be free to pilfer the cabins of settlers along the border. The Senecas, who had provided the Delawares with moral support at least in their war on the English, came along to share in the presents and drink the fire water which would be provided them.

"Honest John" Teedyuscung with an abundance of advice from the Quakers proceeded when the meeting opened to order a showing of the deeds for the purchase of the Lehigh land, known as the Walking Purchase. The proprietary men did all in their power to frustrate the designs of the Quakers, but in spite of all, Israel Pemberton and his Association carried every point. Peace was confirmed with the Delawares on the promise that the dispute over the Walking Purchase would be sent to England for adjudication. This constituted a great political achievement for the Quakers and the Assembly. Benjamin Franklin could now go to England armed with a charge of a scandalous fraud committed by the Proprietors upon innocent and long-suffering natives.[18]

Not all the political history of 1756 and 1757 was being made at the Indian conferences. As would be expected, the enemies of Franklin stepped up their campaign in England to have the Quakers and Germans deprived of their political privileges. In March, 1756, after receiving petitions signed and endorsed by William Allen "for the Inhabitants in General against their Quaker Assembly," the Board of Trade made a report to the Privy Council picturing the Pennsylvania Assembly as a body controlled by pacifists from whom no effective military measures could be expected. "There is no reason to hope that proper or effectual measures will be taken," the paper stated, "while the Majority of the Assembly consists of Persons whose avow'd principles are against Military Services."[19]

Particular pains were taken by the Board of Trade to denounce Franklin's militia law which was, it said, in "every respect the most improper and inadequate to the Service which cou'd have been framed and passed." Letters from Pennsylvania supported this conclusion. Peters wrote that "All concern'd in the Government are Novices, know

---

[17] Ibid., 123-131; Wallace, 459ff.
[18] Thayer, 132-149; Boyd, Indian Treaties, XXVIII.
[19] Col. Rec., VII, 275; Pa. Mag., X, 294.

nothing of military matters, have a rude, insolent & ungovernable People to deal with, averse to discipline, & thro long Ease & Freedom timid as Slaves, & noisy as Bullies." The officers of the militia, he said, "were generally men of no character, & elected on their own solicitation by some of the meanest of their neighbors, & this done, too, in hopes of being taken into pay."[20] Hamilton agreed. Pennsylvanians, he said, needed to be under the strict discipline of a real military code because of the "disoluteness & libertinism of the people."[21]

Charges against Franklin's militia law did not go unanswered. Philadelphia alone, it was pointed out, had a regiment of one thousand men who had been trained to man the fifty cannon which guarded the city. In the counties the militia was affording the people protection, they maintained, and dampening the ardor of the Indians.[22]

Hoping to undermine the people's confidence in Franklin and the militia, the Allen party early in 1756 organized a military association of its own. This was done, they said, in an attempt to try to make up for the deficiences of the popular militia.[23] Surprisingly enough, their organization was in most particulars very similar to Franklin's Association, condemned by them in 1748. Actually, therefore, it was not unlike the existing militia. The Allen party, however, maintained that their organization was but a stop-gap to be used until a real militia act was passed.[24]

In England Thomas Penn, with the aid of his lawyer, Ferdinand Paris, lobbied against the militia law and saw to it that the petitions against the Assembly were widely circulated.[25] In July the Privy Council disallowed the act as being unconstitutional.

After the disallowance of the militia law, the colony depended entirely upon provincial troops, a regularly enlisted corps raised by the Assembly.[26] Since the number which could be recruited and supported in this way was limited, the militia question was not ended. In June, 1757, Governor Denny complained that the militia bill proposed by the Assembly that year was "even more anti-constitutional than that which was repealed by the King."[27] Thomas Penn's comment was that Pennsylvania was still infested with republican ideas which he attrib-

[20] Peters Letter Book, 1755-1757, 22, 27.

[21] Ibid., 27, 110.

[22] Pa. Journal, March 4, 1756.

[23] Pa. Journal, March 25, April 15, 1756.

[24] Ibid., March 11, 1756.

[25] Thomas Penn to James Hamilton, Jan. 27, 1756, Penn-Hamilton Corresp. HSP; Pa. Gazette, May 20, 1756; Pa. Journal, May 13, 1756.

[26] Franklin to Peter Collinson, Dec. 19, 1756, Photostats J. P. Morgan Lib., L. of C.

[27] Col. Rec., VII, 574.

uted in no small part to the influence of Benjamin Franklin.[28] Be that as it may, the Assembly would not make a real militia law, and throughout the remainder of the colonial period the province was without any militia whatever.

At the time the militia act was invalidated, the Privy Council was also considering prohibiting the Quakers holding office during a war. Upon hearing this, London Quakers, of whom Dr. John Fothergill was most influential, became greatly alarmed for the fate of their brethren in Pennsylvania. The Privy Council preferred, however, if possible, to avoid Parliamentary intervention in colonial affairs. An understanding was therefore reached between Lord Granville, President of the Council, and Dr. Fothergill, whereby the former promised to use his influence in preventing Parliamentary action and the latter agreed to ask the Pennsylvania Quakers to voluntarily withdraw from the Assembly.

In Philadelphia, the Pembertons and other leading Friends pledged their support of the plan. In order to signify their sincerity and readiness to comply, James Pemberton and five others resigned at once. These men had consistently voted against all defense measures since the outbreak of the war. No one was more pleased to see them go than Benjamin Franklin. "All the stiff rump except one that would be suspected of opposing the service from religious motives, have voluntarily quitted the Assembly," he wrote to Peter Collinson.[29]

It was soon understood within the Quaker party that all the seats vacated by the Quakers would be filled by certain Anglicans who were staunch supporters of Franklin and his policies. As Peters said, those elected would "be just such as the Quakers and Mr. Frankland pleases to recommend."[30] His prediction was true enough. Thomas Leech and Daniel Roberdeau, the "most violent partisans and creatures of Franklin's that could have been chosen" were elected for the County of Philadelphia. The city chose Col. William Masters "another minion" and close friend of Benjamin Franklin.[31]

In July it was reported that Franklin had gained another political victory by the appointment of Thomas Pownall—a man of considerable influence in England and a personal friend of Franklin—as Lieutenant-Governor of Pennsylvania. Pownall was wished upon the reluctant Penns by the ministry, more concerned with imperial considerations than with the interests of the Proprietors. Pownall was known to favor

---

[28] Stanley M. Pargellis, *Military Affairs in Northern America, 1748-1765*, 384-385.

[29] Franklin to Collinson, June 15, 1756, University MSS., U. of Pa.

[30] Peters Letter Book, 1755-1757, 54.

[31] *Ibid.*, 63, 75-76. Many of the strict Quakers such as Israel Pemberton although opposed to Franklin's policies either voted for his candidates in the hope that they would be moderate and not pass offensive military measures or refrained from voting at all. See Peters Letter Book, 1755-1757, 56-57.

the sole determination by the Assembly of the terms and amounts of all appropriations. Apparently, too, he favored the taxation of the Proprietary estates. He enjoyed a great following among the Quakers as well as among all others in the province, and would, to all appearances, be the kind of governor Pennsylvania had always wanted but never had had.[32]

But Pennsylvanians were soon disappointed to learn that Pownall had refused the position when he found that the Proprietors were as determined as ever to bind him with minute and rigid instructions. Franklin, who voiced the general sentiment in Pennsylvania, declared that Pownall was too honest a man to become the tool of the Proprietors. Pownall himself explained that his refusal was due to his being so bound by instructions that he could not act impartially.[33]

Nearly everyone, however, was hoping that Robert Hunter Morris would not have to be endured much longer. Morris had proved irritable and contentious, unsteady in his policies, and inclined to procrastinate in his duties while he pursued the pastimes which he enjoyed. Much business which rightfully belonged to him fell upon the shoulders of Richard Peters, the Secretary for the Council. With good reason, Peters complained that "my life has been a constant Slavery in being obliged to give such an assiduous attention for fear of some sudden rash Resolves or answers that he is but to apt to make."[34] In his strict obedience to Proprietary instructions, Morris displayed an arrogance infuriating to the people of Pennsylvania.[35] When he left after serving less than two years, Franklin declared that he was the "rashest and most indiscreet Governor" the province had ever known.[36]

Colonel William Denny, who became the Lieutenant-Governor of Pennsylvania in August, 1756, was a stranger to the people in the colony. Forty-seven years of age, a graduate of Oxford, and a former army officer, he seemed a good man for the position. But from the start Denny proved that he had not the qualities for his difficult post. Soon after his arrival, being anxious to please, he naïvely showed his instructions to the House. As a result the Assembly offered him an appropriation bill in direct contradiction to the terms of his instructions.[37] Sensitive and refined in manner, Denny was appalled by the action of the House. But the Assembly, in complete disregard for his

[32] *Ibid.*, 54.

[33] *Pa. Mag.*, XIII, 441; *Pa. Journal*, July 15, 1756.

[34] Peters to John Waddell, Aug. 23-26, 1756, Wharton Letter Book, 1752-1757. HSP.

[35] Peters Letter Book, 1755-1757, 56.

[36] Corresp. of the Penn Family, 1732-1767, 73. HSP.; Smyth, *The Writings of Benjamin Franklin*, III, 276.

[37] Thomas W. Balch, ed., *Letters and Papers Relating Chiefly to the Provincial History of Pennsylvania* (Shippen Family), 63; *Votes*, V, 4298-4306.

feelings, made known that unless "they have their excise bill as usual and a tax on the Proprietary estate, they will grant no supplys let the consequence be never so fatal."[38]   This answer was given when the public money was exhausted and the security of the province endangered.

Before another month had passed, Governor Denny was well initiated into Pennsylvania politics.   In September, he was aroused to the point of threatening to have Franklin removed as head of the colonial Post-Office if he did not slacken in his demands.[39]

Notwithstanding his display of firmness, Denny was persuaded in September to sign a bill for striking £30,000 in paper money with terms contrary to his instructions.   Hamilton and a majority of the Council had, in fact, advised him to sign the bill in view of the pressing needs of the province.[40]

Denny's showing of his instructions to the Assembly proved to be a serious blunder in more than one way.   Coming not long before the annual election, it afforded the Quaker Party with no end of political fuel to use against the Proprietary supporters.   Peters was speaking conservatively when he said that the knowledge of the Governor's instructions had "done great injury to the cause and to the ensuing elections."[41]

Realizing their weakness, the Proprietary party asked Franklin to back a union ticket for Philadelphia in view of the dangers confronting the Colony.[42]   Franklin agreed, knowing full well he could control the Assembly in any event.   But regardless of what Franklin thought, the Quakers would not support the ticket and all of the Proprietary candidates were defeated.   In their places the Quakers elected four candidates of their own, one of whom was Joseph Galloway, soon to become a top man in the Quaker party.

Although the leaders of the Society of Friends kept their promise to their London friends and supported only men outside of the Quaker fold for the Assembly, sixteen Quakers were re-elected.   Four of them

[38] Peters Letter Book, 1755-1757, 79; *Votes,* V, 4308ff.

[39] Peters Letter Book, 1755-1757, 90. Thomas Penn was sounding out the ministry at this time in view of getting Franklin removed from the Post-Office. Thomas Penn to Richard Peters, Feb. 14, 1756, Penn Papers (Exclusive of William Penn, the Founder, Transferred from Soc. Miscel. Coll.). HSP.

[40] Peters Letter Book, 1755-1757, 90-91; *Votes,* V, 4330.

[41] Peters Letter Book, 1755-1757, 91.

[42] The candidates for the Quaker party were Isaac Norris, John Hughes, Daniel Roberdeau, and Joseph Fox. Those for the Proprietary party were Jacob Duché, William Coleman, Phineas Bond and Henry Pawling. The latter were moderate supporters of the Proprietary party. As usual the Allen faction was hopeful of splitting the German vote. Some had hopes also of winning over part of the militia as well as the votes of the mechanics of Philadelphia, Peters Letter Book, 1755-1757, 81-91; Balch, 64; *Votes,* VI, 4383; Balch Papers, Shippen I, 48.

who may not have sought re-election resigned at once. Most, if not all, of the twelve remaining were but nominal Quakers and were as ready as any in the Assembly to support military measures. Isaac Norris who had all along stood shoulder to shoulder with Franklin on defense was the first to be asked to resign. His refusal, of course, set a precedent for the others to follow.

John Smith, the Burlington Quaker, said that the election showed that the people were overwhelmingly behind Franklin and his policies. In particular, he said, it showed their hearty support of the movement to tax the Proprietors and thereby relieve the burden on the people. Not long after Franklin summed up the case against the Proprietors when he said: "Much has the Province suffer'd by this War, some hundreds of Lives lost, many Farms destroy'd, and near £100,000 spent, yet the Proprietor refuses to be taxed, except for a trifling Part of his Estate."[43]

It did Thomas Penn no good to call this the result of "leveling principles," nor for James Hamilton to say that the people of Pennsylvania were possessed with "a mobbish and seditious temper, arising from an excess of liberty."[44] Other observers saw the situation in a different light and recognized the democratic nature of the movement. "The people of this Province," wrote the Rev. Jacob Duché, "are generally of the middling sort, and at present pretty much upon the Level. They are industrious Farmers, Artificers, or Men of Trade; they enjoy and are fond of Freedom, and the *meanest among them* thinks he has a Right to Civility from the greatest."[45]

The new Assembly in December, 1756, presented the Governor with a bill for £100,000 to be raised by a tax on all estates, including those of the Proprietors. The tax, Franklin admitted, would fall heavily upon everyone, but it was absolutely necessary in view of the critical state of the war.[46] Pennsylvania would much prefer to raise funds by issuing bills of credit, he explained, but English opposition to it made direct taxation the only alternative.

Acting in accordance with his instructions calling for tax exemption on all Proprietary quitrents, located unimproved lands, and purchase money at interest, Denny refused the bill. The House, instead of yielding at once, resolved to send Franklin to England to lay the whole matter before the Privy Council.[47] "Heaven and earth," warned William Allen, would now be moved against the Proprietors in London.[48]

---

[43] Franklin to Collinson, Nov. 22, 1756, Photostats, J. P. Morgan Lib., L. of C.
[44] Penn Letter Book, IV, 350-351. HSP; Penn MSS., Add. Miscel. Letters, I, 79.
[45] *Pa. Journal*, March 25, 1756.
[46] Letters from B. Franklin, XLV, 12, APS.; *Votes*, VI, 4459, 4476.
[47] *Col. Rec.*, VII, 401-402; Peters Letter Book, 1755-1757, 133-134; Norris to R. Charles, Jan. 31, 1757, Norris Letter Book, 1756-1766.
[48] Peters Letter Book, 1755-1757, 133.

After attending to this, a new bill for £100,000 was prepared exempting the Proprietors from taxation in order to avoid further delay. But it ran afoul of instructions as to details in the manner of making the appropriation and was refused by the Governor. A third bi'l probably would have met the same fate in March had not Lord Loudoun intervened. Loudoun, commander-in-chief of the British forces in America, advised Denny to sign the bill, regardless of what the Penns might think. Denny obeyed.[49]

While the controversy over taxation was in progress, a heated debate arose over the question of quartering the Royal American regiment under Col. Henry Bouquet. The Assembly had passed an act like the one in England preventing the quartering of troops in private homes. Denny had signed the act while expressing some misgivings as to the ability of the public houses in Philadelphia to meet the needs of the Army. In December, with men on the point of freezing in makeshift quarters, Bouquet persuaded Denny to sign a warrant for the use of private homes until such time as the Assembly provided other quarters.[50]

Within a matter of hours after the warrant was issued, everyone in Philadelphia knew that the Governor had authorized the use of private homes for quartering. Immediately the whole city was in an uproar. At once the Assembly appointed a committee headed by Franklin to investigate the matter. In a violent argument with the Governor which followed, Franklin insulted Denny while accusing him of violating the rights of the people.[51] Hearing of the dispute, Lord Loudoun offered to send another battalion to Philadelphia to enable Bouquet to force his will on the inhabitants.

Loudoun's threat apparently had its effect, for not long after the Assembly found means to appropriate the newly constructed Pennsylvania Hospital for the use of the regiment. In the next year the Assembly built barracks as promised.[52] After the dispute had ended, Bouquet cogently observed that had he gone directly to Franklin instead of the Governor there would have been no trouble. Peters agreed. "This is actually all he [Franklin] aims at," wrote Peters, "and the Governor should really insist on everything going thro' his hands."[53]

Ever since the war began the Assembly had been trying to enact a law for regulating the Indian trade. Morris had refused to sign the

---

[49] Votes, VI, 450ff.
[50] Ibid., VI, 4461ff.
[51] Penn MSS., Add. Miscel. Letters, I, 99; Pargellis, Military Affairs, 369.
[52] Pargellis, Lord Loudoun in North America, 202.
[53] Peters Letter Book, 1755-1757, 127.

bills presented him because the House had virtually divested the Governor of any part in the administration of the law.[54] Such a law would go far in making it possible for the Assembly to control Indian affairs in general—a design of long standing among the leaders of the House.

As the months passed without a law for the Indian trade, the need for one steadily increased. Military officers, on the frontier, like Col. Hugh Mercer were insistent upon the great need for trading posts to draw the Indians into the orbit of the British.[55]

Franklin blamed the Proprietors entirely for the failure to meet the needs of the Indians. He was sorry, he wrote in 1757, that the bill was lost again, but it was of some advantage, he thought, in that the "Iniquitous Views of the Proprs—were so clearly discover'd." "The same spirit that makes them so ardently aim at the disposition of Money not their own," he continued, "is the same that inclined lesser Knaves to rob and pick Pockets. They seem to have no regard for the Publick Welfare, so the private Point may be gained. 'Tis like Firing a House to have an opportunity of stealing a Trencher."[56]

After another attempt to pass an Indian Trade bill failed in November, 1757, the Assembly managed to appropriate £1,000 to buy Indian goods for Fort Augusta at the forks of the Susquehanna. This action was taken in response to letters from army officers citing the urgent need of goods to help induce the Indians to leave the French.[57]

In the spring of 1758 the Assembly prepared another Indian trade bill, whereupon Governor Denny and the House fought for two months over who should be named in the bill for commissioners. Finally, in April, Denny gave in and allowed the House to name the commissioners, provided none of them were members of the Assembly. As a result, the majority were influential Quakers chosen from those who were strong supporters of the Franklin party.[58]

The Indian Trade Act provided for the establishment of provincial stores which would sell goods to the Indians at reasonable prices. It was hoped that this would keep the private traders in line and prevent them from robbing the natives. The act forbade the sale of liquor to Indians altogether.[59]

---

[54] *Ibid.*, 13.

[55] *Ibid.*, 39; Norris Letter Book, 1719-1756, 97; *Col. Rec.*, VIII, 305; *Votes*, VI, 4558.

[56] Franklin Coll., MSS. No. 205. Yale U.

[57] Indians coming to Ft. Augusta complained of being cheated by the private traders in the price paid for their furs. Shippen Papers, III, 59. HSP.

[58] *Col. Rec.*, VIII, 19, 22-25, 29, 50, 68, 71, 74, 77; *Statutes*, V, 320-330; Peters MSS., IV, 91; Penn MSS., Off Corresp., IX, 11.

[59] Norris Letter Book, 1719-1756, 87. Croghan wrote Johnson, Jan. 30, 1759, that "The People of this Province are all running wild after the Indian Trade." *Johnson Papers*, X, 91.

Franklin, who was now in England, found the ministry critical of the act, which was considered a kind of state monopoly. Franklin succeeded in lessening this opinion by pointing out that abuses practiced on the Indians by private traders often led to Indian wars. The public which must suffer and pay the costs of wars brought on by the traders, he said, had the right to regulate the trade in the interest of the common welfare. Furthermore, he shrewdly reminded the Board of Trade that by removing the rum trade, the sale of English manufactures to the Indians would be greatly increased.[60]

During the long dispute over the Indian trade bill, Governor Denny sharply criticized the Assembly for its "Thirst of Power and Fondness to Monopolize all Offices of Trust and Profit."[61]   Although there was much truth in what Denny said, the Assembly was fighting the people's battle against Thomas Penn who was determined to make himself master of the Pennsylvania government. The Reverend Jacob Duché summed up the political strategy of Thomas Penn as follows:

1. To have the negative in all appointments of the Assembly.
2. To establish offices of profit filled by the governor.
3. To increase the fees of all such offices so as to make them more attractive.
4. To establish a militia with appointment of officers by the governor alone.
5. To have a larger appointive council to be constituted as an upper legislative chamber.
6. To have control over the sitting of the Assembly by the power to prorogue or dissolve it at any time.

Some Proprietary partisans, Duché believed, supported this program out of the conviction that the executive arm of the government was too weak in Pennsylvania. Others, he thought, were prompted by personal interests—some perhaps by a combination of interest and conviction. "They say they have studied Politicks in learned Authors," Duché wrote, "and are convinc'd that our Constitution is defective in those Particulars: that the People have too much Power, the Governor too little, hence the lower Sort are not respectful enough to the better Sort, hence the Laws are Lax, and the Execution of them more so." The disposition of public offices they believed was an "inherent Right of the Governor"; and the people were "not fit to be trusted with any Share in it." Balloting, the gentlemen thought, should not be secret so that they could influence the electors in the interest of "better government." An appointed upper house with

---

[60] Franklin Coll., MSS., No. 223. Yale U.
[61] Votes, VI, 4650-51.

legislative powers, they were sure, would put the brakes on the Assembly, imbued as it was with leveling principles.[62]

Against these ideas, Duché said, stood the mass of the people in Pennsylvania who "dread the Growth of Proprietary Power."[63] Indeed sentiment as to the desirability of getting to the root of the trouble by removing the Proprietors was growing. Benjamin Franklin, everyone knew, would do all he could to effect an early removal of the Penns. Isaac Norris, too, seemed in full agreement with Franklin.[64]

In England, Franklin early explored the possibilities of converting Pennsylvania into a Royal province. Richard Jackson, a prominent London attorney, assured him that the change could be made and at the same time retain the constitutional privileges enjoyed by Pennsylvania. As Franklin studied British politics, he became convinced that the change could be made in a reasonably short time if the people of Pennsylvania would insist upon it. Writing to Joseph Galloway, he asked whether in his opinion the people were ready to back demands for a change. Replies from Pennsylvania convinced him that because of a reluctance of the Quakers the time was not ripe for a crusade to remove the Proprietors.[65]

In the October election of 1757, Franklin's party retained control of the Assembly as usual. For the most part the Proprietary party had little heart for the unequal contest. In Chester County, however, the two parties fought a bitter battle. Here the Quaker party was determined to defeat William Moore who had greatly offended the party by his outspoken criticism of the Assembly. They therefore supported Isaac Wayne, father of the Revolutionary general, Anthony Wayne. A sworn enemy of Moore, Wayne declared that ordinarily he would have given £50 not to be in the Assembly, but that on this occasion he would gladly give as much to see Moore defeated. Wayne was elected and got his chance to humble Moore who since August had been charged with malfeasance in conducting his duties as a justice of the peace.[66] In September, the Assembly unsuccessfully petitioned the Governor for Moore's removal, a move which gave rise to a famous libel case to be considered in the next chapter.

Northampton County likewise had an interesting election. William Plumsted, a prominent citizen of Philadelphia who had headed a

[62] *Pa. Journal,* Supplement 694, March 25, 1756.

[63] *Ibid.*

[64] Penn MSS., Off. Corresp., IX, 9. If the Proprietors did not let up on their instructions, Norris told Robert Charles in April, 1757, a rupture was certain to come. Norris Letter Book, 1756-1766, 75.

[65] Minutes of the Meeting for Sufferings, Feb. 24, 1757, Friends Book Store, Phila.; Letters to Dr. Franklin, LXXXVI, 1. APS.; Franklin Papers, Miscel. I, 29. L. of C.; Franklin Coll., MSS., 227. Yale U.

[66] Broadsides, Box 2, Folder K. HSP.

remonstrance against the Assembly, was the Proprietary candidate for
Northampton. Elected the year before, he had been refused his seat
in the House on the charge that his election had been carried by fraud.
The Proprietary party insisted that the charge was trumped up and
arose entirely from spite.[67]

During the campaign of 1757 the Proprietary party had circulated
a broadside, asking the people of Northampton not to allow the
Moravians who supported the Quaker party, to get control of
the county. The Moravians, it was charged, made "use of their Power
to save themselves from their share of the Publick Taxes, and threw
all Places of Profit and all advantages of publick Business, into the
hands of Creatures of their own Society." It was a disgrace, the paper
concluded, for the people of Northampton to have it said that they
had no one but foreigners to represent them.[68] Plumsted was re-elected
and this time was allowed to take his seat unchallenged.

But it was Cumberland County which provided the most interesting
event of all. It happened that Colonel John Stanwix[69] of the British
Army was a man who captivated the imagination and respect of the
American people wherever he went. The frontier was no exception
and Cumberland County showed its esteem for him by electing him
to the Pennsylvania Assembly with William Allen. When the Colonel,
who was also a member of the House of Commons, accepted his new-
found office, all Pennsylvania fairly swelled with pride and satisfaction.
Isaac Norris, the Speaker, declared that Colonel Stanwix was "paying
ye highest Compliment to an Assembly—that ye true Guardians of
English Liberty should concern themselves in our Affairs, & kindly
condesend to partake with us ye care of Protecting ye just Rights of
this Injured oppress'd Colony." Late in November Norris wrote that
Stanwix had not yet presented himself to the House, but that when
he did, the Assembly would rise to the occasion and pay him great
homage and respect.[70]

By this time Governor Denny had been in the colony slightly over
a year and had apparently hated almost every minute of it. For
months his salary had been withheld by the Assembly causing him
to have to borrow from Peters for his living. Denny, in fact, could
claim little respect from anyone. He took some solace in the thought
that all past governors had experienced about the same treatment,
remarking on one occasion that the Assembly was "not so much dis-

---

[67] *Ibid.; Votes*, VI, 4422 ff.
[68] *Ibid.*
[69] Stanwix became a Lieut.-General in 1761.
[70] Norris Letter Book, 1756-1766, 82-84.

pleased with the Person governing, as impatient of being governed at all."[71]

It was not long before Thomas Penn was as dissatisfied with his Deputy-Governor as Denny was with his own position. Penn knew that the latter had refused to defend his instructions, declaring that it was not his duty to fight the battles of the Proprietors or to think up excuses for unreasonable instructions. Peters' comment on Denny was that "he grows sour and peevish, likes no one, and seems to have no affections." In England Thomas Penn was only looking for the first good opportunity to have Denny replaced as his Lieutenant-Governor.

The first two years of the French and Indian war had been crucial ones for the Quaker party. It is altogether possible that the Proprietary party might have won the support of the people and gained control of the Assembly, had not Benjamin Franklin assumed the leadership of the Quaker party. Under his guidance the party grew in popularity as he launched a vigorous campaign for taxing the Proprietary estates. Laws passed under his direction for a system of voluntary military service, financing the war with bills of credit, and other measures were equally popular. The net result of all this was the strengthening of popular government in Pennsylvania. Full well could Thomas Penn reflect on his words to Richard Peters ten years before.

> Mr. Franklin's doctrine that obedience to governors is no more due them than protection to the people, is not fit to be in the heads of the unthinking multitude. He is a dangerous man and I should be glad if he inhabited any other country, as I believe him of a very uneasy spirit. However, as he is a sort of tribune of the people, he must be treated with regard.[72]

---

[71] Penn MSS., Add. Miscel. Letters, 100; Peters MSS., IV 86; *Votes,* VI, 4650; Pargellis, *Military Affairs,* 369.

[72] Pound, 281, or Shepherd, 222.

VI

PARTY POLITICS AND DEFENSE. 1758-1760

IN THE SPRING of 1758 Governor Denny and the Assembly fought the tax question all over again. After twice trying to work out a solution with the Governor, the Assembly bundled together all the legislative correspondence relative to the dispute and sent it to Benjamin Franklin. Then, as in the previous year, it framed a bill exempting the Proprietary estates which the Governor signed. By choosing to exempt the Proprietors totally rather than compromise, the Assembly, Denny charged, had deprived the people of real relief for the sake of eventually having the Proprietors at their mercy.[1]

Most of the money raised by the Assembly went toward aiding General John Forbes who captured Fort Duquesne in November. Forbes had a formidable force consisting of seventeen hundred regulars under Col. Archibald Montgomery and Col. Henry Bouquet and about six thousand provincials from Pennsylvania, Virginia, Maryland, and the Carolinas.[2]

General Forbes was not long in learning, as Braddock had discovered, that the greatest difficulty in launching an expedition against a fort in the wilderness interior was the procurement of a sufficient number of draft horses and wagons to haul the tons of supplies and equipment for the army. In the frontier counties horses and wagons were expensive and not plentiful, and few farmers were willing to hire them out unless the compensation was quite generous. Fifteen shillings per day for a wagon-team of four horses and a driver as set by law was not generally considered to be enough by the farmers. Consequently they proceeded to hide their wagons and teams whenever an army agent appeared.[3]

By May, Col. Bouquet, in charge of procuring wagon-teams, was at his wits' end to know what to do to solve the transportation problem. "Civil authority is so completely non-existent in this county [York]," he wrote, "that, after all the efforts I have made for four days, I have been able to obtain only eight wagons up to the present time."[4] After appealing to the magistrates for press warrants, the results were more encouraging. But the problem was not solved. The fact that a

---

[1] *Votes,* VI, 4796; *Statutes,* V, 337-352.
[2] Letters of Thomas and Richard Penn, 189. L. of C.; Shippen Papers, III, 129, HSP.
[3] *Statutes,* V, 292-293.
[4] *Bouquet Papers,* No. 21652 (1940), 28-29.

horse lost on a previous expedition had not been paid for proved especially embarrassing. Bouquet pleaded with the Army bursar to find some way to pay for "that cursed horse which was drowned last year in the service of the second battalion of R. A. [Royal Americans]."[5] By mid-summer he had procured half enough wagon-teams to start marching. In September he was still waiting for more and feared that the campaign might have to be postponed for another year.[6]

While General Forbes was finishing his preparations for his advance on Fort Duquesne, Pennsylvania held a treaty with a large gathering of Indians at Easton for the purpose of keeping the favor of the friendly Indians and of coaxing as many others as possible into deserting the French. The main objective of the treaty was realized when a month later Forbes forced the French for lack of support among the Indians to abandon the fort and give the country over to the English.

At this treaty political skulduggery reached an all time high in the history of Pennsylvania's Indian relations. The presence of a large delegation from the Six Nations made it possible for the Governor and Council to defeat every move of the Quakers and to control the meeting. To mollify the Six Nations and placate the western tribes, most of the purchase of 1754 was formally restored to the Indians. Word of this concession was at once dispatched to the Ohio Indians who were still undecided as to aiding or deserting the French. Nothing was accomplished about settling the dispute over the Walking Purchase, a problem which remained to plague the Proprietors and to provide political fuel for the Quaker party for some time to come.[7]

While these developments were taking place, the political pot was kept boiling in Philadelphia. Late in 1757 William Moore, after losing the election to Isaac Wayne, was jailed by the Assembly on a libel charge. Moore had long been in the hair of the Quaker party. A firm believer in having a standard militia wherein men must serve or pay for their exemption, he had in 1755 accused the Assembly of neglect of duty in the matter of defense. Next he threatened to raise two thousand men to force the Assembly to provide adequate means of defense for the colony. Therefore in 1757 when charges of misconduct were brought against him as a justice of the peace, his friends said that the motive was one of revenge.

When this and other charges were hurled at the Assembly in a pamphlet written by Moore, he was indicted for libel by the House. Not long after, the Rev. William Smith, who undertook to publish Moore's diatribe in a German newspaper, was likewise charged with

[5] *Ibid.*, 62-66.
[6] Balch Papers, Shippen I, 65. HSP.
[7] Wallace, 551ff; Thayer, 162ff.

libel and sent to join Moore in jail.[8] Attention was now centered upon Smith because of his high place in the Proprietary hierarchy.

After a trial lasting several days, Smith and Moore were sentenced to remain in jail until they made satisfaction to the House for their offense. Smith thereupon asked for copies of the proceedings against him in order that he might hasten an appeal to the Crown, but these were denied him. Then he launched into an "elegant & pathetic Speech" which fairly burned the ears of the Assembly. His words were at once greeted with a tremendous applause from a throng of sympathizers who had crowded into the hall to witness the trial. Instantly the members of the House started from their chairs, calling for assistance to clear the hall and shut the doors. After the confusion had died down, the Assembly set in motion an inquiry into the names of all those who had insulted the House by applauding. Among the offenders charged were such well known men as Thomas Lawrence, William Peters, Richard Hockley, and Thomas Willing. Several saw fit to beg the pardon of the House and their fines were suspended.[9]

Smith and Moore were compelled to stay in jail until April. Hugh Roberts thought the action taken against them had had "the happy effect to make the Scots Clan who were very public in their Clamour against the Conduct of the House, now communicate their thoughts to each other in whispers under the Thistle."[10] During Smith's confinement the Trustees of the College of Philadelphia ordered the twenty-eight enrolled students to attend classes at the jail. A frequent visitor there was Moore's attractive daughter Rebecca, whom Smith married after his return from England in 1759. In April during a recess of the House, Chief Justice Allen released the prisoners on a writ of *habeas corpus*. Smith and Moore were twice again apprehended by the Assembly during the year, but each time were released by Allen as soon as the Assembly adjourned.[11]

Naturally, William Allen was extremely wrought up over the jailing of Smith and Moore. With characteristic vehemence he declared that the action of the Assembly was as illegal as it was arbitrary. "Thus, you see," wrote Allen, "the poor parson was deprived of the common modes of defense by these violent & ignorant men, who claim all the powers of the House of Commons, and greatly go beyond them."[12]

---

[8] *Votes*, VI, 4619ff., 4677; *Pa. Mag.*, LII, 253-258.

[9] *Ibid.*, VI, 4708; Balch Papers, Shippen I, 53; *Pa. Mag.*, LII, 259; Norris Letter Book, 1756-1766, 88.

[10] *Pa. Mag.*, XXXVIII, 288.

[11] Shippen Papers, III, 129. HSP.

[12] Penn MSS., Off, Corresp., IX, 7. Also see Albert F. Gegenheimer, *William Smith, Educator and Churchman*, Chapter V.

Throughout the controversy Smith was accused by his enemies of being altogether an unprincipled man. It was declared under oath that he had said that he was not a supporter of the Proprietary party from conviction and would as soon write for one side as for the other.[13] Whether or not he said this, Smith was plainly on the side where he belonged, judging by his life-long conservatism on political questions. As a college professor he inspired confidence by his learning and literary powers, but outside the classroom it was otherwise. Besides championing unpopular causes, he was considered arrogant, artful, and domineering.

On his trip to England in 1758, James Hamilton carried a sum of money raised by William Allen for appealing the Smith-Moore case to the Privy Council. Presently the case was opened in London with prominent English attorneys representing Smith. The latter was pictured as a victim of Quaker malice because he dared to oppose them and lay bare their wickedness. Franklin, directing the defense of the Assembly, had his lawyers make it clear that the Pennsylvania Assembly was no longer a Quaker body and that Smith and Moore had written a base libel against the House.[14]

It was not until June, 1759, that an opinion in the Smith-Moore case was rendered by the Crown. It was decided that although the writings were libelous, they had not been written against the Assembly which had tried the offenders. When the Assembly of 1757 dissolved itself *sine die* at the close of the term, all matters relating to it were ended. The next Assembly therefore had acted illegally in arresting the men. Furthermore, it was declared, neither the Pennsylvania Assembly nor any other legislative body had the right or power to sit as a court on any case whatever.[15] If it could do this, it would have more power than the House of Commons in England. This opinion, rendered by Crown judges, was accepted by the Privy Council and transmitted to the Governor of Pennsylvania with orders to lay it before the House.[16]

During these proceedings, Smith was in London, pestering his attorneys, as Franklin put it. He returned to Philadelphia in October, 1759, fortified with a doctor's degree from Oxford and with the resolutions of the Privy Council under his arm. When he arrived, there was

---

[13] Franklin Papers, XII, 36. U. of Pa.

[14] Franklin Coll., MSS. No. 216. Yale U.

[15] Peters MSS., V, 76.

[16] *Acts of the Privy Council (Colonial)*, IV, 383-384. Although the Privy Council would have liked to have given the Pennsylvania Assembly much stronger medicine, it did not care to start anything which would lead to Parliamentary intervention. As Franklin said, the Privy Council chose to carry everything by the weight of the prerogative. Franklin Coll., MSS. No. 225. Yale U.

some talk of having him imprisoned again, but the Assembly wisely chose to ignore both Smith and the resolutions.[17]

When Benjamin Franklin sailed for England in 1757 as agent for the Pennsylvania Assembly, people felt confident that he would accomplish much for the province. Franklin, however, realized that it would not be as easy as people imagined. For several years past he had been constantly maligned in England and represented as the arch enemy of imperial defense in America. Consequently, to counteract this feeling, he asked Governor Shirley and other friends to write in his behalf to leading men in England.[18]

Arriving in England, Franklin made steady progress in winning over many influential persons to his way of seeing things. But with Thomas Penn he made no headway. In August Franklin delivered to Thomas Penn his *Heads of Complaints,* a paper aimed mainly at the hated Proprietary instructions and at the tax exemptions demanded by the Proprietors.[19]

After repeated conferences with Thomas Penn, Franklin reported to Galloway early in 1758 that his patience was all but exhausted. He was of the opinion that Penn was deliberately stalling by refusing to discuss anything without first obtaining an opinion from the Attorney-General.[20] About this time Ferdinand Paris, attorney for the Proprietors, told Franklin that instructions to the Governors were essential for the protection of Proprietary interests. As for taxation, he argued, it would be absurd to allow people who were, according to the charter, a kind of feudal tenants of the Lord-Proprietor, to tax the rents of the overlord.[21] Such words were maddening to all Pennsylvanians who cared not a particle for the anachronisms to be found in William Penn's charter. Months later Thomas Penn rendered an answer to the *Heads of Complaints* which, according to Franklin, was no more than a studied piece of obscurity and uncertainties.

---

[17] Moore, who was quite lost sight of by the dust kicked up by his illustrious colleague, was deprived of his office of justice of the peace by James Hamilton in 1759. Coming from a Proprietary man, this was a severe blow to Moore. William Franklin told his father that Hamilton had sacrificed Moore in the hope of gaining popular support for his administration. More likely, Hamilton, who tried to be fair in his dealings, felt that there was some truth in the charges against Moore. Five years later, when John Penn became Governor, Moore was reinstated upon the solicitation of his friends. This came at a time when the Proprietary party was striving desperately to gain more support by use of the patronage. Letters to Dr. Franklin, LVIII, Part 1, 32. APS.

[18] Letters to Dr. Franklin, XLVI, Part 1, 13. A letter from Governor Shirley (late commander-in-chief of His Majesty's forces in America) who was in disrepute in England, especially after the fall of Oswego in 1756, would, in reality, do more harm than good.

[19] See Votes, VI, 4926 for *Heads of Complaints,* or *Col. Rec.,* VIII, 278.

[20] Franklin Coll., MSS. No. 207. Yale U.

[21] *Col. Rec.,* VIII, 279-281.

At this Franklin informed his friends that there would presently be published a true account of Pennsylvania history which should help their cause materially.[22] This publication, entitled *An Historical Review of the Constitution of Pennsylvania,* was dedicated as a political gesture to the Speaker of the House of Commons. Franklin said that he did not write it, although his son, William, furnished much of the material and otherwise aided the author. The author, whose name was kept secret, was Franklin's close friend and advisor, Richard Jackson, a rising London attorney.[23] The book appeared in 1759 and was circulated with noticeable effect among the ministers of state and other influential persons in England.[24]

By 1758 the cost of the war was bearing down heavily in Pennsylvania. Isaac Norris declared in April, 1758, that the tax load was assuming dangerous proportions. By now almost the entire burden was falling on the eastern counties, as the back country was too impoverished to meet its assessments. Cumberland County, in fact, defaulted on its taxes between 1755 and 1760 and finally had the entire five-year tax canceled by the Assembly.[25]

But regardless of heavy taxes and much distress, the devouring needs of war continued to press upon the province. To meet the demands of General Jeffrey Amherst, who asked Pennsylvania to supply him with twenty-seven hundred men, the Assembly decided in March, 1759, to raise £100,000 in bills of credit to be funded by a tax on all property including the Proprietary. Denny refused to sign the measure without the exemptions specified by the Penns. This time, however, both General Amherst and General Stanwix stepped into the dispute and advised Denny to approve the bill. In spite of warnings from the Council, Denny followed the advice of the Generals who promised to protect him in case the Proprietors caused him any trouble.[26]

---

[22] Franklin Coll., MSS. No. 229. Yale U.

[23] *Ibid.,* MSS. No. 223 and 226. One of Franklin's letters about this time fell into the hands of Thomas Penn. In it he compared Penn to "a low Jockey who triumphed with Insolence when a Purchaser complain'd of being cheated in a horse."

[24] Pemberton Papers, Etting Coll., II, 41.

[25] *Col. Rec.,* VIII, 474; Norris Letter Book, 1756-1766, 90-91.
Cumberland County had lost population as well as property by the war. Many people had even moved out of the province to safer areas to the southward. Norris Letter Book, 1756-1766, 90-91. Not everyone in the West had been impoverished by the war. Some few, in fact, had made great fortunes out of it. Norris suspected some of these men had advised the county officers to default on the tax. It may be possible that William Allen who owned much land in Cumberland County had a hand in the defalcation. *Ibid.,* 92.

[26] Shippen Papers, IV, 31. HSP.; Norris Letter Book, 1756-1766, 102.

Under the law for the first time property of the Penns became subject to taxation on the same terms as all other property.[27] When the act was transmitted to them, the Proprietors at once asked the Privy Council to disallow that part of it which violated their instructions. Their attorneys termed the tax an injustice on the Proprietors who were, they said, at the mercy of popular government in Pennsylvania. In spite of all that Franklin or Jackson could do or say, the Board of Trade ruled against the colony, but the Privy Council was not so hard to deal with. That body offered Franklin a compromise whereby the Penns' surveyed but uncultivated lands would be assessed no higher than the lowest rate at which similar lands belonging to the inhabitants were assessed.[28] Franklin agreed and promised to have the Assembly amend the act accordingly. That body, however, refused to honor the agreement made by their agent.

It was generally believed after Denny signed the tax measure that he would be at once dismissed by Thomas Penn. Already William Allen had written Penn voicing the hope that his brother-in-law, James Hamilton, could be persuaded to become Lieutenant-Governor again. Allen warned that the appointment of another person like Denny or Morris might be disastrous for the Penns. Hamilton, on the other hand, would inspire confidence and strengthen Proprietary government.[29]

But the greatest difficulty, Allen knew, lay in getting Hamilton to consent to serve again. Hamilton "loved his ease too much, and did not care to have his peace of mind disturbed." Allen therefore concentrated his letters on Hamilton who was in England, appealing to his sense of patriotism and his love of the province.

After much coaxing, James Hamilton told Penn that he would consider the appointment. Penn then sent him a summary of his intended instructions. Upon reading the paper, Hamilton learned that the Proprietors wanted him "to prevent the Assembly from including any part of our Estates in any tax to be by them raised." If pressed hard he could, however, permit a tax on the Proprietary rents and quitrents but none whatsoever on "any vacant lands whether appropriated or not, nor on any fines or purchase moneys."[30]

Firmly resolved not to take the appointment under terms which were sure to embroil him at once with the Assembly, Hamilton candidly answered: "I find the present Instructions so little calculated for healing, or narrowing the disputes which subsist, that it hath a direct

[27] *Statutes*, V, 379-396.

[28] *Col. Rec.*, VIII, 552-554.

[29] Norris Letter Book, 1756-1766, 100; Penn MSS., Off. Corresp., IX, 9; Peters MSS., V, 23.

[30] Letters of Thomas and Richard Penn, 191-192. L. of C.

tendency further to influence and widen them." Hamilton was determined to let Thomas Penn know exactly how Pennsylvania felt about the question. The Royal charter did not exempt the Penns from taxation, he said. Neither was there any provision made for an exemption by William Penn or any other party. The largeness of the Proprietary estates, rather than being an argument against taxation, as the Penns seemed to think, constituted one of the best reasons for it. In the last analysis, Hamilton concluded, the Penns could claim either full exemption or none at all. The latter he was sure was the right answer. "I have not met with a single person either here, or there who was not, in his judgment on the side of the Assembly in this point, provided the Proprietors suffered from no discrimination," he informed Thomas Penn.[31]

In August, Hamilton bluntly told Penn that he had not solicited the appointment and would not accept it unless he was permitted to approve laws for taxing the Proprietary estates on the same terms as other property in the province. Confronted by Hamilton's firmness, Thomas Penn gave in and modified his instructions accordingly.[32] Hamilton thereupon accepted the office and set sail for America.

In the spring of 1760 the Pennsylvania Assembly sent its new Governor a bill for raising £100,000 in bills of credit to be funded by a tax on all property of a specified nature. Hamilton thought the measure proper enough if it were amended to provide commissioners to whom the Proprietors could appeal questionable or excessive assessments upon their property. The alleged injustice done the Penns by the assessors of Cumberland County in 1759, Hamilton declared, justified his request. The Assembly refused to comply whereupon Hamilton signed the bill under protest.[33]

The Cumberland assessors were not without an answer to the Proprietary charges. They declared that their accusers either did not understand the method of assessing in Cumberland County or had wilfully misrepresented the facts. In order not to over-estimate the immense Proprietary holdings in Cumberland County, they had, they explained, taken the pains to call in Col. John Armstrong, the Deputy-Surveyor.[34]

[31] Penn MSS., Off. Corresp., IX, 101-102.

[32] Letters of Thomas and Richard Penn, 193. L. of C.

[33] Penn-Hamilton Corresp., 1748-1774, 41. HSP.; Votes, VI, 5112, 5123, 5128-29; Statutes, VI, 7-22.

[34] Penn-Hamilton Corresp., 1748-1774, 41; Lamberton Scotch-Irish Coll., I, 37. HSP. A committee of the Assembly in 1761 reported that the Proprietary tax for the previous year was only £566 while that on the inhabitants was £27,103. Votes, VII, 5148, 5216.

In September, 1760, William Allen introduced General Robert Monckton's request for four hundred men for garrison duty on the Pennsylvania frontier. The House postponed the question until the meeting of the new Assembly in October. Norris warned Hamilton that it was rather unlikely that the Assembly would raise the men considering the high tax already burdening the people. It was evident that, with the French and Indians no longer an immediate menace to the colony, little further military aid could be expected from Pennsylvania. Governor Sharpe of Maryland reported himself faced with the same situation, now that his colony was no longer in danger.[35]

When the Assembly met in October, it exhibited no more interest in General Monckton's needs than had its predecessor. "Now Canada was taken and the War over in America," there was no need for raising the men, one of the members candidly explained.[36] After a short session of two weeks, the Assembly adjourned. Hamilton was disgusted. He felt sure nothing would be done in January when the Assembly met again. In fact he was convinced that the Assembly had only voted the £100,000 appropriation earlier in the year in the belief that he would surely veto it.[37]

When the Assembly met in January no move was made to raise men for the service until it was announced that the British troops would soon be withdrawn from the Pennsylvania frontier. Three hundred men were then raised by the Assembly for garrison duty.[38]

In February, acting upon orders from England, General Amherst requested Pennsylvania to supply several hundred more men for the current year. The House voted the proposition down although only by a vote of fifteen to twelve.[39] Upon receipt of this news, Amherst, who by now had lost all patience with American legislatures, sent Hamilton a stinging condemnation of the Pennsylvania Assembly. In the hope of shifting the blame, the Assembly responded by voting £30,000 for raising five hundred troops. The bill was made as inconsistent with Crown and Proprietary instructions as the Assembly could devise, and it was of course rejected by Hamilton. In all haste the House then quickly adjourned. In England the Earl of Egremont sized up the situation with the remark that Pennsylvania would grant no further assistance now that war was "removed from their own Doors."[40]

[35] Chalmers MSS., Phila., I, 40-41, 46, 48, 53. NYPL.

[36] *Ibid.*, 46-48.

[37] *Ibid.*, II, 1.

[38] *Votes*, VI, 5171, 5210, 5218.

[39] Chalmers MSS., Phila., II, 18.

[40] *Ibid.*; *Votes*, VI, 5251; *Pa. Arch.*, 4th ser., III, 191-192.

The cessation of hostilities on the Pennsylvania frontier after the capture of Fort Duquesne in November, 1758, left the Proprietary party without an issue with which it could hope for success in attacking the policies of the Quaker party. The latter had continued to champion the popular causes: paper money, taxation of the Proprietary estates, and voluntary military service. Franklin had kept the Proprietors on the defensive in England while his party had humbled the Proprietary leaders in the province. Not until 1763 would the Quaker party again have cause to view with alarm the rise of political opposition in Pennsylvania.

VII

THE WESTERN PROBLEM. 1760-1764

THE CAPTURE of Fort Duquesne in November, 1758, having brought hostilities to an end on the Pennsylvania frontier, the province was free to go ahead with western expansion and development. As early as 1760, Peters noted that the settlers were extending themselves all along the road to Pittsburgh, regardless of Indian rights to the land. The Rev. Thomas Barton of Lancaster also noted that many of those who left Pennsylvania during the Indian raids were flocking back and buying up land. Good land was everywhere in great demand and high in price except on the extreme frontier.

Although the suffering had been great on the exposed frontier, there were many in the West, especially in the Lancaster area, who had profited much by the war. At Lancaster farmers sold provisions to the Army contractors at high prices, the tavern keepers did a thriving business, and wagonmakers, saddlers, blacksmiths, and other tradesmen found the demand for goods and services greater than their ability to provide for them. Naturally many Pennsylvanians who had profited by the war were not at all displeased to learn that England was considering sending ten thousand troops to America for garrison duty after the war.[1]

To help those impoverished by the war, Pennsylvania in 1759 passed a special relief act. This law permitted the Loan Office to make larger or additional loans to persons who had suffered severe losses by the war. Unfortunately the law was disallowed by the Privy Council on the theory that it was economically unsound. Besides passing this law the province canceled taxes and the Proprietors canceled quitrents and interest due on war-ravaged property.[2] Acts such as these disprove the thesis that the frontier people suffered discrimination at the hands of an eastern oligarchy in Pennsylvania.

Of substantial relief to the Pennsylvania taxpayer was the British policy of reimbursing the colonies for part of their war expenditures. England did this in order to encourage the raising of troops in America so that it might be saved the heavier cost of transporting more men

---

[1] Norris Letter Book, 1756-1766, 92. Joseph Shippen thought that Pennsylvania should have no objection to the Quartering Act provided some American officers were appointed. William Allen thought the presence of British troops tended to maintain the provincial currency at a high rate with sterling. *William Allen's Letter Book*, 37; Shippen Papers VI, 5. HSP.

[2] *Statutes*, V, 427-443; Lamberton Scotch-Irish Coll., I, 37. HSP.

to America.[3] During the years 1760-1763 Pennsylvania was able to pay the ordinary expenses of government out of this fund.[4]

Until discontinued in 1762, the Loan Office provided the provincial treasury with a sizable revenue. In 1758 alone, the province gained £2058 from interest on mortgages handled by the Loan Office. Thereafter the amount declined as the mortgages matured. New mortgages could not be made, for the law provided that after 1756 bills of credit coming into the possession of the Loan Office had to be retired.[5]

In 1760 the Assembly failed to provide the Loan Office with a new lease of life when the Privy Council disallowed an act for re-emitting the £80,000 originally vested in the office. The Council contended that Pennsylvania had too much paper money, having emitted £485,000 in bills of credit during the war. So great, however, was the sentiment in Pennsylvania for a Loan Office that it was re-established by the Assembly in 1773. The law passed by Parliament in 1764 prohibiting the use of paper money as legal tender in all the colonies was met by not making the bills legal tender.[6]

Thus it is clear that paper money and the Loan Office were considered almost inseparable in Pennsylvania. As in former years the powerful merchant class, believing that paper money stimulated business, defended it on all occasions, enlisting in their aid their correspondents in England. In 1760 when paper money was under fire in all branches of the British government, Daniel Mildred, merchant, sent word to Philadelphia that London merchants had signed a petition in behalf of Pennsylvania currency which he was confident would carry weight in Court.[7]

Notwithstanding the near universal support of paper money in Pennsylvania, there were a few of the very wealthy citizens who were critical of it. In 1759 the Pennsylvania Council advised a reduction of the amount of currency to ward off a rise in the exchange rates and "the Ruin of Orphans, Merchants, and Trading part of this Province, and Great Injury to the English Merchants."[8] William Allen was one of those who feared that his wealth was menaced by paper money. In 1759 he told David Barclay & Sons, London bankers, that he was sending to England as much money as possible for investment. A year

---

[3] Root, 324; *Pa. Arch.*, 4th Ser., IV, 17-19, 65-66, 70-71.

[4] Prov. Papers, XXXVI, 31, Harrisburg; Root, 324.

[5] *Votes*, VI, 4859; *Statutes*, V, 14.

[6] Root, 216-219; *Col. Rec.*, IX, 599; Penn MSS., Off. Corresp., IX, 184; *Statutes*, VIII, 284. £150,000 in bills of credit were created in 1773. See Pemberton Papers, X, 75, for the Philadelphia merchants views on paper money.

[7] *Bouquet Papers*, No. 21645 (1941), 148; Balch Papers, Shippen, I, 118.

[8] *Col. Rec.*, VIII, 358.

later, Barclay reported that he had purchased for Allen three percent
consolidated annuities worth £1500 at par.[9]

With Franklin in England and Isaac Norris growing feeble with age,
the leadership of the Quaker party fell to Joseph Galloway, an Episcopalian of Quaker antecedents. Opportunistic and ever watchful for
whatever might enhance his fortune in life, Galloway had early attached
himself to Franklin and the Quaker party. In his zealous championship
of the anti-proprietary and other popular causes, the people overlooked
his natural conservatism and supported him as ardently as either
Franklin or Norris.

For a time before Norris retired from politics, Galloway had the
unpleasant experience of finding the elder statesman outwardly peevish
and jealous of his growing popularity. William Franklin advised Galloway to ignore it as much as possible, coming as it did from a sick old
man who took "umbrage at any whom he thought likely to interfere
with his Power."[10]

Having failed to win over permanently very many people during the
war, the Proprietary party now reverted once more to the rather small
body of gentlemen of former years. Only William Allen in the Assembly
in 1761 opposed continuing Franklin as a Pennsylvania agent in
England. Allen did his best to keep partisanship alive, seldom letting
an opportunity escape to drag politics into any question before the
House. When Sir William Johnson at last brought the dispute over the
Walking Purchase to a close at Easton in 1762 in a way which cast
little credit on either the Assembly or the Quakers, Allen alone defended
Johnson and the Proprietors with "such a torrent of Obstreperous
Jargon as might have been heard in a still morning to ye Jersey shore."[11]

Allen admitted in 1762 that a political calm had settled upon Pennsylvania, but added that Franklin's expected return to the province
would stir things up again. Franklin, he said, had an "almost insatiable
ambition" which had been whetted by basking among the Lords and
Ladies of England for five years at the expense of the province. Hamilton agreed with Allen that politics would not long remain calm after
Franklin was back from England.[12]

As on previous occasions, the next great upsurge of political activity
in Pennsylvania occurred in 1763 as a result of war. The new war was
another Indian uprising known in history as Pontiac's Conspiracy.
Although the late war between the English and the French had decided

[9] *William Allen's Letter Book,* 37-43. This was only a fraction of Allen's English
investments.

[10] Norris Letter Book, 1756-1766, 115; Penn MSS., Off. Corresp., IX, 186.

[11] *Pa. Mag.,* V, 63. (From "Fragments of a Journal Kept by Samuel Faulke.")

[12] *William Allen's Letter Book,* 49; Penn MSS., Off. Corresp., IX, 186.

the ownership of the Ohio Valley, it left in its wake a very unsettled Indian situation. During the French and Indian War, the Indians, aware that an English victory would place them at the mercy of the conquerors, had viewed with despair the rising tide of British arms. With the capture of Fort Duquesne by Forbes in 1758 the Indians were compelled to make peace and to give lip service to the English.

At the Treaty of Easton in 1758 the English had promised with a solemnity equal to their insincerity that, after the French were vanquished, the soldiers would be withdrawn and the forts demolished in the western country. In 1760 General Amherst again assured the Indians that their rights would be respected and that squatters would be ejected from the Indian lands. But the Indians wanted more than promises and they grew daily more disgruntled as the forts were kept in their midst and the white people continued to press upon them.[13]

Everyone on the frontier realized the seriousness of the Indian problem. After one experience with an Indian War none looked forward to another. In February, 1760, the inhabitants of Berks County sent a petition to the Assembly for a law to prevent persons from encroaching on the Indians. "Certain People," the petition read, "during the late hunting Season, have gone in Companies far into the Indian Country, in pursuit of Deer and other Game, to the great Damage and Displeasure of the Indians."[14] Similar petitions followed from other parts of the frontier. As a consequence, in April, the Assembly passed a law providing heavy penalties for violating the rights of the Indians.[15]

At a treaty with the Indians at Easton in August, 1761, the natives again complained of settlers on the unpurchased lands west of the Alleghenies.[16] Some months later in an effort to quiet them, Col. Bouquet proclaimed from Fort Pitt that no persons could hunt or settle west of the Alleghenies.[17] At about the same time the Privy Council adopted the principle of a definite boundary for the entire Indian frontier by stating that grants of land west of the Alleghenies henceforth could be procured only through the Crown.[18] This provision was incorporated in the Royal Proclamation (1763) prohibiting settlement beyond the mountains unless sanctioned by the Crown.

Besides trying to protect the Indians in their rights, Pennsylvania continued in its efforts to win their good will by affording them a fair

---

[13] Prov. Papers, XXX, 18-19, 23-24, 81, Harrisburg; Franklin Coll., MSS. No. 226, Yale U.

[14] Votes, VI, 5097.

[15] Ibid., VI, 5097, 5120, 5126, 5129.

[16] Col. Rec., VIII, 643.

[17] Bailey, 223; Bouquet Papers, No. 21648, Part I (1942), 3; Pa. Arch., 1st Ser., III, 571-574.

[18] Documents Relative to the Colonial History of the State of New York, VII, 478-479.

exchange for their furs at provincial stores.[19] In addition, large sums were spent by the Assembly for presents and for restoring English prisoners carried off by the Indians during the late war. Furthermore, the Indians were not pressed to allow the use of the West Branch of the Susquehanna for the Ohio trade, although merchants of Philadelphia were very anxious to utilize this means ot transportation.[20] Certainly the Pennsylvania government and the British authorities were trying to find a solution to the conflicting interests of the Indians and the white people.

However, in spite of all that was being done to satisfy the Indians, it was apparent at Pittsburgh that the relations between the two races were steadily deteriorating. The truth was that neither laws nor proclamations could prevent encroachments by the white people and the Indians could not be restrained from retaliating. James Kenny, agent for provincial stores at Pittsburgh, noted in 1762 that the Indians returning from a treaty at Lancaster were still dissatisfied and disgruntled.[21] So menacing did the Indians appear by this time that Kenny lived in perpetual fear of being caught in a massacre.

In May, 1763, Bouquet warned Amherst that the Indians were alarmed by the news that France had ceded all her lands in North America east of the Mississippi to the English. But Bouquet, who had a low opinion of the Indians, thought that "their dislike can be of little consequence" and that a few presents and a little flattery would reconcile them. A few weeks later when Pontiac's warriors made their surprise attacks on the English forts, Bouquet and Amherst were enraged by their duplicity and savagery. "The vermine," exclaimed Bouquet, "should be exterminated."[22]

Having received disquieting reports from the frontier throughout the month of June, Hamilton finally summoned the Assembly.[23] Just before the House convened, word arrived that a full scale Indian war had broken out, that Presque Isle, Le Boeuf, and Venango were all lost, and that Pittsburgh and Ligonier had been strongly attacked.[24] Upon

---

[19] In June, 1763, Gov. Hamilton at the suggestion of the Commissioners for Indian Affairs sent orders to Col. James Burd at Fort Augusta to build a house for sheltering Indians, enlarge the store, erect a smoke house for curing venison, ferry Indians across the river when signaled by them, and assist the agents in seizing liquor in possession of the private traders. Shippen Papers, VI, 11. HSP.

[20] *Votes*, VI, 5350.

[21] Thayer, 185.

[22] *Bouquet Papers*, No. 21634 (1940), 161, 172, 203, 204. Col. Mercer echoed the sentiment of the frontier when he wrote: the "Clamour of the Delawares, the Perfidy of the Shawnese, the Noise of the Tawaw, and the Treachery of the Mingo, and in short—the Damnation that is attendant on the whole Race of Barbarians." *Ibid.*, No. 21648, Part I (1942), 149

[23] *Votes*, VI, 5425-28; *Bouquet Papers*, No. 21634 (1940), 181-183.

[24] *Col. Rec.*, IX, 35, 63.

meeting, the Assembly acted promptly by voting to raise seven hundred men exclusive of a few already in the service. Hamilton was satisfied and agreed with the Assembly that the force was large enough to protect the frontier.[25]

Faced by a fierce and wily foe, Bouquet did not at all share the complacency of Hamilton and the Pennsylvania Assembly. Hearing that the Assembly had adjourned until September without providing stockades on the frontier as he advised, he was furious. Equally ex- asperating was the fact that the Assembly had refused to put the provincial troops under his command as Amherst had directed. Instead they were sent to the frontier in small parties to protect the harvest. Hamilton declared that, had he not complied with the wishes of the Assembly, the populace would have risen and pulled down his house.[26] Virginia and Maryland likewise refused to place their provincial troops under the command of the British. Bouquet and Amherst now agreed that the war, if it were to be won, would have to be waged by British troops alone.[27]

In September Governor Hamilton reported to the Assembly that the provincial troops had been stationed at various points on the frontier, with the result that most of the harvest had been saved. He admitted, however, that the attention of the Indians had been diverted to Bouquet's troops marching to the relief of Pittsburgh. He warned the Assembly that the Indians might return to range and plunder the frontier notwithstanding their defeat by Bouquet at Bushy Run in August.[28]

Following the recommendations of Hamilton, the Assembly resolved to keep the troops in service and to raise a sum of £25,000 in bills of credit for their maintenance. But Hamilton refused to accept an appro- priation in the form of paper money. Thereupon the Assembly angrily adjourned to await the verdict of the election. The new Assembly, composed of about the same membership, met as was the custom on October 14. Sensing that further delay was impossible, the House appropriated £24,000 from funds at its disposal. Hamilton signed the measure, after which the Assembly adjourned until January 16.[29]

Meanwhile, the Indians returned to the attack on the frontiers of Pennsylvania. Already Bouquet had reported that nearly six hun-

[25] Votes, VI, 5431.

[26] John Watts to Sir William Baker, July 22, 1763, N. Y. Hist. Soc. Coll. (1928), 159.

[27] Bouquet Papers, No. 21649, Part II (1942), 32, No. 21634 (1940), 271.

[28] Votes, VI, 5435-36.

[29] Ibid., VI, 5478-84. £12,000 came from the remainder of Parliamentary reëmburse- ment, £7,000 from a sum previously granted Philadelphia for defense, £4,000 from the Indian trade fund, and £1,000 from the duty on negroes.

dred of the inhabitants had been killed or captured.[30] In order to bring the war to a speedy close by attacking the Indian towns, General Amherst levied quotas for troops upon all the colonies under attack. Pennsylvania was asked to contribute one thousand men. Sentiment in the province was now strongly in favor of aiding the British in striking at the Indian strongholds on the Ohio and to the westward.[31]

Governor John Penn, who had succeeded Hamilton, called the Assembly together for a special session in December to consider the General's request. It was at this time that Benjamin Franklin resumed his seat in the Assembly after an absence of five years. Franklin favored giving the Indians a thorough beating, but he was equally determined that the Proprietors should pay their share of the cost. It was to counteract such a move that Thomas Penn had appointed his nephew in the place of Hamilton whom he considered not partisan enough for the crisis which confronted the Proprietors.

Without the least hesitation the Assembly resolved to raise the men requested by Amherst. Then it took under consideration the raising of £50,000 for the King's use. Not wishing to run afoul of the Proprietary instructions again, it requested early in 1764 information from the Governor before undertaking to draft the measure. Penn restricted his reply to quoting paragraphs eleven and twelve of his instructions requiring all payments to the Proprietors to be in sterling or the rate of exchange.[32]

Finding the Governor not very helpful, the Assembly was at a loss, as one member said, to know how to proceed, being desirous to avoid running into a long dispute over this question as on former occasions.[33] It was not long, however, before the Assembly had prepared a bill in true Franklin style for emitting £50,000 in bills of credit to be funded by a tax on all property including the Proprietary holdings.

By this time Franklin was quite aware that the new Governor in spite of his youth was capable of holding his own with the Assembly. The son of Richard and grandson of William Penn, the founder, John was a near-sighted, quiet, middle-sized Englishman who wanted to please, but who would not be driven into making concessions. Realizing that it was impossible to please both the Assembly and his uncle, he decided to adhere strictly to his instructions, come what may.

After much delay the supply bill reached the Governor on February 25. A fortnight later he returned it to the Assembly with objections

---

[30] *Bouquet Papers*, No. 21649, Part II (1942), 45, 104; Peters MSS., VI, 14. Bouquet became as disgusted with the people on the frontier as with the Assembly. "I meet everywhere," he declared, "with the same Backwardness, even among the most exposed of the Inhabitants." *Bouquet Papers*, No. 21634 (1940), 223.

[31] *Col. Rec.*, IX, 99.

[32] *Votes*, VII, 5514.

[33] *Pa. Mag.*, V, 68.

relative to the provisions for taxing the Proprietary estates. After arguing the disputed points for three weeks longer, the Assembly abruptly adjourned with a note to the Governor that the House would be pleased to convene whenever he was ready to approve the measure as prepared by the Assembly. It was adjourning, it explained, in order for members to consult their constituents upon a question so vital to the province.

The crux of the dispute was that the Assembly demanded that the located but uncultivated lands of the Penns should be assessed in a manner which bore some relation to the value of the property. The Penns insisted that in assessing the land the exact wording of the Privy Council's formula of 1759 should be applied. This order stated that "the located uncultivated Lands belonging to the Proprietaries, shall not be assessed higher than the lowest Rate at which any located uncultivated Lands belonging to the Inhabitants shall be assessed." The Assembly modified this in the appropriation bill to read: "that the located uncultivated Lands belonging to the Proprietaries of this Province shall not, by Virtue of this Act, be assessed higher than the lowest Rate at which any located uncultivated Lands belonging to the Inhabitants thereof, under the same Circumstances, of Situation, Kind and Quality, shall be assessed." Franklin claimed that this construction was the true meaning and intention of the Privy Council.[34]

Everyone in Pennsylvania, William Logan said, was of the opinion that the Assembly had done well to agree to all the Governor's amendments except this one.[35] William Peters admitted that everyone, including the Provincial Council, was in sympathy with the Assembly and thought the Proprietary terms altogether unreasonable. What justice could there be, asked the Council, in demanding that the best of the Proprietary lands could be taxed no higher than the very worst of that of the people?[36] John Watts, a prominent citizen of New York, told General Monckton that in his opinion "the Assembly appears to be indisputably in the right" although he wondered how either party to the dispute had the heart to hold out. "But party rage is a sad Fury," he observed.[37]

When the Assembly met in May, rather than let the defense of the province suffer any longer, it at once passed a supply bill in accordance with the Governor's amendments.[38] In the meantime Thomas Penn had decided to concede the points in dispute for fear that Pennsylvania

[34] *Votes,* VII, 5568-90. See especially page 5578.
[35] Smith MSS., VI, 137. Ridgway Lib.
[36] Penn MSS., Off. Corresp., IX, 226.
[37] "Letter Book of John Watts, 1762-1765," *N. Y. Hist. Soc. Coll.* (1928), 243, 258.
[38] *Col. Rec.,* IX, 187-188; *Votes,* VII, 5616-17. As early as the middle of March most of the troops had been raised. *Votes,* VII, 5575.

might be converted into a Royal province because of the growing dislike in England of the way he exercised his governing powers. Instructions to this effect were dispatched to Pennsylvania thus bringing to an end one of the bitterest controversies in colonial history. More surprising than the concession itself was the fact that Penn now admitted that there was some justice in what the Assembly had so long sought to achieve.[39]

While the tax question was being fought out, the old controversy over the militia reappeared. As before, Franklin and the Assembly insisted on having a democratic militia law like that of 1755, while the Governor and his Council steadfastly opposed it. None therefore could be passed.[40] On this question Pennsylvania was not much different from the other colonies. Everywhere, in fact, the traditional militia system as handed down from England, was giving way before the rising power and independent spirit of the American yeoman farmer. Governor Sharpe of Maryland told Bouquet that under the Maryland law the men and their officers, and not the Governor, controlled the militia.[41] Governor Fauquier of Virginia reported that about the same thing existed in his colony.

Within the settled parts of Pennsylvania there lived some half-civilized natives who had relatives among the enemy. Suspicion was early aroused that some of them were giving aid to the warring Indians. After several complaints were registered against the "Moravian" Indians at Bethlehem, the Governor, in November, for fear that they might be harmed, ordered their removal to Philadelphia.[42]

Determined not to let any others get away, a band of frontiersmen swooped down on a small number of Indians (mostly women and children) living at Conestoga near Lancaster and in two attacks, one at Conestoga itself and the other in Lancaster where a remnant had been taken for refuge, killed them all.[43]

These unfortunate victims of frontier rage were a remnant of the Susquehannock tribe. Because they were dependents of the Six Nations, it was feared in Philadelphia that their murder might bring on a war with this powerful Indian confederacy.

The Conestoga massacre showed the explosive nature of conditions on the frontier where week after week the people were harried by a merciless foe while the Governor and Assembly did nothing but argue

---

[39] Penn MSS., Off. Corresp., IX, 252; Letters of Thomas and Richard Penn, 286½. L. of C.; *Votes*, VII, 5556ff.

[40] *Votes*, VII, 5542ff.

[41] *Bouquet Papers*, No. 21650, Part I (1942), 109.

[42] Penn MSS., Off. Corresp., IX, 208.

[43] Rhoda Barker's Journal. HSP. On the day of the massacre there was a company of Highlanders in Lancaster who would have defended the Indians had they been called upon. But no magistrate could be found to sanction the use of the troops. Graeff, 191-192.

in Philadelphia. George Bryan declared that the West considered itself "deserted by the Government" and was "dreadfully incensed."[44] Their anger rose to white heat when they thought of themselves without food, shelter or defense, while over one hundred Indians were being provided for by the province at Philadelphia. The indignation spread like a "contagion" out of the West and eastward into Philadelphia itself. When the Assembly prepared a bill for bringing the murderers of the Indians to trial "such a Clamour [arose] in ye House and out-of-doors" that the measure was set aside after the first reading.[45]

Not long after the massacre of the Indians at Conestoga it became known in Philadelphia that a large number of frontiersmen were massing to march on the city to kill the Indians there and overawe the Assembly. Some of the rioters, who were known as the Paxton Boys, wildly swore that they would kill Israel Pemberton, the friend of the Indians, and Joseph Fox, a prominent member of the Assembly, who as Barracks Master had charge of the Indians being sheltered.[46]

Under the leadership of Franklin, Philadelphia prepared to defend itself against the Paxton Boys who were soon marching upon the city more than five hundred strong. Orders were issued by the Assembly (which had quickly passed an act for suppressing riots and tumults) for the rioters to disperse in the King's name under penalty of death.[47] Before the mob arrived, the city was quite prepared to defend itself. Even some of the younger Quakers volunteered their services and appeared on the streets with guns.

By the time the marchers had reached the vicinity of Philadelphia many of the demonstrators, especially the Germans, had been persuaded to return to their homes, leaving only about two hundred and sixty rioters, most of whom were Scots Irish. Even the ardor of these champions of the West cooled considerably when they learned that the Indians were guarded by three companies of Royal Americans. Nevertheless, Philadelphia was practically in a state of panic as the rioters were hourly expected to fall upon the city.[48]

But the episode had a much less exciting ending. With the rioters nearing Germantown, a committee headed by Franklin went out to meet them and make peace. At Coleman's tavern a meeting was held with James Smith, Matthew Smith, James Gibson, and other leaders of the Paxton Boys. Col. John Armstrong, who had been in Philadelphia to see the Governor, acted as moderator. Dr. Wrangle, a prominent Lutheran minister, used his influence with such Germans as were still with the rioters to reach an understanding.[49]

[44] George Bryan's Memoranda of Events, 1764. L. of C.
[45] Pa. Mag., V, 67.
[46] Thayer, 187-189.
[47] Statutes, VI, 325-328.
[48] Pemberton Papers, XVII, 10; Graeff, 197-199.
[49] The Journals of Henry Melchior Muhlenberg, II, 21-23.

With tongue in cheek, the spokesmen for the West declared that they had no intention of hurting anyone and only desired to escort the Indians beyond the "borders" of the province. To make their words seem more impressive, they talked of giving a bond of £10,000 to guarantee the safety of the Indians. No one, of course, was deceived by this talk, but to pacify the rioters they were persuaded to send some of their leaders to Philadelphia to inspect the Indians (most of whom were old men, women and children) to convince them that none had participated in the war. The Paxton men then presented a petition from three of the western counties asking that the West be given representation in the Assembly proportional to its population. The present situation it was said was "oppressive, unequal, and unjust, the cause of many of our Grievances."[50]

Although apologists for the actions of the Paxton Boys were not wanting, Allen, Hamilton, and other leaders of the Proprietary party had too great a fear of anarchy to condone their action. As John Penn said, there was nothing which could "justify the madness of these people in flying in the face of government."[51] Franklin described the frontiersmen as no more civilized than the barbarians at whose hands they suffered. On a similar occasion, Allen told the people of Cumberland County that inasmuch "as they were Christians they were worse than the Indians."

The common people, however, except for the Quakers and other pietists, let their hatred of the Indians overcome their sense of justice in their approval of the deeds of the Paxtonians. This was true for both the East and the West. John Penn told his uncle that the people of Philadelphia "are as Inveterate against the Indians as the Frontier Inhabitants."[52]

There were some who thought that the Quaker interest in the Indians proceeded from ulterior motives.[53] Some historians have given credence to the charge that the Quakers protected the Indians because they hoped to derive great profits from the fur trade when the war closed.[54] But there is really no evidence to support this conclusion. Very few if any of the Quakers who were most forward in protecting the Indians were in any way concerned in the western trade. They were motivated, it would seem, by humanitarian principles and a desire to preserve the good name of the Quaker province.

On the frontier, if anyone was so bold as to criticize the activities of the Paxton Boys he was almost certain to be "thrashed to bits."[55]

---

[50] *Col. Rec.,* IX, 138; *Votes,* VII, 5549-55; Pemberton Papers, XXXIV, 128.
[51] Penn MSS., Off. Corresp., IX, 238.
[52] *Ibid.*
[53] *The Journals of Henry Melchior Muhlenberg,* II, 18-19.
[54] Charles Lincoln, *The Revolutionary Movement in Pennsylvania, 1760-1776,* 108.
[55] William Logan to John Smith, Jan. 21, 1764, John Smith Corresp., 1740-1770. HSP.

In reality it would have been hard to find a man out there who was not in full sympathy with the rioters. Governor Penn declared that every man in Cumberland County was a rioter at heart and that ten thousand of the King's troops could not bring one to trial.[56] Penn couldn't get the name of even one man concerned in the massacre of the Indians although almost anyone on the frontier knew any number of them. Apparently all the justices of the peace and sheriffs had either made themselves scarce when the massacre took place or had actually connived with the Paxton Boys. Col. John Armstrong, who condemned the murder of the Indians when corresponding with the Governor, spoke otherwise when conversing with his frontier neighbors.

The pamphlet war which accompanied and followed the Paxton riots was as bitter as the fighting on the frontier was bloody. The motives of the Quakers, as on former occasions, were misrepresented and their leaders reviled. Israel Pemberton's career during the past eight years was raked over and the worst possible construction placed upon it. He was even accused of exciting the Indians to acts of violence against any settlers who encroached on their land.[57] When some of the younger Quakers joined the defenders of Philadelphia their enemies called this pulling off "the mask."[58] The apologists for the Paxton rioters saw in the Quakers a handy scapegoat, knowing all too well that there was no real defense for the massacre of the defenseless Conestoga Indians. Quaker pacifism in 1763-1764 was no more the cause of Pennsylvania's troubles and political disputes than during the previous war, but it was used again to try to undermine Franklin and the Quaker party.

Before the summer of 1764 was gone the Indian power was broken and the war terminated. But the political repercussions which were set in motion by it were far from ended. Already Franklin had initiated a movement to convert Pennsylvania into a Royal colony. The original motive however had to be abandoned when the Penns conceded the dispute over the taxation of their estates. Henceforth the campaign was waged on the assumption that the Proprietary government was too weak to maintain law and order in Pennsylvania. The loss of much popular support during the preceding months had greatly frightened the Quakers and their adherents. With their control of the legislature threatened by the rising power of Proprietary-Presbyterian politics, the best defense was to assume the offensive. The Quaker party must seek control of the executive by converting Pennsylvania into a Royal government.

---

[56] Penn MSS., Off. Corresp., IX, 238.

[57] *The Apology of the Paxton Volunteers, 1764.* HSP. Consult the Rare Book, Room of the NYPL for a collection of contemporary writings on the Conestoga massacre.

[58] *Ibid.*

Quaker Party Politics, 1764, as Pictured by Their Opponents.

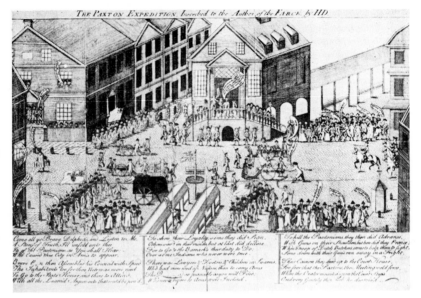

CARTOON DEPICTING THE DEFENCE OF PHILADELPHIA AGAINST THE PAXTON BOYS, 1764.

CARTOON REPRESENTING FRANKLIN AND THE QUAKER PARTY AS THE SOURCE OF
PENNSYLVANIA'S WOES, 1764.

VIII

THE MOVEMENT FOR A ROYAL GOVERNMENT.
1764

THAT Franklin had long desired to see Pennsylvania converted into a Royal province was a well known fact in political circles. Franklin saw clearly the mistake of having the governing powers of the province in the hands of the principal landowners. Because of this Pennsylvania had come to experience the evils of Proprietary instructions which not only protected the vested interests of the Penns, but also deprived the province of a voice in any number of questions which vitally concerned it. In Franklin's opinion Proprietary government had undermined and destroyed in Pennsylvania the essential rights of freeborn Englishmen.

In studying the reaction in England to a change in the Pennsylvania government, Franklin had found that opinion generally favored such a plan. The feeling that Proprietary governments were undesirable was of long standing. The Crown had, in fact, regretted the granting of the proprietorship to William Penn from the start. Efficiency, financial considerations, and defense all called for the creation of more uniform administrative districts in America.[1]

This being the case, it is to be wondered that Penn succeeded in regaining his colony after losing it to the Crown between 1692 and 1694. It was not long before William Penn became dissatisfied with the role of proprietor and with the continued heavy financial burdens which it entailed. Negotiations were finally entered upon for the sale of the province to the Crown, but Penn died before the transfer could be made.[2]

It was about this time that the Board of Trade recommended that the Crown acquire control of all the chartered colonies which it considered "an anomaly in the imperial system."[3] Thereafter, the proprietary question was almost a perennial one. But the heads of the British government, who could seldom be brought to a decision on anything which could be postponed, did nothing about it.

When Franklin first became convinced that Pennsylvania had much to gain by a change from a Proprietary to a Royal colony is not known.

---

[1] Root, 50, 267.

[2] Arthur Pound, *The Penns of England and Pennsylvania*, 269; Bigelow, ed., *The Works of Benjamin Franklin*, III, 337-338.

[3] Root, 144-145.

By 1757, however, when he sailed for England as agent for the Pennsylvania Assembly, he entertained no doubts of its desirability. During the next five years while in England, he did what he could to promote the change. When he returned to Pennsylvania in 1762, it is very possible that he had decided to launch a drive for a change in government at the first opportunity. In any event, within a year after his return, he had a full-scale movement under way for converting Pennsylvania into a Royal province.

Everyone in Pennsylvania knew that Franklin was the chief promoter and director of the movement to oust the Proprietors. William Allen heard Franklin say to some members of the House that they must "wage an eternal war against the Proprietary." Franklin, continued Allen, had long been "the chief author and grand abettor of all the seditious practices in this Government, and [had been] continually infusing into the people's ears his Republican, Anarchical Notions."4 John Penn thought that Franklin was motivated particularly by a personal dislike of Thomas Penn engendered by his "ill-nature" and "black heart."5

Franklin always insisted, however, that personal feelings did not enter into his crusade against the Proprietors. "You know I have many enemies," he confided in his daughter Sarah in 1764, but "all indeed on the public account—yet they are enemies, and very bitter ones."6 His own interest and those of the Proprietors, Franklin declared, had never clashed. His motives, he told Col. Bouquet, arose solely from the belief that Pennsylvania could not hope for internal peace and good government so long as the Proprietors remained at the head of the government.7

When John Penn refused to sign the Assembly's tax bill early in 1764, it was soon apparent that Franklin would launch a movement to solve the problem by going to the root of it and removing the Proprietors as the governing head of Pennsylvania. In March when the Assembly adjourned until May in order to consult their constituents on the momentous issues, John Penn admitted that the movement had already gathered considerable power and was daily becoming more ominous. Still he steadfastly refused to disregard his instructions and sign the bills insisted upon by the House. By this time tempers in the Assembly had risen to such a pitch that many swore they would never again do business with a Proprietary governor. Already there was talk

---

4 Penn MSS., Off. Corresp., IX, 282, X, 1.
5 *Ibid.*, IX, 220.
6 Bigelow, III, 257.
7 *Bouquet Papers,* No. 21650, Part II (1943), 158.

of pulling down the Proprietary arms over the Speaker's chair and replacing them with the King's.[8]

Not all who joined in the movement to eject the Proprietors were prompted by the same motives. Many were most concerned with the seeming inability of the government to enforce law and order and thought that a Royal government would check the rise of lawlessness in Pennsylvania.

One such person was William Logan whose recent brush with the Paxton Boys at Germantown had convinced him that no one was safe under Proprietary government. Logan had gone out to meet the rioters as a member of the Council. Upon arriving he was recognized by one of them who shouted "There's that scoundrel Logan, that Quaker!" At this, the mob rushed toward him. Quite shaken he leaped onto his horse and made straight for Philadelphia.[9]

Fear of anarchy was not the only motive which compelled adherents of the Quaker party to line up with Franklin for a change of government. James Pemberton echoed the thoughts of many when he said that, unless the province had a strong government, the Scots Irish Presbyterians would throw the colony into anarchy in the hope of emerging as the political masters of the province.[10] The Reverend Hugh Neill, an Episcopalian minister at Oxford, Pennsylvania, impartially summed up the rising tension throughout the province as primarily the outgrowth of "the political squabble that is now on foot between the Quakers and the Presbyterians."[11]

There was still another motive operating, and one which, with many of the politicians, may have been the strongest. This was the opportunity which a change in government presented for winning new posts of honor and profit. William Allen, as early as March, declared that Franklin's politicians were already parceling out among themselves the various offices which would be available if their scheme succeeded. The deplorable situation facing Pennsylvania, thought Allen, was but the natural and inevitable outgrowth of popular government.[12]

Thus it was evident to all that the executive and judicial offices of the province, which in the past had been occupied by Proprietary appointees, were at stake. These offices were the magnet which had

---

[8] Penn MSS., Off. Corresp., IX, 216; William Logan to John Smith, March 17, 1764, Corresp. of John Smith, 1740-1770. HSP; *Votes*, VII, 5593-95.

[9] William Logan to John Smith, 1764, Corresp. of John Smith, 1740-1770. HSP; *Journals of Henry Melchior Muhlenberg*, II, 22-23.

[10] Pemberton Papers, XXXIV, 30, 134. In 1742 when the Quakers had fears that the Proprietary party might capture the Assembly, there was talk of converting to a Royal government.

[11] Guy S. Klett, *Presbyterians in Colonial Pennsylvania*, 255; Sparks, VII, 281; Broadsides, Box 2, Folder B. HSP.

[12] Penn MSS., Off. Corresp., X, 1.

long held the Proprietary party together when it was possible to elect
only a few gentlemen to the Assembly.

For nearly thirty years William Allen had, practically alone, determined who would fill the high appointive offices in the province.
So powerful was Allen that when John Penn had the courage to appoint
Alexander Stedman associate judge for the Supreme Court, he brought
upon himself a sharp rebuke from Thomas Penn for not following
Allen's advice. John tried to defend himself by explaining that he had
consulted Benjamin Chew and Edward Shippen who were close friends
of Allen. He also tried to reduce his uncle's reliance on the Chief
Justice by informing him that many people thought that there was
too much regard "shown to all of Allen's recommendations" for every
office that fell vacant.[13]

But William Allen's power over the patronage continued unabated in
spite of criticism. In 1765 Allen had James Tilghman appointed secretary of the land office; Benjamin Chew who held the office of Attorney-
General on his recommendation was appointed Register-General for
the probate of wills that same year. Other appointments suggested by
Allen followed in rapid succession. Thomas Willing was appointed
judge of the Supreme Court, Andrew Allen Attorney-General on Chew's
resignation, Edward Shippen Prothonotary of the Supreme Court, and
so on.[14]

The lesser Proprietary offices were numerous and of great value in
affording party workers among the people. In checking the names of
the justices of the peace, notaries of the public, and county clerks, few
but Proprietary partisans are to be found. In 1774 there were two
hundred and seven justices of the peace in Pennsylvania, all of whom
were appointed by the Governor. Among those of Lancaster County
are to be found such well known Proprietary men as James Burd,
Edward Shippen, Isaac Saunders, Emanuel Carpenter, and Dr. Adam
Kuhn; for Philadelphia County are Samuel Mifflin, Jacob Duché
George Bryan, John Allen, George Clymer, and Samuel Powell.[15]

Aligned with the Proprietary office-holders, according to the testimony of Charles Thomson, were all the tavern keepers in the province
who received their licenses from the Governor. The colony, Thomson
observed, was in fact overrun with taverns. In these places, he said,
people became debauched and were thus fit subjects to bow to the
tyranny of the Proprietors.[16]

[13] *Ibid.*, IX, 218, 252.

[14] *Ibid.*, IX, 186, X, 3, 98, 116.

[15] Penn-Hamilton Corresp., July 13, 1752, HSP. Aitken's Register and Calendar,
1774, Hazard Family Papers. HSP.

[16] Letters to Dr. Franklin, I, Part 2, 112. APS.

The question arises whether or not the inner clique of the Quaker party (Franklin, Galloway, Abel James, John Hughes, and the Whartons) had a motive apart from the others for desiring to remove the Penns. Could it be that they were seeking to maneuver themselves into a position whereby they could make immense profits in land speculation? Did they, in other words, believe they could force the Proprietors to sell their holdings to the Crown and then contrive to secure for themselves vast tracts as Crown favorites? William Allen and John Penn had so low an opinion of Franklin that they believed him capable of going to any extreme to gratify his craving for power and wealth. If they had suspected that he was aiming at the Proprietary lands as well as the governing of Pennsylvania, they would have made reference to it in their letters. But there are none.

One letter written by William Franklin to his father in 1767, when they still had hope of realizing a change of government, might possibly be construed as conveying an ulterior motive on the part of Franklin. William disagreed with his father that the Assembly should have a say along with the governor in the disposition of land. The only difference, said William, when the Assembly had a hand in its disposal, would be that the private interest of every member of the Assembly would have to be satisfied before any land could be released.[17]

Franklin's desire to have the Pennsylvania Assembly have a voice in the disposition of land in no way argues that he was scheming to enrich himself at the expense of the Proprietors. To all appearances he was arguing solely for the right of the people of the province to have a voice in the disposition of the unappropriated land. Perhaps he was more naïve than his son in supposing that a more democratic handling of the land problem would be accompanied with greater regard for the public interest. It was this same concern for the public interest which constituted one of several reasons why Franklin insisted upon taxing the Penns as all others were taxed in the province. Tax money was the immediate aim, but in the long run he wanted to make it quite impossible for the Proprietors to speculate on land by withholding it from sale indefinitely. This policy, as practiced by the Penns, left large areas undeveloped in many parts of the country and was a serious hindrance to the development of the province.

The movement for converting Pennsylvania into a Royal Colony apparently had little or no connection with the Vandalia project which was rapidly taking form during these years. After receiving a land grant by the Crown for losses from Indian depredations during the Pontiac uprising, Galloway, the two Franklins, Abel James, Hughes, and the Whartons hit upon making great fortunes out of acquiring a

---

[17] *Ibid.,* II, Part 1, 88. APS.

huge tract of land on the Ohio.[18] Already Samuel Wharton, as cunning
a contriver as ever took a hand in land speculation, had persuaded his
French and English employees of his fur trading business in the Illinois
country to sign a petition for a Crown colony beyond the Ohio.[19] In
England, Franklin let no opportunity escape for promoting the enterprise. Before long Franklin and Jackson were busily engaged in drawing up a charter for the colony which would comprise twenty million acres. But the grant was slow in materializing and Franklin was
still waiting for action when the Revolution broke out and all thought
of it had to be put aside.[20]

It may seem quite inconsistent for Franklin to advocate the over-
throw of the Penns and at the same time be seeking the control of a
vast area beyond the Ohio. But Franklin appeared to think that there
was nothing inconsistent in what he was doing. Vandalia, if it became
a reality, would be a Royal colony with the government and the property interest separate as in New Jersey. That this might prove to be
theory rather than fact in the new colony Franklin was pleased to
ignore. Everyone knew that Samuel Wharton, the principal stockholder, was hoping to become the Governor of Vandalia.

To the side of the defenders of the Proprietors and the Charter of
Liberties came many like the lawyer, John Dickinson, who had no
ulterior interests and who opposed the change because they considered
it unwise and likely to cause the loss of freedom and valuable privileges
conferred by William Penn's Frame of Government. Another who
shared this opinion was Israel Pemberton who feared the power of the
Crown and a loss of religious liberty under a Royal government. Pres-
byterianism, Pemberton said, was less dangerous than Anglicanism if
Pennsylvania became a Crown colony. Still another was Isaac Norris
who also turned his back on his party and refused to support the movement for the change.[21]

Pemberton had the backing of many Quakers, although by no means
a majority, and could count upon the support of the German sects led
by Christopher Sauer. But by far the largest group which rallied to
Proprietary government was the Scots Irish who blamed the Assembly
(which they identified as a Quaker stronghold) for all their recent
misfortunes. They had no particular love for the Proprietors but none
at all for the King's government, which they associated with their
miseries experienced in Ireland. Associated likewise with the Proprie-

[18] Galloway to Franklin, Oct. 17, 1768, Letters to Dr. Franklin, II, Part 2. APS.
[19] Prov. Papers, XXXVII, 10. Harrisburg.
[20] John Baynton's Letter Book, 1769-1770, 91-96. Harrisburg; Letters to Dr.
Franklin, IV, 66. APS.; Franklin Coll., MSS. No. 384. Yale U.
[21] Pemberton Papers, XVII, 103. Isaac Sharpless, *History of Quaker Government in
Pennsylvania*, II, 70-71.

tary party were many of the German Lutherans and the Reformed. In some sections the Germans opposed a change in Pennsylvania's government; in other places, they supported the movement to establish a Royal colony.

Notwithstanding the widespread opposition, Franklin seems to have had a majority of the people on his side. Franklin's prestige, indeed, was so great among all classes in Pennsylvania, that almost any cause he supported was certain to have popular acclaim. Political rallies were held and petitions sent throughout the province for signing by both parties. John Penn noted that the Franklin party had "procur'd some names by the Assistance of Punch and Beer for they kept open house at first at a Tavern for all the Blackguards in Town, by which means a few Ship Carpenters and some of the lowest sort of people were prevailed upon to sign it."[22] Even on the frontier, except for Cumberland County, where the Scots Irish predominated, Franklin found support. At Easton a Proprietary man admitted that the "Petition for an alteration in the Government meets with Considerable Success, particularly on the frontiers, who are made to believe they will then be better protected."[23]

In May, when the Assembly reconvened, Franklin introduced his petition (signed by thirty-five hundred persons) to the Crown praying for a change of government. A committee of eight was chosen to consider it, of whom four were from western counties. So strong was opinion in the House for a change of government that when the resolution to adopt the petition came to a vote, only John Dickinson and the three Proprietary men, William Allen, John Montgomery, and Isaac Saunders voted against it.[24]

The Conestoga massacre, the march of the Paxton Boys, the dispute over taxation and defense, and the movement for the change in government, all happening simultaneously or within a few months, sent political heat in Pennsylvania to unprecedented heights. Soon the streets were alive with pamphlets and broadsides let loose by the contending parties. Franklin, of course, was the principal target of the Proprietaries. Especially irritating was a charge that he had misapplied provincial funds (the Crown reimbursements to the colony) when these were placed in his care in England. This was a questionable charge and even William Allen had acknowledged that Franklin had done his best to carry out the orders of the House.[25]

---

[22] Penn MSS., Off. Corresp., IX, 219.

[23] Bigelow, III, 334-335; Pa. Arch., 1st ser., IV, 175.

[24] Charles Stillé, The Life and Times of John Dickinson, 62.

[25] Letters to Dr. Franklin, I, Part 2, 129. APS.; Pa. Mag., XXXV, 329, 441-443; Paul L. Ford, ed., The Writings of John Dickinson, I, 153.

Franklin's friends and supporters fared no better. John Hughes, a wealthy ex-baker, was accused of stealing old land warrants and surveys from a chest in the State House. With the legal aid of Galloway, it was said, he planned to lay claim to immense tracts of land long in the possession of men who had honestly bought and paid for them. Thus when Pennsylvania became a Royal colony and Galloway was Chief Justice and Franklin the Governor, these papers, they warned, would prove "more fatal than Pandora's Box to many good Men."[26] As for Galloway, the Proprietary writers declared, it was he who had meanly snatched an office from an old man who depended upon it for his livelihood. Likewise Joseph Fox had solicited the office of Barracks Master, and then contrived to have the Moravian Indians confined there to augment his fees.[27]

The Proprietary leaders and their supporters came in for the same kind of treatment at the hands of the Quaker party. Chief Justice Allen became intensely wrought up when the Assembly in a letter to Richard Jackson said in effect that "Justice could not be obtained in the Province owing to the Proprietary influence." This was a "scandalous" reflection on the integrity of the judges and magistrates, declared Allen, and demonstrated how little Franklin and Galloway cared about the truth. The House, in fact, soon backed down when Allen demanded it to produce specific examples of favoritism in the Courts. It feebly drew attention to the possibility that there was always the danger of the Proprietors being favored by judges appointed by them.[28]

No one during these turbulent days came in for more slander than Israel Pemberton. His former friends were especially vitriolic in their treatment of him, feeling as they did he had deserted them for the enemy. One cartoon pictures him as riding a Scots Irishman and leading a "Dutchman" by the nose. In a libelous verse entitled "King Wampum" the writer graphically described an affair he was alleged to have had with a pregnant squaw (who stole his gold watch) at one of the Indian conferences.[29] Apparently his provokers felt that they had splendid caricature material, for in a broadside two years later he was labeled a "Presbyterian Indian Colonel." The sheet was as mean and cutting as could be imagined, especially in that there was an element of truth in the description of his personal traits. It claimed that he early exhibited a propensity for vice and low cunning, that he used to steal marbles from his schoolmates, that he had cheated his brothers out of part of their inheritance, that he had practiced dis-

---

[26] *Pa. Journal* (Supplement), Sept. 27, 1764; Broadsides, Box 2, Folder R. HSP.
[27] Broadsides, Box 2, Folder R.
[28] *William Allen's Letter Book,* 56-57.
[29] Joseph Shippen to Edward Shippen, April 11, 1764, Edward Shippen Papers. L. of C.; King Wampum. APS.

honesty as a merchant, and then, with his record behind him, he had feigned reform and thought of himself as a saint. With this introduction it went on to put the worst possible construction upon his activities during the French and Indian War.[30]

It was not long before the controversy permeated the churches and schools and all kinds of associations. Anglican as well as Quaker congregations were rent by it. Smith and Duché allowed political rallies to be held in Christ Church and St. Peters. Anglicans who supported Franklin accused them of playing into the hands of the Presbyterians who were determined on becoming the political masters of the province.[31] It may in fact seem strange that Smith and Duché as Anglican clergymen came out in opposition to the change which presumably would be advantageous to the Episcopacy in Pennsylvania. On the other hand it would have been very embarrassing for them to have deserted their friends and have gone over to Franklin whom they had condemned for so many years.

The College of Philadelphia, now quite dominated by Presbyterians under the leadership of Francis Alison, the vice-provost, used its influence to undermine Franklin, even to the point of indoctrinating the students.[32] Professor Hugh Williamson wrote a pamphlet against Franklin entitled *What is Sauce for a Goose is also Sauce for a Gander*. His colleague, John Ewing, bitterly attacked Franklin in a preface to a speech delivered by Dickinson. Schoolmasters as well as the college professors entered the fray. David James Dove who ran a private school wrote a vicious attack upon the Popular party entitled *The Quakers Unmasked*.

Franklin's pamphleteers answered the attacks upon them as regularly as they appeared. The Mayor and Common Council of Philadelphia, composed of Proprietary men, were labeled a tight political ring which controlled the city elections. This junto, it was charged, never properly accounted for the money derived from licenses and fees from market stalls, ferries, wharves, and vendues, amounting to over £3000 annually.[33] Then there were also the Proprietary minions in the Land Office, it was declared, who had enriched themselves by dabbling in land. That there was truth in this accusation was shown by the fact that Penn for this reason had to remove the Rev. William Peters as secretary for the Land Office the next year.[34]

---

[30] Broadsides, 1764. HSP.
[31] MSS. and Scrap Book, 87, Collectanea of J. Thompson. HSP.
[32] Edward P. Cheyney, *History of the University of Pennsylvania*, 110-113.
[33] Broadsides, Box 2, Folder R; Sparks, VII, 279.
[34] *Ibid.;* Penn MSS., Off. Corresp., IX, 292, X, 17.

Thus ran the charges and counter charges. Neither party attempted to stick very closely to the truth and as Franklin said, the "slightest indiscretions were magnified into crimes" in order to gain political advantages. Franklin tried hard to keep religion out of the dispute but without much success as "great pains is taken to lug it into the squabble."[35]

Not all the writing provoked by the movement to convert Pennsylvania into a Royal colony was of a slanderous nature. The issue in fact provoked the best thinkers of the province to enter into an exhaustive and penetrating debate concerning the respective merits and limitations of the Proprietary and Royal types of government. Benjamin Franklin and Joseph Galloway initiated the discussion by a searching analysis of the question. John Dickinson answered them in an equally cogent and penetrating treatment of the issue.

Franklin, who wrote the preface to Galloway's essay, alone refrained from personal abuse, and made, with an abundance of humor and wit, and sarcasm, a strong case for a change to a Royal form of government. Drawing freely from the history of the colonies, he gave his arguments an air of objectivity. In no small measure he based his arguments on the supposition that the Crown could not maintain a close survey of the colony as the Proprietors were in the habit of doing by the fact that the ministry was too busy with more important matters. Similarly the Crown governor would be a much freer agent than a Proprietary deputy bound by strict and onerous instructions.[36]

To remove the fears of dissenters who were afraid that a Royal government would lead to the establishment of the Anglican Church in Pennsylvania, he reminded his readers that the Crown itself had repeatedly disallowed colonial laws restricting the freedom of religion. After Massachusetts had lost its charter, he pointed out, the British Government did not impose the Episcopalian Church upon the colony.

The weakest part of Franklin's essay is found in his charge that Proprietary government was too weak to maintain order and that a Crown government would rectify this condition.[37] This was hardly consistent with his argument that Pennsylvania would enjoy a greater degree of home rule under a Royal government. Galloway candidly admitted that he wanted British regulars stationed in the colony to help in keeping law and order. Franklin, however, said that a change would not affect the number of King's troops in the province for, if more were needed, they would be sent regardless of its form of gov-

[35] Bigelow, III, 291.

[36] *Ibid.*, III, 310-356; Carl Van Doren, ed., *Letters and Papers of Benjamin Franklin and Richard Jackson, 1753-1785,* 68-85.

[37] Bigelow, III, 350-353.

ernment. Franklin's strangely illogical reasoning was probably due to a fear of losing support if he were as candid as Galloway.[38] Yet there was something unreal about the whole approach of these men to the problem of lawlessness in Pennsylvania. John Penn was undoubtedly right when he said that it would take ten thousand Regulars to seize one Paxton man and that this would mean nothing less than civil war.[39]

With fine irony Dickinson made it clear that he was not defending Proprietary government in the hope of reward. Unlike some others he had not "juggled in dirty cabals, about the offices of chief justice and attorney general." This would have been enough but Dickinson, like Galloway, marred his brief by spending much time in defaming the characters of his adversaries. He raked over again the charge that Franklin misused his trust as agent for the colony in England and made sarcastic allusions to Galloway and other dignitaries of the Quaker party.

In setting forth his principal reason for opposing a change in government, Dickinson emphasized the dangers of such a move to the liberties of the province. Franklin and Galloway were unrealistic, he argued, in thinking that Pennsylvania's charter privileges could be preserved in a Royal government. For example he asked in what colony other than New Jersey could a Quaker be a witness in criminal cases or hold office? In none, he answered, and only in New Jersey because there were not enough other persons to perform the functions required to carry out the laws.[40]

Surprisingly enough, Dickinson or other critics of a change in government made little mention of the new British colonial policy fast shaping up in England. This program aimed at stricter British control of American affairs. A conversion of Pennsylvania into a Royal colony would, it seems, have served to implement this program. Dickinson and Allen may have said little about this matter for fear that their words would be misrepresented in England and thus do more harm than good. Already the Allen party, especially the Presbyterian wing of it, was being represented in England as a disloyal and lawless band of men who might soon be seeking independence for the sake of carrying out republican ideas.[41]

In the Assembly, Dickinson found it impossible to do anything to help the Proprietary cause. Having been denied the privilege of registering a protest against the proposed change in the Journal, Dickinson

---

[38] Smyth, IV, 385; Bigelow, III, 299, 303, 352, 353.
[39] Penn MSS., Off. Corresp., IX, 238.
[40] Ford, I, 34-35, 39, 44-45, 108.
[41] Penn MSS., Off. Corresp., IX, 290.

worked hard throughout the summer to get petitions to every part of the province for signing.[42] Allen's return from England late in the summer was encouraging to Dickinson who with John Montgomery and Isaac Saunders had been the only opposition in the House.

In September, the Assembly adjourned to allow its members to conduct the campaign for the crucial election on the first of October. Franklin professed to be confident of victory pointing to the thirty-five hundred signers of his petition and of the many who were only waiting an opportunity to sign it. Allen, however, thought that Franklin was not as sure of the result as he appeared to be. This, he surmised, accounted for his sober demeanor of late, a soberness which was not at all relieved by a letter from Lord Hyde upbraiding him for his conduct in the Assembly during the recent Indian war. When questioned about the letter, Franklin promptly answered that no matter what others might think he had no intention of being "Hyde Bound."[43]

In the campaign of 1764, the Presbyterians presented as united a political front as the Quakers had ever shown. Having recovered from the division wrought by the Great Awakening, they were everywhere viewed as the most powerful single group in Pennsylvania. In order to stimulate political action to the utmost, the Presbyterian ministers and elders held a convention in Philadelphia, from which circular letters were sent to all their congregations in Pennsylvania. In every parish, Presbyterian ministers, spurred by Francis Alison, the "Presbyterian Pope," turned their pulpits into political rostrums.[44]

The Presbyterians found an energetic organizer in the person of Samuel Purviance, Jr., a merchant who kept a store on Front Street near the drawbridge, where he specialized in brandy and wine. Purviance set to work with great zeal forming committees of correspondence in all the counties in Pennsylvania.[45] Composed of the most active partisans to be found, the committees spared no pains to incite the people of all denominations to vote for the Proprietary-Presbyterian ticket.

Purviance, who spent over £300 of his own money on the election, knew how to handle frontier politics. He told Col. James Burd at Lancaster to spread the word that the Presbyterian men would come to the polls well armed and if the least partiality were shown, they would "thrash the sheriff, every inspector, Quaker and Mennonist to

[42] Ford, I, 61-63; *Pa. Journal*, July 19, 1764; Thomas Penn to Joseph Shippen, April 10, 1765, Edward Shippen Papers. L. of C.
[43] Penn MSS., Off. Corresp., IX, 256; Bigelow, III, 333-334.
[44] L. R. Harley, *Life of Charles Thomson*, 61-62; *Klett*, 256.
[45] Penn MSS., Off. Corresp., X, 96.

jelly." If anyone not qualified tried to vote, he advised his friends to have the mob deliver him a chastisement.[46]

Purviance not only supplied the Proprietary leaders with much advice on how to conduct the election but also had suggestions as to the type of candidates which should be selected. He advised Burd to put up at least two Germans to attract the vote of that important group. Lawyer George Ross, Episcopalian and English in descent, would have to be dropped to please the Scots Irish.[47]

Burd answered Purviance within a week. After trying to work out a compromise with the Quaker party wherein both sides would choose four candidates pledged to oppose changing the government, the Proprietary-Presbyterian party held a rally at Crawford's Tavern at which candidates were selected for the "New Ticket" as the anti-Franklin coalition was called.[48]

Foremost on the "New Ticket" for Lancaster was Isaac Saunders, long one of the principal Proprietary politicians in the West. In the Assembly, of which body he had been a member for several years, he was cordially despised by the Franklin party which accused him of secretly relaying everything that happened in the House of the Governor.[49] In Lancaster he had many enemies but could count upon the support of a powerful political ring which fed upon Proprietary patronage. In this way Saunders, who operated a ferry over the Susquehanna, found Proprietary favor very helpful. William Allen obligingly asked Thomas Penn not to grant a ferry license to a would-be competitor of Saunders', as it was "but common Policy for government to encourage their friends." In no place was this practice more necessary than in Pennsylvania, Allen assured Penn.[50]

In Philadelphia the "New Ticket" put on a campaign of no less intensity than at Lancaster. Thomas Willing, the Mayor of the city, was put up against Franklin. Slow and easy-going George Bryan was slated for the other seat by the Proprietaries. John Hunt, a prominent English Quaker, arrived in time to help Israel Pemberton persuade Friends to vote for Willing and Bryan or to stay away from the polls.[51] Isaac Norris, the venerable Speaker, after years of resisting the Proprietors, drew back now that the final test had come and refused to follow Franklin. Proprietary politicians now praised him as loudly as they had abused him in former years. Politics is like religion,

---

[46] Penn MSS., Off. Corresp., X, 96; Balch, 211.
[47] Shippen Papers, VI, 107. HSP.
[48] Ibid., VI, 109.
[49] Ibid., VI, 129.
[50] Penn MSS., Off. Corresp., IX, 272.
[51] Ibid., IX, 266; Balch, 206.

pithily observed Franklin: "repentence and amendment, though late, shall obtain forgiveness and procure favor."[52]

The Proprietary party worked hard in Franklin's own vineyard, the mechanics and tradesmen of Philadelphia. Although the heads of most of the mechanic associations announced that they would stand by Franklin, the "New Ticket" captivated many votes from among the individual craftsmen.[53]

William Allen associated himself with his old enemy Israel Pemberton and assured the Quakers that the Presbyterians were not aiming to dominate politics in Pennsylvania. The Quakers could name the candidates for office, for all the Presbyterians cared, he declared, so long as they were anti-Franklin men. As the election day approached Allen looked ahead with confidence. He was sure that his party would command the votes of all the Presbyterians, almost all of the Lutherans and Reformed among the Germans, about half of the Episcopalians, and a sizable number of Quakers.[54]

All was excitement in Philadelphia on the day of the election. Party workers milled about the throng of voters and much money was spent by both sides to buy votes. William Logan, working feverishly for Franklin, declared that if he lost, the Quakers were undone. From early morning the electors waited in long lines to cast their votes. By midnight they were still coming, the aged and the lame in litters and chairs, and the tardy farmers from their distant homes. When the polls were finally closed nearly four thousand votes were counted for the county and thirteen hundred for the city.[55]

To the dismay and chagrin of the Quaker party both Franklin and Galloway were defeated. So close had been the vote, however, that Franklin would have won had some last-minute voters been allowed to cast their ballots. Although mortified by the outcome, Franklin "died like a philosopher." Galloway, on the other hand, could not hide his feelings and died an agonized death "like a Mortal Deist, who has no Hopes of a Future Existence."[56]

Franklin chiefly blamed William Allen for his defeat and to soothe his nettled pride publicly derided Allen in a pamphlet entitled *Remarks on a Late Protest Against the Appointment of Mr. Franklin as Agent for this Province.*. Directly addressing Allen, Franklin reminded him

---

[52] Bigelow, III, 340.

[53] *Bouquet Papers*, No. 21651 (1943), 44.

[54] Penn MSS., Off. Corresp., IX, 270, 282. Judging from the burial figures there were more Anglicans in Philadelphia by this time than any other denomination. See Proud Papers, Historical Notes and Memoranda Respecting Philadelphia, 24-25. HSP.

[55] *Pa. Mag.*, XX, 207.

[56] *Ibid.*, IX, 274; William B. Reed, *Life and Correspondence of Joseph Reed*, I, 36-37; Bigelow, III, 360-361.

that with all his wealth and affluence he could not get elected from the county or city in which he resided and was best known. Allen consequently had been obliged to seek his seat in the Assembly as a representative of a remote frontier county. In contrast, Franklin insisted that he never solicited a vote in his life and was re-elected to the Assembly during his entire six years stay in England, and this in spite of the incessant and malicious attacks by Allen upon his character and reputation.[57]

In Philadelphia County as in the city the "New Ticket" did very well. Five of the eight seats were won in the county, one going to Henry Kepple, a German Lutheran, whose election stirred the pride of that denomination.[58] But outside of the Philadelphia area it was different, except in the Scots Irish counties of Cumberland and York. In Lancaster County the "Ticket" elected only Isaac Saunders. It elected none from Chester, Bucks, Northampton or Berks and could command in all only twelve of the thirty-six votes in the Assembly.[59]

Although disappointed at not gaining control of the Assembly, many of the Proprietary leaders felt encouraged by the election. Joseph Shippen noted that the gains made in Philadelphia had "caused the greatest dejection of spirits in those of the Quaker party and their friends."[60]

It has often been said by historians that the Quaker party would not have won this election or probably any other election during this period, had there existed a fair system of representation and equal suffrage laws in the province. But this is not the case. More equal representation in 1764 would have made the contest very close, but Franklin's party would in all probability have kept control of the Assembly by a small margin. However, most of the dissatisfaction which was the cause of this alarming loss for the Quaker party evaporated during the following year. In 1765, in fact, the Franklin party made a strong comeback and even defeated Dickinson, the leading crusader against a Royal government.[61]

---

[57] Bigelow, III, 356-370.

[58] *Journals of Henry Melchior Muhlenberg*, II, 123.

[59] When the Scots Irish in Lancaster failed to elect the sheriff, some of the wildest of them fell upon the successful candidate who was a German. The latter fled leaving his horse to have his ears cut off by the mob. Sparks, VII, 280.

[60] See Charles Lincoln, *The Revolutionary Movement in Pennsylvania, 1760-1776*, 44ff; *Pa. Mag.*, LXXI, 28-32.

[61] Pemberton Papers, XXXIV, 128, James Pemberton to John Hunt, April 11, 1764, Pemberton Papers, Box 3; Sparks, VII, 281.

The East found some reason for justifying unequal representation in the fact that the frontier counties paid only a small part of the tax burden of the province. In 1773 both the city and the county of Philadelphia remonstrated against this situation. The tax delinquency of the West, it was said, had thrown the burden almost entirely upon the East. Philadelphia (county and city) had already paid

The fact that the Quaker party could have held its own if representation had been based on population does not of course justify keeping it uneven. Franklin admitted that the West and the city of Philadelphia were under-represented and he apparently was willing to see the discrepancy rectified. But not so most of the Quakers and many of the Anglicans, who were now thoroughly frightened by the rising power of the Presbyterians. Like James Pemberton, Thomas Wharton voiced their feelings when he said that "the natural increase of the Presbyterians, and the vast numbers yearly arriving among us," made it imperative to seek a Royal government to escape Presbyterian domination.[62]

Thus it is true that Franklin's crusade to convert Pennsylvania into a Royal colony, which had its inception, in Franklin's mind at least, from the abuse practiced upon the colony by the Proprietors, was seized upon as a possible protection against forces at home as well as abroad. Only a few weeks before the election, "rioters" had reappeared in Philadelphia from the West with a petition for more representation. Although it may have been five yards of paper all in the same handwriting, as William Logan said, it was nonetheless disquieting.[63] By this time Presbyterians such as George Bryan, Gilbert Tennent, Francis Alison, and John Ewing were picturing the Assembly's plan to convert Pennsylvania into a Royal colony as "no more than an artful scheme to divert the attention of the injured frontier inhabitants from prosecuting their petitions, which very much alarm them."[64]

---

nearly £9,000 above its quota while the West continued to default on taxes. In 1772 the three eastern counties paid nearly £19,000 under the eighteen-penny tax. Only about £8,000 was gathered from all the other counties. *Votes*, VIII, 6861-6873, 6921, 6985, 7048, 7052.

It is not true that the Assembly purposely gave the western counties only one or two representatives at the time they were created as counties so as to maintain political power in the East. Most of these counties had a very small population at the time they were established and to have given them any more would have made them over represented. In the early days, in fact, these counties did not want more than one or two representatives because of the cost involved. For this and other reasons western counties very often chose residents of Philadelphia to represent them in the Assembly. Countyhood was a luxury and there are cases where people petitioned the House not to create a new county because of the expense involved. Furthermore, if more new counties had been created and their representation been high in numbers, more than likely the Quaker party would have benefited by it. Dr. Thomas Graeme recognized this when he suggested in 1750 that new western counties with few representatives would be of advantage to the Proprietary party by confining most of the German vote to the West and thus depriving the Quakers of their vote in the crucial eastern counties. *Votes*, VIII, 6751, 6757, 6913, 6924; *Pa. Mag.*, XXXIX, 446-447; *Pa. Gazette*, January 21, 1771; *Statutes*, V, 7072.

[62] Letters to Dr. Franklin, I, Part 2, 111, APS.

[63] Smith MSS., VI, 137. Ridgway Lib.

[64] Sparks, VII, 282.

Although John Penn was besought by many of his friends in the days preceding the election to remove all justices who favored a change in government, he moved cautiously for fear of making more enemies than friends. This policy was approved by Allen and Hamilton.[65] But after the election the politicians could no longer be restrained. William Franklin declared that as a reward to the Presbyterians "Mr. Bryan & Mr. Alexander Huston, two fiery Bigots, are appointed Justices for the City and County [Philadelphia]."[66] In Chester County, William Moore was made president of the Council of Justices. Other Proprietary men favored with judicial commissions at this time were Thomas Willing, John and Thomas Lawrence, Jacob Duché, William Coxe, Samuel Shoemaker, William Humphreys, James Biddle, Peter Evans, and Henry Harrison. John Dickinson, however, who had suffered much abuse for championing the Proprietary cause, was not rewarded by the Governor because Benjamin Chew, the Attorney-General, had such a dislike for him.[67] Among those removed from office for supporting Franklin were John Morton, John Potts, and Henry Pawling.[68]

With the convening of the new Assembly on October 14, the majority resolved to present the petition for the change of government to the Crown and to send Franklin to London to assist Richard Jackson in this important matter.[69] The minority doggedly fought Franklin's appointment. As an alternative they proposed Dr. John Fothergill, the famous Quaker physician, for the Pennsylvania agency. But he would not do, for the Quaker party knew that he was much influenced by Israel Pemberton and had joined with those opposing the change.

Next the Proprietary party tried to stop the resolution for presenting the petition by pointing out that the Penns had conceded the most important points in dispute, thereby removing the cause for changing the form of government. All failing, William Allen got up and begged the House not to send Franklin to England. His appeal was of no avail and the appointment was speedily confirmed.[70]

---

[65] Penn MSS., Off. Corresp., IX, 252.

[66] Letters to Dr. Franklin, LVIII, Part 1. 32. APS. So great was the wrath of the inhabitants at Moore's appointment that only through the persuasion of John Morton, the Chief Burgess of the Borough of Chester, could the justices be brought together to hold Court.

[67] Penn MSS., Off. Corresp., IX, 276.

[68] Letters to Dr. Franklin, LVIII, Part 1, 32; Part 2, 112, 115.

[69] Votes, VII, 5682ff.

[70] Bouquet Papers, No. 21651 (1943), 44; Bigelow, III, 363-364; Pemberton Papers, XVII, 103; Ford, I, 153; Penn MSS., Off. Corresp., X, 274.
    The last time Franklin was in England, the opposition said he had cost the colony £6,000 by mishandling funds received from the Crown. Besides this he had been paid £5,000. Franklin answered that he had only followed the directions

As the Assembly did not have money enough on hand to send Franklin, a group of merchants quickly raised £1100 as a loan to the House. On the day of his leaving, a great cavalcade of more than three hundred citizens accompanied Franklin to Newcastle to see him embark. There amid waving flags and booming cannons, Franklin bid his friends farewell. Deeply touched, Franklin exclaimed to a friend standing by, "God bless them and all Pennsylvania."[71]

Politics in Pennsylvania did not lose any of its tenseness after Franklin was gone. Isaac Norris, sick of politics and not well physically, declined to accept the speakership again. When his resignation was delivered to the House, John Hughes at once nominated George Ashbridge, a strong Franklin man. About half of the Assembly immediately stood up for Ashbridge, but Dickinson managed to make himself heard above the excitement and commotion. With all the powers at his command he beseeched his colleagues to ask Norris to reconsider before anything further was done. At this suggestion "Uproar, Rage and Confusion filled the Room." Joseph Fox shouted that the House would not "be deceived by such Tricks." But somehow Dickinson managed to get a short adjournment. After the House reassembled it proceeded calmly to nominate and elect Joseph Fox as Speaker. Thus during the adjournment Dickinson and his friends had succeeded in securing a shift from Ashbridge to Fox, who was known to be more moderate and less firmly attached to Benjamin Franklin.[72]

Franklin had hardly set sail before there appeared on the streets an answer to his attack on William Allen. The latter had asked Dickinson to write one, but he had declined not relishing another round of mudslinging. The answer which appeared was a joint effort of Alison, Ewing, Smith, and Edward Shippen. As was usual, it aired all the gossip and accusations which could be thought of against Franklin and his friends.[73]

Much mirth was provoked when John Hughes, the ex-baker, whom the Proprietary men had dubbed the "Welsh Squire," posted a notice in the *Pennsylvania Gazette* asking Allen or any other gentlemen responsible for the pamphlet to pay £5 to the Pennsylvania Hospital for every statement which could be proved false. Hughes for his part would give £10 for every statement proved true. In the next issue

of the House regarding the Crown reimbursements and had borne a large part of his expenses out of his own pocket. Be that as it may, in 1762, Allen prevented having a second sum granted by the Crown placed in Franklin's hands. *William Allen's Letter Book,* 49.

[71] Bigelow, III, 257.
[72] Norris Letter Book, 1756-1766, 144-145.
[73] Letters to Dr. Franklin, LVIII, Part 1, 33. APS.

of the newspaper, Hughes' opponents countered his challenge by offering to bet him ten pies or cakes against five pies or cakes.[74]

The "Welsh Squire," however, was a much more dangerous person than William Allen or any of his friends recognized. Already he had taken it upon himself to write to the ministers of state charging Allen and the Proprietary leaders of disloyalty to the Crown. Proof of this, he asserted, was their opposition to a Royal government. Certainly Hughes was a busybody, a trait which presently helped to make him the most despised man in Pennsylvania.

While Pennsylvania was caught up in an unprecedented political upheaval, the people throughout the colonies followed with deep interest the course of events. Franklin had admirers everywhere and anything he did or said was certain to attract attention. The Maryland Assembly, which had a habit of taking its cues from Pennsylvania, now began to consider a petition to the King for changing it from a Proprietary to a Royal colony. In this regard the Maryland leaders had an interview with Franklin before he left for England. "It is extraordinary," commented John Penn, that "this man cannot be contented with what he is doing in this Province."[75]

When Franklin arrived in London, he found Richard Jackson very cool toward his petition for a Royal government. Franklin probably was not very surprised, for word had reached Pennsylvania some months before that Jackson no longer was in favor of a change. This was one of the principal reasons, in fact, why Franklin was sent abroad. Allen, on his return to Philadelphia, had done his best to impress upon the Assembly Jackson's reasons for opposing a change. Just before the election Allen had had a letter from Jackson published in the *Pennsylvania Journal* in which his reasons were presented.[76]

Jackson, whom Samuel Johnson called the "All Knowing," was one of the best lawyers in England at the time. He was counsel for the South Sea Company and Cambridge University, and after 1770 became an advisor to the Board of Trade. Being close to British politics, Jackson realized how dangerous was Franklin's plan in the face of the new colonial policy rapidly taking form in England. "The mischiefs and dangers to Pennsylvania in particular," he warned Franklin in a letter in November, "and to all America in general, are inconceivable to one, who had not been in England a good part of the past year."[77]

Franklin was not long in learning after his arrival that sentiment was much against him. Many said the petition proceeded from a

---

[74] *Pa. Gazette,* Dec. 20, 1764, Dec. 27, 1764.
[75] Penn MSS., Off. Corresp., IX, 274.
[76] *Pa. Journal,* Supplement No. 1138, Sept. 27, 1764.
[77] Sparks, VII, 272-275.

"malevolent heart" and not from a right way of thinking.[78] It may
seem strange that the British ministry did not welcome the chance to
convert another colony into a Royal province especially in view of
the new colonial policy. Consistency, however, was not one of the
virtues of the British government in the Eighteenth century.

The petition for a change of government was never officially presented by Franklin for Crown consideration. In February, 1765,
Franklin got nowhere when he approached some of the ministers on
the question.[79] The next year the Privy Council read over some correspondence relating to the question and then put them aside *sine die,*
which the President of the Council laconically described as meaning
"for ever and for ever."[80] But with individual ministers, Franklin
thought that he was making some headway. In 1766 Lord Shelbourne
told him that he thought the Proprietors should voluntarily give up
the colony.[81] Franklin even heard that Thomas Penn might be given
a peerage as an incentive to giving up the colony.[82] In 1768, however,
Franklin was disappointed in his talks with Lord Hillsborough, the
Secretary of State for the Colonies. Before long he was convinced that
Hillsborough could not be trusted and would probably side with the
Penns in a showdown.[83]

The fact that Franklin and his followers did not abandon the plan
for a change of government after the Stamp Act controversy broke
upon the colonies left them open to the charge that they were motivated by self-interest. Many of the Quakers who had favored a Royal
government grew cool when the Stamp Act issue arose. By that time
many people rightly considered it an out-dated question. In March,
1766, James Pemberton noted a growing disposition among the people
not to quarrel with the Governor.[84]

William Allen read the signs of the times much clearer than Franklin
or Galloway when he observed in September, 1765, that the Stamp
Act would be repealed and that Pennsylvania would see no change in
government. Allen surmised that Franklin had offered to support the

---

[78] Smith MSS, VI, 161. Ridgway Lib.

[79] Bigelow, III, 372-374. A rumor arose in Philadelphia that Franklin was endeavoring to persuade Springett Penn (a grandson of William Penn by his first marriage
and not one of the Proprietors) that he was the rightful heir to Pennsylvania.
If recognized as the rightful heir by the Crown, he would come to the colony as
governor, it was said. Penn MSS., Off. Corresp., IX, 298.

[80] *Pa. Journal,* Feb. 27, 1766.

[81] Franklin to Galloway, Oct. 11, 1766, Franklin Papers, William L. Clements Lib.
(Yale U. Transcripts); Smyth, V, 23.

[82] Letters to Dr. Franklin, I, Part 1, 66. APS.

[83] Smyth, V, 97-99; Franklin to Galloway, Aug. 20, 1768, Franklin Papers, William
L. Clements Lib. (Yale U. Transcripts.)

[84] Pemberton Papers, XXXIV, 140; *Pa. Mag.,* LIII, 156-157.

Stamp Act in exchange for Grenville's aid in securing a change of government for Pennsylvania. Both, he thought, had failed now that the King had been forced to change the ministry.[85]

In 1767 after the excitement of the Stamp Act had abated, Galloway and his friends succeeded in reviving interest in removing the Proprietors. The Townshend Acts, which Parliament enacted that year, furnished him with a new argument for converting Pennsylvania into a Royal colony. The duties, explained Galloway, would be used to pay governors, judges, and other Royal officers in the colonies. Unless Pennsylvania became a Royal colony, therefore, it would derive no benefit from the taxes which it paid under the Acts.[86]

The next year the old scare of frontier lawlessness reappeared in Pennsylvania. Two white men killed a number of defenseless Indians. The murderers were caught and put in the Carlisle jail to await trial. When it was learned that Chief Justice William Allen had issued a warrant for bringing the prisoners to Philadelphia for examination, a band of men broke into the jail, and set the prisoners free.[87] Hamilton felt sure Franklin would dress up the affair so as to put the Proprietors in the worst light possible even though every one knew it was "no more in the power of the Government to bring the Offenders to punishment, than to raise the unhappy sufferers from the dead."[88]

But Franklin had changed his mind considerably about the matter of law and order in America. No longer was he confident that a mere change of government from a Proprietary to a Royal form would put an end to lawlessness on the frontier. In answer to Galloway's lament over the sad state of law and order in Pennsylvania, Franklin replied that riots were commonplace occurrences in London and that no one in England would be a bit startled to hear of mob action in America. In a letter to John Ross, Franklin told of the riots incited by Wilkes, of violent strikes for higher wages, of soldiers firing on the populace, and of a general unrest in England which seemed to menace the very existence of the nation.[89]

The sad state of English politics and government, Franklin said, made it impossible to correct abuses even when such were apparent to

[85] Letters to Dr. Franklin, LVIII, Part 1, 35. APS.

[86] *Ibid.*, II, Part 1, 98.

[87] *Votes*, VIII, 6141ff; Penn MSS., Off. Corresp., X, 138; Shippen Papers, VI, 196. HSP. "Some lawyers," Allen wrote Thomas Penn, "chiefly one [George Ross who happened to be in York at the time] represented it as an oppressive illegal measure to have the prisoners carried out of the county and that it was with an intention to have him tried in Philadelphia which was a great invasion of their liberties——. This lawyer harangued people in the court at York which was sitting & got them excited & convinced even some of the justices." Penn MSS., Off. Corresp., X, 138.

[88] Letters to Dr. Franklin, II, Part 2, 143. APS.; Penn MSS., Off. Corresp., X, 156.

[89] *Pa. Mag.*, XXVI, 298; Bigelow, IV, 163.

all. What hope was there, he asked, for an intelligent handling of English problems, to say nothing of American with "the ministry divided in their counsels with little regard for each other, worried by perpetual opposition, in continual apprehension of changes, intent on securing popularity—and with little time or inclination to attend to our small affairs, whose remoteness makes them appear still smaller."[90] In these words can be found the principal reasons for Britain's failure to solve the problems of imperial relations upon which the fate of the empire rested.

As late as 1768 Franklin received instructions from the Pennsylvania Assembly to work for a change of government.[91] Yet, as everyone knew, the Penns and the colony had resolved their differences which had long kept the province in a state of agitation. Even the fear of Presbyterian domination had subsided as the colonies became locked in a great controversy with the mother country over taxation. But all this did not deter the Quaker junto from continuing its quest for a Royal system of government. Galloway and his friends would not be content, it would seem, until they had control of all branches of the government and occupied the appointive as well as the elective offices in the province.

The movement to change Pennsylvania from a Proprietary to a Royal government had far reaching consequences. The next chapter will show that it may very well have been an important factor in the attitude which Franklin and the Quaker party leaders took toward the Stamp Act and the great constitutional dispute with Great Britain. But of greater significance, it would seem, was its influence on the Proprietary-Presbyterian party. For the first time William Allen's party had a cause to defend which appealed to a large number of people. The next year his party led the resistance to the Stamp Act. From then on until the movement for independence set in, the great majority of leaders in the revolutionary movement came from the Proprietary-Presbyterian party.

---

[90] Smyth, V, 132-133.
[91] *Votes,* VII, 6290.

IX

THE STAMP ACT. 1765-1766

B EFORE the passage of the Stamp Act, the British Parliament had already entered upon its new post-war approach to British-American relations. The war had revealed the looseness of the empire and its failure to act as a coordinated unity in time of emergency. Colonial governments were the objects of censure by the ministry for not cooperating sufficiently with the home government and with the other colonies. All this proved the need, it was said, of bringing the colonies more directly under the control of the British government. Under more ordinary circumstances the government could be depended upon to procrastinate, but after the Seven Years' War public opinion would not allow it to let things drift. The British debt was colossal and there arose a general feeling that the colonies should assume at least part of the current cost of defending and garrisoning British North America.

As early as February, 1763, only a few days after the Treaty of Paris was ratified, Charles Townshend, in the capacity of First Lord of Trade, announced the new plans for British colonial government. The program consisted of stricter enforcement of laws pertaining to the colonies, a greater extension in the scope of the navigation laws, and duties and taxes to be applied to the cost of colonial defense.[1]

The next year when most Pennsylvanians had their attention riveted upon the turbulent domestic politics, George Grenville, now Chancellor of the Exchequer and First Lord of the Treasury, went ahead rapidly in his program for the American colonies. Lumber, pot-ashes, whale fins, logwood, and iron were added to the list of American goods enumerated for exclusive shipment to Great Britain. An entirely new feature, however, was seen in the Sugar Act which lowered the duty on foreign molasses from six to three pennies per gallon. Whereas the former duty was a prohibitory one for the purpose of regulation, the new duty was as stated in the preamble of the act, intended to be a source of revenue. Still more frightening to the colonists than the tax itself was the knowledge that the act carried provisions for strengthening the Customs Office and the Admiralty Courts in America.[2]

---

[1] William MacDonald, *Select Charters*, 273-281.

[2] Claude Van Tyne, *The Causes of the War of Independence*, 126-127, 135; MacDonald, 272-281; George Beer, *British Colonial Policy*, 274-286. Merchants of Boston, New York, and Philadelphia all petitioned their legislatures to remonstrate against the new laws. Prov. Papers, XXXIV, 12.

111

The new duties under the Sugar Act were much disliked throughout the colonies, especially in New England which would suffer most. Nevertheless, it produced none of the uproar and defiance which accompanied the passage of the Stamp Act the next year. A stamp act for the colonies had been discussed by the Treasury during the late war, but no action had been taken. In 1763 Townshend had proposed a stamp act as part of his new program for America. The next year Grenville carried forward plans for the measure, announcing in March his intention of introducing it at the next session of Parliament. The colonies were thus given time to propose an alternative plan if they cared to do so. As nothing was offered by the colonial agents other than keeping the old requisition system, the Stamp Act became a law with but slight opposition in Parliament. The measure required revenue stamps on all legal and commercial documents, newspapers, almanacs, pamphlets, and on playing cards and dice. The taxes derived from the act were to go toward maintaining ten thousand troops which the ministry was planning on sending to America.[3]

The role which Benjamin Franklin played during the planning and passage of the Stamp Act became a matter of great political importance in Pennsylvania. The Proprietary men became convinced as events unfolded that he had secretly encouraged the ministry to pass the act. There was, in truth, a good deal to excite suspicion. Only a month before he left for England in November, 1764, William Allen asserted that Franklin had a plan in mind for taxing America which he intended to present to the Crown. By this means, Allen believed, Franklin hoped to "ingratiate himself" with the ministry and thereby secure a change of government for Pennsylvania without delay.[4]

The Proprietary men soon were in possession of intercepted letters between Franklin and his friends in Philadelphia which proved to their satisfaction that he was guilty of promoting the detested Stamp Act. It was not long before they had pieced together the evidence and come out with a full explanation of what had happened in England. Franklin, it was said, had long advocated a stamp tax as the best means of raising revenue in America. As early as 1755 it was rumored he had acquainted General Braddock with his views on taxing America. The

---

[3] Van Tyne, 142; MacDonald, 281-305. Although relief to the Exchequer was the real motive for sending more troops to America, the late Indian war (1763-64) led by Pontiac, which was quelled mainly by the British Regulars, was used to justify the plan. Most of the troops were never sent.

[4] Penn MSS., Off. Corresp., IX, 290. See Edward Shippen to Jasper Yeates, May 15, 1775, Balch Papers, Shippen, II, 25, HSP. It is possible that Allen made reference to Franklin's ideas on a colonial loan office and not to a stamp act. Franklin did propose to Grenville a colonial loan office in lieu of taxing America. Interest earned by the loan office would be at the disposal of the Crown. Grenville turned a deaf ear to the plan.

genesis of the Stamp Act they reasoned as follows. The act as now passed by Parliament had been nurtured in Bute's administration, when Franklin was closely associated with this favorite of the King. It was Lord Bute who had shown his regard for Franklin by obtaining for his son William the governorship of New Jersey. Although Bute had been forced out of the King's circle of advisors by the insistence of Grenville after he had resigned from the ministry, the change did not in any way alter Franklin's position with the ruling circle. He was then in fact prepared to indulge in some horse trading. Franklin would back the Stamp Act, and in exchange Grenville would do what he could to push through a change of government for Pennsylvania at the first opportunity. This assumption on the part of the Proprietary men finds some support in that on one occasion Pitt presumably said that the ministry had been led into the tax by an American who hoped to obtain a reward.[5]

In any event one may wonder why Franklin was not able to do more in defending the colonies. James Logan (Junior) wrote from London in April, 1765 that he believed the act would have been deferred if the Colonies had petitioned against it.[6] Yet most of the colonies had sent their agents what amounted to petitions for presentment to the ministry.[7] Israel Pemberton said in May that none of the agents "adventur'd to present their petitions, the House of Com⁸ being determined the sovereignty of the Parliament of Great Britain shall not be disputed."[8] Franklin's failure to act may also seem strange in view of his great weight in governing circles. Capt. Barnsley said in 1767 that "he saw our Benj. Franklin always twice a Week, that he has as Great a Levee as a Minister of State, & is advised with & consulted by ye Ministry, on all affairs relative to America."[9]

Certain it is that William Allen and his friends had an abundance of circumstantial evidence to support their conclusions. They knew that Franklin had sent Thomas Wharton a pamphlet vindicating the Stamp Act and that he had nominated John Hughes for the office of Stamp Collector for Pennsylvania. In choosing Hughes, Franklin was but paying a political debt to one of his most loyal supporters in the province. "It was my interest, assiduity, and influence," declared

---

[5] *Pa. Journal*, Sept. 18, 1766. See V. W. Crane, "Benjamin Franklin and the Stamp Act," *Col. Soc. of Mass.* (1932), XXII, 56-77, for a vindication of Franklin.

[6] William Logan to John Smith, April 12, 1765, John Smith Corresp., 1740-1770.

[7] *Votes*, VII, 5628, 5643.

[8] Pemberton Papers, XVIII, 3. John C. Miller states that the colonial petitions were laid aside by Parliament having adopted a rule against having petitions read on money bills. Miller, 118. Van Tyne, on the other hand, says that Grenville carefully concealed them from Parliament. Van Tyne, 141.

[9] William Logan to John Smith, Aug. 13, 1767, Corresp. of John Smith, 1740-1770. HSP.

Hughes in a letter which Thomas Bradford intercepted, "that sent Dr. Franklin [to England] for a change of government."[10] But Franklin, the Proprietary leaders believed, had more in mind than simply paying a political debt in nominating Hughes for Stamp Collector. Hughes was a resolute and determined man and Franklin knew, they reasoned, that he would do all in his power to execute the Stamp Act. Certain it is, that as late as July, 1765, Franklin believed the Stamp Act would not be repealed. "Such Things once done," he assured Charles Thomson, "are seldom given up."[11]

Most damaging to Franklin's reputation was a letter he sent John Hughes after hearing of the intense opposition to the Stamp Act in America. "If it continues, your undertaking to execute it may make you unpopular for a Time," Franklin wrote, "but your Acting with coolness and Steadiness, and with every circumstance in your Power of Favor to the People, will by degrees reconcile them. In the meantime, a firm Loyalty to the Crown & faithful Adherence to the government of this Nation, which it is the Safety as well as the Honour of the Colonies to be connected with, will always be the wisest course for you and I to take, whatever may be the Madness of the Populace or their blind Leaders."[12]

But the case against Franklin does not end here. When Coxe, the Stamp Collector for New Jersey (whom Franklin had also appointed), resigned, Franklin told Hughes to have his son apply for the office. About this time, William Franklin, who was corresponding regularly with his father, called for troops to help enforce the act in New Jersey.[13] Meanwhile, Galloway, who also closely followed Franklin's advice, appealed to the people of Pennsylvania to accept the stamps and remonstrate afterward. The assurance of Galloway and others in Pennsylvania that Franklin was doing all in his power to get the act repealed had the appearance of a smoke screen against the wrath of the people.

In London, when merchants of Bristol at the insistence of Philadelphia tradesmen visited Franklin in the interest of repeal, they found him cool and reserved. A little later, when Parliament met in January, 1766, and called for papers and petitions from America, Franklin obligingly produced the letters of Hughes and Galloway which pic-

---

[10] Broadsides: Six Arguments Against Chusing Joseph Galloway for Assemblyman, 1766. HSP; Penn MSS., Off. Corresp., X, 80; Letters to Dr. Franklin, I, Part 2, 138. APS.

[11] Pa. Journal, Sept. 18, 1766. Franklin to Thomson, July 18, 26, 1765, Thomson Papers. L. of C.

[12] Franklin to Hughes, Aug. 9, 1765, Hughes MSS. HSP. Franklin prefaced this admonition by saying that he was doing all he could to get the law repealed.

[13] Pa. Journal, Sept. 18, 1766.

tured Pennsylvania in a state of rebellion engineered by William Allen, the arch conspirator.[14]

A few weeks later, however, Franklin saw Grenville falling, and repeal certain. Thereupon, it may be, he was obligingly offered an opportunity to whitewash himself by an examination before the bar of Parliament. If Franklin had had a hand in promoting the act, the least Grenville could do was to offer him a chance to escape. In his examination before Parliament, Franklin said that the law could not be enforced in America. Yet it was he who had told Grenville less than a year before that the tax could be collected in spite of some expected opposition, and it was he who had had his friends appointed to collect the tax.[15]

Franklin's defense of himself may appear rather weak against the array of evidence against him. In July, 1765, he wrote to his friend Charles Thomson: "Depend upon it my good neighbor, I took every step in my power, to prevent the Passing of the Stamp Act,—but the Tide was too strong against us."[16] Later he explained that Grenville had called the American agents to his office a few days after the act was passed and asked for suggestions for stamp collectors, inasmuch as the ministry wanted to please America as far as possible. "By this plausible and Apparently candid Declaration," wrote Franklin, "we were drawn in to nominate and I named for our Province Mr. Hughes." "None of us," he continued, "foresaw or imagined, that this Compliance with the request of the Minister would or could have been called an Application of ours, and adduced as a proof of our *Approbation* of the Act we had been opposing."[17]

To strengthen Franklin's defenses, extracts from several letters by prominent men in England were published in the *Pennsylvania Gazette* asserting that Franklin did his best to prevent the passage of the Stamp Act. Yet it seems entirely possible that most if not all of these letters had been written at the suggestion of Franklin. Certain it is that he solicited Dr. John Fothergill to write for him. Fothergill was without doubt sincere in what he said, but it is doubtful that he had

---

[14] Penn MSS., Off. Corresp., IX, 290; *Pa. Journal,* Sept. 18, 1766. Of Franklin, Joseph Shippen wrote: "His not doing the least Service to the province during his present Agency in England but on the Contrary his yielding to the late Measures of imposing Taxes & Burthens on the Colonies, and his acceptance of Posts for his Friends to execute the Stamp Act, the very thing he was instructed to oppose, are matters which seem to open the Eyes of many that were before blinded in his Favor." Penn MSS., Off. Corresp., X, 13.

[15] *Pa. Journal,* Sept. 18, 1766.

[16] Franklin to Thomson, July 18, 1765, Thomson Papers, I, L. of C.

[17] Smyth, VI, 200-201.

any first-hand testimony other than what Franklin was pleased to give him.[18]

In Pennsylvania, as in all the colonies, opinion was overwhelmingly opposed to the Stamp Act. Even the Quakers added their voices to the general clamor against the act, which was declared to be unconstitutional. Israel Pemberton not only signed the petition against the Stamp Act, but considered organizing a company to manufacture cloth. To Franklin's surprise even Thomas Wharton, one of the inner-circle members of the Quaker party, refused to endorse the act. When Franklin sent him a pamphlet vindicating Parliament for passing the law, Wharton answered that he was as much opposed to the measure as anyone in America. Wharton told Franklin that America could not raise the specie to pay the tax and any attempt to enforce it would drive America into manufacturing the goods which were customarily imported from England.[19]

With the principal leaders of the Franklin party evincing a spirit of equivocation or even approval of the Stamp Act, an opportunity was presented for the Proprietary party to become the leaders in a popular cause. Still, until after the news of the actual passage of the act, William Allen was not at all sure that it would have any bearing on domestic politics. As late as March, 1765, Allen admitted that there was "no standing against the torrent of Franklin's party." When word came of Franklin's arrival in London with his petition for a Royal government, all Philadelphia seemed to turn out in the streets in jubilation and the bells rang all night long.[20]

Just how much party consideration motivated the Proprietary leaders in opposing the Stamp Act is difficult to judge. Certainly their stand was hardly consistent with their former profession as the upholders of prerogative and authority. The Rev. William Smith confessed that he usually sided with government, but on this occasion he could not condone what was patently a breach of English liberties. No one could doubt but that Dickinson was motivated by principle rather than party considerations but what about Allen, Chew, Shippen and a host of others? Was Allen against the Stamp Act because he saw a chance to ruin Franklin in Pennsylvania or was it because Parliament had all but ruined his iron business by recent legislation, or was it, as he said, because the act was an invasion of American constitutional rights? Although party interests wielded great weight with William Allen and he was indeed very provoked at his losses in the iron business, it seems quite safe to assume that he would not have

---

[18] *Pa. Gazette*, May 8, 1766; Penn MSS., Off. Corresp., X, 35, 39.
[19] Letters to Dr. Franklin, I, Part 2, 138. APS.
[20] Penn MSS., Off. Corresp., X, 7.

opposed the Crown for either party or personal considerations.[21] Allen had too great a respect for England to do that, as is evident from the fact that when the die was cast in 1776 he risked losing most of his fortune when he turned his back on independence and sailed for England.

For a time the Quaker junto and Franklin entertained the hope that the colony would divide openly on the issue of the stamp tax, with the Quaker party standing for loyalty and cooperation with Great Britain. Galloway published an article which he called *Americanus* in which he condoned Parliament in passing the act. Britain, he said, was so heavily taxed that it could not bear the mounting imperial expenses. Why should Americans object to paying their share, every cent of which would be spent in America? True, Americans preferred to be taxed only by their own legislatures but this method, as everyone knew, had not been very successful. The stamp tax was probably too high, but at least it was equitable in that no colony could dodge its responsibility.

It was sheer folly, Galloway continued, to think that America could bully England into denying itself the right to tax the colonies. America's protest should rest solely upon the plea that the tax was too heavy and would cripple commerce and thus prove harmful for both England and the colonies. Perhaps, he said, a union of the American colonies would provide a means whereby America could tax itself in lieu of the method adopted by Great Britain. He was glad to hear that Massachusetts had taken the lead in calling a Congress to consider the whole problem; through such action he hoped a solution could be found.[22]

If Galloway thought that he could keep his authorship of the article a secret, he was doomed to disappointment from the start. Soon his opponents were publishing, with appropriate comments, those parts of his article which placed him in the most unfavorable light, as an enemy of American liberty. Other articles answered *Americanus*. These generally insisted that the colonies must stand firm on their constitutional rights if they valued their liberties and hoped to preserve them.[23]

---

[21] *Ibid.*, X, 9; See Shippen Papers, L. of C.

[22] Letters to Dr. Franklin, LVII, Part 1, 34. APS.; Sparks, VII, 298. In Jan. 1766, Galloway told Franklin that he was writing a pamphlet which he would call "Political Reflections on the Dispute between Great Britain and her Colonies respecting her Right of Imposing Taxes on them without their Consent." He was going to show it to William Franklin, he said, before having it published. Letters to Dr. Franklin, I, Part 2, 116½. APS.; Sparks, VII, 305.

[23] America, it was said, could not possibly pay the stamp tax. Pennsylvania for example, had an unfavorable balance of trade with Great Britain, amounting to over £300,000 sterling on which it paid five percent interest. In an economy such as this England was asking the colonies to pay a tax which would amount to one-fifth of the land tax of England. *Pa. Journal,* Sept. 19, 1765.

When the Assembly met in September, Galloway, although not a member, was accused of contriving to prevent the appointment of delegates to the Stamp Act Congress in New York. If this accusation is true, he failed miserably. The Assembly appointed a committee dominated by the leading Proprietary men in the House to draft instructions for the Pennsylvania delegation which would presently be chosen. Galloway must have squirmed when he read the names of the committeemen: Allen, Dickinson, Saunders, Bryan, McConnaughly, Taylor, and Morton—the most fiery opponents of the Stamp Act in the House and nearly all leaders of the Proprietary party. It may be, however, as was said at the time, that Galloway was able to persuade the House to soften the resolutions proposed by Dickinson's committee.[24]

To attend the New York meeting, the House appointed Joseph Fox, Speaker of the Assembly, and John Dickinson, John Morton, and George Bryan, four bitter opponents of the Stamp Act.[25] Party politics, however, may have been active in making this choice. Dickinson and Bryan were dangerous rivals to the Quaker party as had been shown in the last election. Why not, then, get them safely out of the province during the next election which was soon to be held? If that was planned, it was a shrewd move: neither Dickinson nor Bryan was re-elected that year to the Assembly.[26]

During the month of September preceding the annual election, the Proprietary party stepped up its campaign against the Quaker party. William Allen accused Franklin on the floor of the House with being the greatest enemy in England to the repeal of the Stamp Act.[27] This produced a great uproar with the members such as James Pemberton and George Ashbridge demanding that Allen produce proof of what he said or be expelled from the Assembly. It may be that Allen was spared the censure of the House only by the abrupt adjournment of the meeting by Joseph Fox, whom everyone knew had grown very cool toward Franklin during the past year.

About the middle of September, at a great mass meeting held at the State House, it was resolved that John Hughes must resign his commission as tax collector without delay. Led by James Allen,

---

[24] *Pa. Mag.*, XXVI, 290.

[25] Sparks, VII, 299; *Votes*, VII, 5767-69; *Pa. Mag.*, XXVI, 290.

[26] At the Convention there was great disagreement as to what course should be pursued by the colonies. The president of the meeting was Timothy Ruggles, an arch Tory, who became a brigadier general in the British Army during the Revolution. But the Radical majority including such well-known men as Dickinson, Otis, and Gadsden, after eleven days of debate, succeeded in having adopted a Declaration of Rights and Grievances and petitions to the King, Lords, and Commons.

[27] Penn MSS., Off. Corresp., X, 13.

son of the Chief Justice, and other well-known gentlemen, the mob "whooping and hollowing" surged through the streets until it arrived at Hughes' house. The redoubtable Hughes, so sick he could hardly stand on his feet, stood them off with loaded guns. He had not received his commission, he said, so how could he be asked to resign?[28]

Baffled by Hughes' defiance some of the mobsters shouted that they should get at the real source of their troubles and pull down Franklin's house. White with fright, Deborah Franklin saw a huge crowd of men (estimated at eight hundred) appear before her house. But they were the White Oaks, Franklin supporters, arrived in time to place themselves between her and the patriotic mob.[29]

As the election date approached, both parties worked feverishly to win votes. The Proprietary party tried to impress it upon the people that the Stamp Act was a domestic issue and not merely a dispute with England. The inhabitants had for so long looked upon Allen's party as the "Court" party and Franklin's as the "people's party" that it was difficult for them to see it in any other way. Even Charles Thomson, who was violently opposed to the Stamp Act, still thought of the political contest as "between the Court party & the people."[30] Many people still seemed to think that the principal issue facing Pennsylvania was the question of the change of government which the great majority still seemed to favor.

Once again Samuel Purviance took a prominent part in directing the campaign for William Allen's "New Ticket." In a letter to James Burd, Purviance revealed party tactics in the eastern counties:

> I met some of our Friends at Chester Court and there concerted some measures for dividing the Q—r (Quaker) Interest in that County. I went lately up to Bucks Court in order to concert measures for their Election in pursuance of which we have appointed a considerable meeting of the Germans, Baptists, & Presbyterians to be held next Monday at Nesheminy [Neshameny].

A certain number of Presbyterians, Baptists, and Germans of Philadelphia, he continued, planned to attend the meeting in an endeavor to form a common front against the Quaker party. If the "New Ticket" could carry Bucks County, Purviance felt sure of being able to "recall our dangerous enemy Franklin with his petition."[31]

---

[28] Shippen Papers, VI, 125. HSP.

[29] Deborah Franklin to Benjamin Franklin, Sept. 22, 1765, Franklin Papers, Bache Coll. APS.

[30] Thomson to Hooper, Oct. 8, 1765, Clifford Corresp., XXVII, Pemberton Papers. HSP.

[31] Shippen Papers, VI, 127, 129. HSP.

As for carrying Lancaster County, Purviance was not at all optimistic. However, he advised Burd to leave out James Webb and to put up Dr. Adam Simon Kuhn or some other popular Lutheran or Calvinist German. To help convince the Germans of the iniquity of Benjamin Franklin and his party, Purviance sent some anti-Franklin literature published by Christopher Sauer.

At the instance of William Allen, Governor John Penn again brought the weight of proprietary patronage to the aid of the "New Ticket." Just before the election, charters of incorporation were granted to the Lutheran and German Reformed churches. This was done, Penn confessed, "with a view to engage these people to vote against the Quaker faction." For the same reason he granted the borough of Reading a license to have a market and a fair "by which means Mr. Ross [of the Quaker party] lost his seat in the Assembly."[32]

Once again the closest and hottest contest was right in Philadelphia. Neutral observers cast prediction to the winds and awaited the returns with the greatest interest. Shortly before the election, over twenty-six hundred Germans in a move to avoid the extra fee imposed by the Stamp Act, appeared before Chief Justice Allen to be naturalized.[33] The naturalization fee of two dollars was paid in most instances, it seems, by the Quaker politicians whom John Penn said spent an enormous sum of money to win the election. John Hughes, of course, was left out of the ticket by the Quaker party, but leaders like James Pemberton insisted upon having Galloway. In this respect, John Penn may have been right when he said that "there is no resisting the Intrigues of the Yearly Meeting."[34]

In spite of all the optimism of the Proprietary party, the election was an overwhelming victory for the Quaker party or "Old Ticket," as it was now often called. Philadelphia County swung back in line with practically every man elected a strong Franklin supporter. Joseph Galloway was among those chosen for the county. John Dickinson was not returned, a fact which alone attested the complete rout of the Proprietary party. In the city James Pemberton tied George Bryan and then beat him in a run-off election. Of small comfort was the fact that Thomas Willing was elected by the Proprietaries.

---

[32] Penn MSS., Off. Corresp., X, 17.

[33] *Pa. Arch.*, 1st ser., IV, 242-243; Shippen Papers, VI, 129, 135. HSP; *The Journals of Henry Melchior Muhlenberg*, II, 271. The candidates for naturalization had to swear that they had lived in Pennsylvania for seven years and had not been absent from the colonies for longer than two months during that period. Each had to present a certificate to show that he had "taken the Sacrement of the Lord's Supper" within the last three months. Next an oath of allegiance to the King was taken. Then when the naturalization fee of two dollars was paid, his papers were delivered to him.

[34] Penn MSS., Off. Corresp., X, 17; Shippen Papers, VI, 125. HSP.

Fortune favored the Quaker party in Lancaster when Isaac Saunders was defeated "and a better man placed in his room."[35] Bucks County, in spite of the grand strategy of Samuel Purviance, likewise returned all Franklin men.[36] In the new Assembly the Allen party was not represented by more than seven or eight members.

Only four or five days after the election, the ship arrived from England with both the hated stamps and Hughes' commission. All Philadelphia was immediately in a great uproar. Thomas Bradford long after told how he beat the drums through the streets. When stopped by magistrate Samuel Shoemaker, who wanted to know the cause of all the commotion, he told him to go to the Coffee House if he wanted to satisfy his curiosity.[37] A crowd quickly gathered at the State House where, leading merchants and lawyers took turns in "haranging the people from the State House steps." While they spoke, muffled bells tolled in the steeples.[38]

Prominent among the speakers was a man who was destined to soon become second only to Dickinson as a leader of the Pennsylvania Whigs. This was Charles Thomson, merchant and elder in the Presbyterian church. Thomson had come to Philadelphia from Ireland as an orphan at the age of ten. Educated by Francis Alison in his academy at the New London Crossroads, he had afterward spent nearly ten years teaching school. He first appeared in public eye in 1756 when he was chosen by Teedyuscung, upon the suggestion of Israel Pemberton, to be the clerk for the Indians at the Treaty of Easton. The Indians liked the straightforward youth, whom they called "the man who tells the truth." In 1760 Thomson gave up teaching, entered trade and prospered.

The most prominent leaders heading the protest meeting, other than Thomson (who still backed the Franklin party), were of course men associated with the Proprietary party. Among these were William Allen's four sons, John, Andrew, James, and William, John Dickinson, James Tilghman, Robert Morris, Archibald McCall, John Cox, William Richards, and William and Thomas Bradford. Most of these were presently chosen by the meeting to call upon John Hughes and demand his resignation.[39] When Hughes saw this delegation approaching, headed by the Allens, it is no wonder that he thought the

---

[35] *Pa. Mag.,* XXXVIII, 296.

[36] Letters to Dr. Franklin, LVIII, Part 1, 35. APS.

[37] Thomas Bradford's Narrative, Bradford MSS. HSP.

[38] The Lutheran church bell was not rung, for Muhlenberg feared that the Germans might be blamed as the English had a habit of egging on the Germans and then blaming everything on them. *The Journals of Henry Melchior Muhlenberg,* II, 273.

[39] L. R. Harley, *The Life of Charles Thomson,* 65; *Pa. Journal,* Sept. 4, 1766; Peters MSS., VI, 41.

whole uprising against the Stamp Act was the work solely of the Presbyterians. Most of the magistrates including Governor Penn and
Chief Justice Allen had by this time conveniently left town, leaving
matters in the hands of the meeting.

It seems a pity that Hughes' fortitude and courage could not have
been expended at this time on a better cause. Hughes was the man
who in 1757 had led a party of men to Wyoming to build cabins for
Teedyuscung's Delawares. Only after one of his workmen was killed
and scalped by the enemy, and Hughes was unable to hold his men
longer, did he abandon the project and return to Philadelphia. As a
politician he had been a man of considerable power, having a following
(which may have had for its core the Welsh communities) that had
never failed him before 1765.

Sick as Hughes was, he refused again to resign his commission and
would concede only that he would not attempt to carry out the law
until it was enforced in the other colonies. The crowd at the State
House received the report from Hughes with threats and jeers, but
the leaders persuaded the people to allow Hughes a few more days to
reconsider. That night Thomson went to see his friend Hughes to try
to persuade him to resign before the inhabitants resorted to violence.
But Hughes was adamant. The resistance of the colonies, he declared,
was rebellion, instigated by the Presbyterians. What he wanted, he
told Thomson, were troops to enforce the law.[40] Soon the delegation
paid Hughes another visit, but he would not yield although he was
hourly in danger of mob violence. Meanwhile, tempers cooled a little
when the stamps were returned to the ship which brought them.

By this time Hughes had utterly ruined any chance that he might
have had to regain favor with the people of Pennsylvania. Soon
through the efforts of Hugh Williamson who was in England studying
medicine, copies of Hughes' letters to Franklin and the British officials
were obtained and forthrightly published in the *Pennsylvania Journal.*
Other letters were stolen by young Bradford from the post office.
Hughes sued the Bradfords for printing the letters which he claimed
were garbled. The printers retaliated by charging that Hughes' action
constituted a wanton attack upon the freedom of the press.[41] When
the day of the trial came, several thousand people appeared with the
publishers, but there was no Hughes present to press the suit. The
case was dismissed.[42]

---

[40] *Pa. Journal,* Sept. 5, 12, 18, Oct. 10, 1765, Sept. 4, 1766.

[41] *Pa. Gazette,* Sept. 11, 1766. Galloway admitted that Hughes wrote many letters to
the Stamp Commissioners and the Treasury who allowed them to become public.
Letters to Dr. Franklin, II, Part 1, 49. APS.

[42] Thomas Bradford's Narrative, Bradford MSS. HSP.; *Pa. Journal,* Sept. 4, 1766.

In December a meeting of the Heart and Hand Fire Company voted to drop Hughes from the rolls, unless he resigned at once "without any equivocation, evasion, or mental reservation."[43] But Hughes, the self-styled "Son of Liberty," was determined to go through with it. Even Galloway had by then given him up as a stubborn, indiscreet man who had lost all sense of reason.[44] Nevertheless, Hughes was at least consistent and not altogether unrealistic in his thinking. To the British ministers he prophesied that unless Britain remained firm and enforced the Stamp Act at all cost, her "empire in North America is at an End."[45]

Believing that he had been deceived and deserted by his friends, especially Franklin, Hughes became soured and cynical. Five years later, a friend chancing to meet him on the Lancaster road, found him unchanged. However, he inquired about both Benjamin and William Franklin and asked to be remembered to them. He lived secluded on his farm, shunned all his old friends and spent much of his time writing letters to the British ministry full of descriptions of the iniquity and disloyalty of his countrymen.[46] It may be wondered if John Hughes had much consolation when, in 1769, his loyalty was rewarded by the ministry with an appointment as collector of the port of Piscataqua. Shortly thereafter he was put in charge of the customs at Charlestown [Charleston?] where he died in 1772.[47]

While the dispute with John Hughes was in progress, the Philadelphia merchants met at the Court House and unanimously adopted resolutions (like those already adopted in some of the other colonies) not to import goods from England until the Stamp Act was repealed. Next they dispatched letters to England canceling orders and urging their British correspondents to labor for the repeal of the act. Meanwhile, they worked feverishly to get their ships and cargoes to sea before the Stamp Act went into force. By November 4 every ship had either left the port or was cleared for sailing. The next morning their sailing papers would have to bear the hated stamps or violate the law.[48]

It was not long, however, before the suspension of all business requiring stamps began to produce an intolerable situation. Charles Thomson wrote:

> The Confusion in our City and Province, and indeed thro the whole Colonies are unspeakable—The Courts of justice and the

---

[43] *Pa. Journal,* Dec. 19, 1765.
[44] Letters to Dr. Franklin, II, Part 1, 49, 53. APS.
[45] *Pa. Journal,* Sept. 4, 1766.
[46] Letters to Dr. Franklin, II, Part 2, 156. APS.
[47] *Pa. Journal,* Aug. 3, 1769; *Pa. Gazette,* Feb. 20, 1772.
[48] Shippen Papers, VI, 133. HSP.; T. Clifford to J. Harper, Oct. 8, 1765, Clifford Corresp., XXVII, Pemberton Papers; *Pa. Gazette,* Nov. 14, 1765.

offices of Government are all shut; numbers of people who are
indebted to take advantage of the times refuse Payment and
are moving off with all their effects out of reach of their Creditors.[49]

In similar words Galloway described the state of affairs:

> No Business can be legally Transacted, no Lawsuits prose-
> cuted, no vessels sail, no securities for money taken. The mer-
> chant of course will not purchase Flower, The Miller wheat,
> the farmer cannot pay the Labourer, nor can the Labourer get
> Bread, etc.

All this, thought Galloway, was brought on the Americans by themselves and their mad leaders. "Tis a pity," he said, "that the Innocent
and loyal must suffer with the Guilty & Disloyal."[50]

The inevitable step was taken to put an end to this situation in
December, when people began doing business without stamps. The
members of the Philadelphia bar met and resolved that they would
conduct business without the use of stamps. Only Joseph Galloway
and John Ross opposed the resolution. What John Ross said may have
been amusing but it didn't help Galloway much, for Ross was more in-
toxicated than usual. Galloway gave as his reason that it would be
best to wait until the judges signified that they would hold court
without the use of stamps.[51]

Even before the lawyers took action some of the merchants went
ahead with their business without the use of stamps. Thomas Clifford,
a wealthy Quaker merchant, told one of his captains who was ordered
to clear without stamps to beware of having his ship seized in the West
Indies.[52] Within a month the lawyers and magistrates all over the
province were conducting business without stamps. An unconstitutional law, everyone declared, was not binding upon the people and,
furthermore, they were in duty bound to resist actions of both Crown
and Parliament which violated the sacred rights of freeborn Englishmen.

In February, 1766, Franklin had his famous hearing before the
House of Commons in which he made amends for any past indiscretions.[53] By February 27 he could write Charles Thomson that repeal

---

[49] "The Thomson Papers," *N. Y. Hist. Soc. Coll.*, XI (1878), 7.

[50] Letters to Dr. Franklin, LVIII, Part 1, 36. APS.

[51] Richard Peters, Jr., to Joseph Yeates, Nov. 26, 1765. Yeates Papers, 1762-1780;
Address of J. Galloway, Dec. 20, 1765, Thomson Coll., 91. HSP.

[52] Clifford to Harper, Dec. 1765, Clifford Corresp., XXVII, Pemberton Papers; *Pa.
Gazette*, Feb. 6, 1766, Feb. 20, 1766.

[53] Bigelow, III, 407.

seemed almost certain.[54] Within a few weeks after he wrote the act was repealed.

When news of the repeal reached Philadelphia, there was great rejoicing in the city. Following Franklin's advice, who desired Pennsylvania to make a good impression on the ministry (which had been told that repeal would but make the Americans more insolent), the leaders of the Quaker party endeavored to keep the city as quiet as possible. But it was useless. "The chief justice, mayor, and recorder with several others of the magistrates, were spoken to but to no purpose—the city was illuminated by the proprietary party," wrote Galloway.[55] The latter, however, was too biased to be a good reporter. John Penn, Thomas Wharton and others agreed that the celebration was kept within bounds and that William Allen used his influence toward that end.[56] A big banquet was held at the State House where public-spirited individuals pledged to give their recently purchased homespuns to the poor and to appear on the King's birthday in new English broadcloth.[57] Out in Lancaster, where George Ross "promoted a great drunken bustle," the rejoicing was as hearty if less dignified.[58]

During the excitement over the Stamp Act, Benjamin Rush complained that Philadelphia was cursed with "a sett of men who seem resolved to counteract all our efforts against ye Stamp Act, and are daily endeavoring to suppress the spirit of Liberty among us. You know I mean the Quakers."[59] This charge was not at all fair to the great majority of Quakers who were as bitterly opposed to the act as anyone else. Galloway, Hughes, Franklin, and Samuel Wharton were all Episcopalians. Hardly without exception the great names among the Quakers—Israel and James Pemberton, John Reynell, Thomas Clifford, Thomas Wharton, Samuel Pleasants, James and Henry Drinker—all heartily entered into the nonimportation resolves and petitions to the London merchants. Almost every merchant in Philadelphia signed the agreement and the large majority of them were Quakers.

Still it is true that the Quakers, as was their way, were a moderating influence and tended to restrain the more aggressive elements, especially the Presbyterians. James Pemberton may have been right when he

---

[54] Franklin to Thomson, Feb. 27, 1766, Thomson Papers, I., L. of C. With clever irony Franklin put an article in a London newspaper to the effect that America had about two hundred and fifty thousand men capable of bearing arms, but since one Englishman was as good as five Americans, it would take only an army of fifty thousand to quell the colonies in a three or four year contest at a cost of ten or twelve million a year! See *Pa. Chronicle*, Feb. 23, 1766.

[55] Sparks, VII, 317.

[56] Letters to Dr. Franklin, II, Part 1, 19. APS.

[57] *Ibid.*

[58] Shippen Papers, VI, 143. HSP.

[59] L. H. Butterfield, ed., *Letters to Benjamin Rush*, I, 18.

declared that the Presbyterians, if not restrained, would have turned to violence during the set-to with Hughes.[60] Exaggerated as Galloway's words may be, there was something prophetic when he wrote in 1766 that "A certain set of people [Presbyterians], if I may judge from all their late conduct, seem to look on this as a favorable opportunity of establishing their Republican Principles, and of throwing off all connexion with their Mother Country."[61] At close range, John Ross saw the whole West, not alone the Presbyterians, as altogether "Republican" and the people "all Governors."[62]

Taking the long range view, John Penn could not help thinking that the Stamp Act had demonstrated that the question was not whether England could hold the colonies but whether she could hold them longer by indulgence or by severity. The latter course he now believed would lead to an early wrecking of the Empire.[63]

---

[60] Pemberton Papers, XXXIV, 137.

[61] Letters to Dr. Franklin, I, Part 2, 116½. APS.

[62] Letters to Dr. Franklin, I, Part 2, 142. APS.; Sparks, VII, 305.

[63] Penn MSS., Off. Corresp., X, 33.

X

ECONOMIC AND DOMESTIC ISSUES. 1760-1775

A s ALREADY SHOWN, people on the Pennsylvania frontier blamed the East for their suffering during the Indian wars. After the wars this feeling tended to be dispelled although, naturally, there remained in the minds of many a lingering resentment. Differences in national origin, religion, language, and especially social position, gave rise to distrust and jealousy in the minds of both easterners and westerners. Certain divergent economic interests had also a tendency to produce sectional ill-feeling. But this last factor has been considerably exaggerated in history. It would be sounder, it appears, for the historian to stress the common economic interests of the East and the West which tended to alleviate and in time remove much of the distrust and ill-feeling.

Some historians have made much of an alleged discrimination in legislation on the part of the East against the West. In a previous chapter it was shown that the Assembly, rather than discriminating in taxation, went so far as to cancel the taxes in war-torn areas and passed laws to alleviate the conditions of sufferers in other ways. Neither was there discrimination against the West in the spending of money for internal improvement. The representatives of the agrarian interest of the eastern counties, it is true, didn't care to see provincial funds used for building roads in the west, but they were consistent, at least, in saying that roads were a local problem for each county to solve. The eastern counties had built their roads, let the West do the same. The Philadelphia commercial interest, however, took a favorable view toward spending provincial funds for internal improvement in that their prosperity depended to a large degree upon the growth and expansion of the West.

After the French and Indian War there was a great outburst of interest in internal improvements in Pennsylvania. The early American wars all had the tendency to reveal forcibly the need for more and better transportation facilities. The customary western expansion, which followed swiftly upon the close of each war, further emphasized the need for roadways into the west. After 1763 the frontier rapidly gave way and receded toward Pittsburgh. Immigration from Europe again set in and swelled the tide of settlers seeking new homes beyond the Susquehanna. All Pennsylvania was interested in improving trans-

portation facilities but numbers of questions arose as to how it should
be realized.

That Pennsylvania did not give much attention to the problem of
internal improvements in the west before 1763 does not prove that the
people were not interested in the question.   Before 1755 the trans-
Susquehanna region was too little developed to afford the outlay of
expensive roads and the province was not wealthy enough to undertake
the building of them ahead of actual needs.   During the period of war
few roads other than those for military needs could be constructed, so
great was the expenditure for war.

The old belief, however, that the problem of internal improvement
was a local one remained to retard progress after the war was over.
In 1761 an act was passed for the improvement of navigation on the
Schuylkill.   The project, however, was to be financed by subscriptions
from persons most interested.[1]   Not long after, the Assembly began
matching local subscriptions with provincial donations.   In this way
during 1772-1773 the House voted sums ranging from £200 to £1000
for roads and river navigation.[2]

Petitions for roads, bridges, canals, dredging streams, and for ferries
came before the Assembly in ever greater numbers after about 1769.
They came from all parts of Pennsylvania, east as well as west, from
farmers and mechanics, from merchants and lawyers, from the rich
and from the poor.   In 1770 Philadelphia merchants were instrumental
in obtaining an order from the Governor and Council for a new road
sixty feet wide to be laid out between Lancaster and Philadelphia.[3]

By 1772, Pennsylvania's thinking on the problem of internal improvement had made great advances.   Many canals in connection
with its larger rivers were already being planned, while better road
construction was receiving the careful attention of all public-minded
persons.   Franklin advised his friends in Pennsylvania not to go ahead
with canals without first procuring a construction engineer from Europe.
Mistakes in building canals were very costly, he explained, as was
recently learned in Ireland.   For one thing, he advised building the
canals parallel to the rivers rather than attempting locks in the rivers
which would not stand against floods.[4]

A far-sighted writer in 1772 advocated building a turnpike (a type
of road which was being introduced in Europe) between the Susquehanna and Philadelphia at an estimated cost of £110,000.   To most
Pennsylvanians this was an unheard-of sum to be expended for one

[1] *Statutes*, VI, 93-99.

[2] *Votes*, VIII, 6844, 6917, 6953.

[3] *Col. Rec.*, IX, 699-703.

[4] Franklin to Rhodes, Aug. 22, 1772, Franklin Coll. Yale U.

road. The author, however, thought that the province had attained sufficient population and wealth to undertake the project.[5]

From Lancaster County the Reverend Thomas Barton emphasized the need for better transportation facilities in 1773. A great land boom was in progress west of the Susquehanna, he said, with prices in the "new purchase" (1768) doubling in twelve months.[6] Many persons both in the east and in the west were troubled by the fact that much of the trade of the Susquehanna valley was being conducted with Baltimore which showed signs of becoming a serious rival to Philadelphia for the trade of all of central and western Pennsylvania. Baltimore was actually nearer to a large section of Pennsylvania, but the Philadelphia market was generally considered a better one by the inhabitants. For this reason the western farmers kept asking for improved roads and ferry facilities leading to the Pennsylvania metropolis.

Realizing that Philadelphians were worried about keeping their western trade, the West held the threat of going to Maryland as a club over eastern business interests. Western petitioners for better roads were instructed in 1770 to inform the Assembly "that the Marylanders have been among us, and have measured the distance from the highest navigation to us, and say it is only 28 miles—but we dispise them with all their offers provided we receive proper incouragement from the Philadelphians."[7] Two years later, a petition from Lancaster County asked that a bridge be built across the Schuylkill to facilitate trade between the East and the West. The bridge planned would cost about £8000, it was thought. This improvement, the petitioners believed, would alone cause much of the grain, flaxseed, hemp, iron and other products going to Baltimore to be sent to the Philadelphia market.[8]

Discerning observers noted many factors concerning the question of trade which were often overlooked. Maryland kept improved only one road leading to the Susquehanna region, while Pennsylvania was obliged to maintain several longer and more expensive roads. Topography was also in favor of transportation lanes to the south, there being no ferry service required in going from York to Baltimore.[9] On the other hand it was noted that the road into Maryland was very bad and the Maryland legislature did not appear interested in improving it. Baltimore itself suffered from having a very shallow harbor: it was

---

[5] *Pa. Gazette,* March 5, 1772.
[6] Penn MSS., Off. Corresp., XI, 77.
[7] Prov. Papers, XXXIX, 52, XLII, 6. Harrisburg.
[8] *Votes,* VIII, 7172, 7174, 7179, 7205.
[9] *Pa. Chronicle,* April 5, 1773.

not more than five feet deep and necessitated the building of wharves four hundred feet out into the bay.[10]

This analysis, however, did not go unchallenged. The road to Baltimore was no worse than those to Philadelphia and the Maryland legislature was no more apathetic toward internal improvements than the Pennsylvania Assembly, declared one writer. Furthermore, Baltimore's harbor was not so bad as represented and the Philadelphia merchants should not be lulled into a false sense of security by such reports. The best proof of the threat of Baltimore to Philadelphia, the writer said, was the fact that its trade had increased ten-fold in as many years. It was an indisputable fact, he concluded, that the majority of the farm land west of the Susquehanna was from twenty to seventy miles nearer to Baltimore than to Philadelphia.[11]

Although both areas had a need for internal improvements, the people on Pennsylvania's northern frontier and those in the West were more apt to disagree and argue than to work together. The farmer of Northampton County often sent his produce to New York via Esopus or by the Raritan-Perth Amboy route. Usually, however, Philadelphia was preferred over New York as a market for their goods. Petitions from that region, as would be expected, stressed the Lehigh-Delaware navigation. Northampton people could not see the necessity for improving the roads leading into the trans-Susquehanna region. The farmers west of the Susquehanna, declared one booster of the Lehigh Valley, were "lazy, licentious, and lawless." Why should the province build roads into that region, when the people there were scarcely able to support themselves and had nothing to sell worth the mentioning?[12]

Perhaps the most sensible article written on the inter-colonial trade question appeared in 1767. The author, unlike most writers on economic subjects, was able to discover an element of humor in the problem of trade and transportation. He told his Philadelphia friends:

> I would recommend for the more certainly securing our superiority, that a wall like that in China, be built on the line of the two governments, and that creeks and rivers which may happen to intersect the said wall, be so filled and obstructed that no bark may pass: the expense of this undertaking may at first seem great, but when we consider the money will all be laid out amongst our dear selves, we shall no more begrudge it, than the miser would the purchase of a strong box to keep his money. And perhaps it might not be amiss to employ some ingenious mechanic, to fix secondary gates in the said wall, so contrived that the Marylanders could come in amongst us with their money, but not return with it.

[10] *Ibid.*, Feb. 10, 1772.
[11] *Ibid.*, Feb. 24, 1772.
[12] *Ibid.*, Jan. 1, 1770.

After this pungent introduction, the writer, a self-styled "freetrader," proceeded to point out that the people of Maryland purchased vast quantities of goods from Philadelphia and other parts of Pennsylvania. He argued that Pennsylvania's transportation facilities should certainly be improved, but not for the purpose of crushing or working a hardship upon a neighbor. "Let the farmer," he declared, "carry his produce where he can make most of it, without a partial regard to this or that province." In conclusion, he stated, "We are one grand empire and the good of the whole will be wished for by every generous mind."[13]

The vendues or public auctions of pre-revolutionary times have, like the question of internal improvements, often been cited as a cause for much political and economic discord in the province. The importance of this has likewise been exaggerated. There is no doubt that auctioneers were obnoxious to the great majority of merchants and shopkeepers of Philadelphia.[14] Most certainly they would have been outlawed if these merchants and shopkeepers could have had their way about it. But it is wrong to assume that this class had a throttle hold on the Assembly and could consequently bring pressure to bear on the vendues. The merchant class supplied much of the leadership in the Assembly, but it could not dominate it to the detriment of the rest of the people of the colony. The Assembly divided differently on many separate issues, but the dominant economic interest represented was not the merchant class but rather the great agrarian interest of the province. For example, it was not the Philadelphia merchants who showed reluctance to have funds appropriated for internal improvements for western counties but the agrarian interest of Bucks, Chester, and Philadelphia counties. The farmers in these districts could control the Assembly with their twenty-four representatives out of the thirty-eight, whenever their interest was at stake.

This explains why there were ten vendues operating in the suburbs of Philadelphia in the early 1770's and none in the city itself. The merchants and shopkeepers could control the mayor and aldermen of the city, but were unable to compel the Assembly to prohibit the vendues in the counties.[15] However, the Assembly was not adverse to regulating the vendues for protection against the danger of selling stolen goods. By an act of 1729 a vendue master was appointed to supervise the auctions. Further regulations were proposed by the Assembly in 1773, but were refused by the Governor.

---

[13] *Ibid.*, Feb. 9, 1767.

[14] In 1770 associated storekeepers agreed not to buy goods at vendue if sold in lots below a specified amount. This was to stop retailing by vendue and hurt the small shopkeeper who bought from the vendues in small amounts. *Pa. Chronicle*, April 16, 1770.

[15] *Ibid.*, Feb. 24, 1772.

In 1774 when the Assembly was petitioned by the booksellers of Philadelphia to prohibit the sale of books by vendue, a committee reported that it could find no just reason for not allowing the merchandise to be sold in this manner.[16] Even among the merchants, especially the wholesalers, there were more than a few who approved of the vendues. In general, most importers depended upon them to dispose of their odds and ends, surpluses, and damaged goods. There were certain merchants who by 1774 were importing solely for the vendue trade.

An impartial observer in 1772 summarized the arguments in favor of and against the vendues. First of all, he said, they provided a living for several families. Secondly, they afforded merchants of little capital with quick sales and gave more substantial ones a place to dispose their surpluses. The most essential service, however, was that the vendues helped in keeping prices down. On the other hand, he admitted that they encouraged thieving, were the cause of occasional losses to importers, and encouraged extravagance and unnecessary buying among the people.[17]

Like the shopkeepers and merchants, the mechanics and processors harbored monopolistic tendencies. In 1763 the carters of Philadelphia accused the wheelwrights of fixing the price of fellies. In the same year the tanners of Lancaster were charged with forcing up the price of leather.[18] But matters such as these in colonial days were for the most part local questions without any appreciable significance in the course of provincial politics.

When Parliament in 1764 passed the law prohibiting the use of paper money as legal tender in all the colonies, the resentment was as widespread as it was intense. No act of Parliament before the passage of the Stamp Act called forth so much criticism in the colonies.[19] The next year, when a post-war depression hit the colonies, people everywhere attributed it to the paper money law.

---

[16] *Votes,* VIII, 7072.

[17] *Pa. Chronicle,* Feb. 24, 1772.

[18] *Votes,* VI, 5394-95.

[19] According to Franklin, Parliament was moved to pass the Paper Money Act in the belief that the large quantity of Virginia money had caused British merchants substantial losses. Franklin explained that short crops caused a rise in price which the merchants attributed to an inflationary rise resulting from the paper money. Smyth, V, 188. Thomas Penn apparently approved of the Paper Money Act. John Watts wrote Gen. Monckton, Nov. 10, 1764, and said, "You mention Mr. Penn being an Advocate for this Doctrine [no paper money], the reason is plain, he is an enormous Landholder, too much for any One Subject, and if his Tenants have nothing to tender, Silver & Gold they cannot have, they become in a manner his Slaves, instead of Tenants because they lay at his Mercy." "Letter Book of John Watts," *N. Y. Hist. Soc. Coll.* (1928), 310.

Thomas Clifford expressed the general feeling about the economic situation when he wrote in 1765:

> Our paper Currency is annually sinking, & must soon be extinct, we are restricted from making any more, Duties are laid on divers of our imports, to be paid in Silver before the goods are landed, the avenues of Trade to supply us with silver all shutt up, Business greatly suffers already for want of a proper medium, a stamp act starring us in the Face—.[20]

Daniel Roberdeau, who conducted an extensive West Indian trade, in like vein lamented that he had a fortune "but not in Cash, Money is so very scarce."[21] Galloway was of the opinion that unless England allowed America the use of paper money as legal tender, the colonies would be forced to resort to the manufacture of nearly everything used in the country.[22]

In Pennsylvania there were a few individuals who believed that the prohibition of paper money had little or nothing to do with the economic recession. William Allen pointed out that Pennsylvania still had over £300,000 in bills of credit which had several years to run. The depression, he knew, had fallen upon Europe as well as America, and its causes were to be found in the law of supply and demand.[23]

In the hope of stimulating business, a group of Philadelphia merchants undertook to issue circulating notes carrying five per cent interest payable in nine months. The majority of the merchants, however, were of the opinion that these notes endangered the standing of the provincial currency. Soon, over one hundred merchants signed a protest and agreed not to accept the notes.[24]

In 1767 Pennsylvania was happy to see the Assembly issue £20,000 of non-legal-tender bills of credit in order to pay the provincial debt. Further issues amounting to £56,000 were made in 1769, 1771, and 1772 and furnished some relief to the money stringency in the colony.[25]

Being a firm believer in a controlled paper money system, Franklin directed much of his attention while in England to this important ques-

---

[20] Thomas Clifford to Hyde and Hamilton, Nov. 23, 1765, Clifford Corresp., XXVII, Pemberton Papers.

[21] Daniel Roberdeau's Letter Book, 75. HSP.

[22] Letters to Dr. Franklin, I, Part 2, 116½. APS.

[23] In answer to Allen, the advocates of paper money pointed out that much of the Pennsylvania currency was in use in New Jersey and Maryland. All of it would be retired by 1773 leaving the colony without a medium of exchange. Pa. Gazette, Aug. 7, 1766.

[24] Pa. Gazette, Dec. 11, 1766.

[25] Penn MSS., Off. Corresp., X, 98; Votes, VII, 6023; Statutes, VII, 100-107, VIII, 15-22, 204-220, 284-300. As on previous occasions, there were British merchants who sided with America on the paper money question. One group, in 1767, with the advice of Franklin, petitioned the Board of Trade for the repeal of the act. Pa. Gazette, May 28, 1767, July 30, 1767; Pa. Chronicle, June 1, 1767.

tion. When the Stamp Act was being considered, he said that he had presented Grenville with a plan for an American currency as an alternative to the Stamp tax. Franklin suggested a General Loan Office for a continental currency on the pattern of the Pennsylvania system which had functioned so well. The interest money from the Loan Office business, he suggested, could be used by the Crown for its American expenses. Grenville, Franklin said, paid not the least attention to his proposal having apparently made up his mind to have the Stamp Act.[26]

Franklin patiently waited for a favorable opportunity to convince the British government of the great need for an American currency. He was still waiting for that time to come, when the Revolution put an end to the hope that England would find a solution to the problems which faced the empire. With independence declared, Pennsylvania and the other colonies seized with alacrity the liberty of establishing a legal-tender paper money.

The question of an Anglican bishop for America became a subject of at least secondary importance in the period prior to the Revolution. A spirited dispute over the question occurred in Pennsylvania in the year 1768 when zealous churchmen put on a campaign to convince people of the need for establishing a bishopric in America. The principal protagonists were the leaders of the Anglican church on the one side, and an equally alert number of Presbyterians and Congregationalists on the other.

It had long been suspected in Pennsylvania that the Reverend William Smith of Christ Church had a secret ambition to become the first Anglican bishop for America. John Reed wrote Franklin in 1761 that this was Smith's intention and that the Presbyterians of New York were already considering steps to oppose the establishing of such an office in America.[27] William Allen, likewise, early became convinced that Smith was one of the principal promoters of the project and that he hoped to be the possessor of the first American "mitre."[28] It may well be that Smith, during the Stamp Act upheaval, kept himself on the sidelines for fear of giving offense to British officialdom and hurting his chances of heading the Anglican Church in America.

The year 1768 was marked by a series of articles in the *Pennsylvania Gazette* advocating a bishop for the colonies. The writers argued that the Episcopalian Church needed the power to consecrate ministers in America to put the church on an equal footing with other churches in the colonies. The Presbyterians, they charged, were contriving to

---

[26] Franklin to Galloway, Oct. 11, 1766, Franklin Coll., William L. Clements Lib. Transcripts. Yale U.

[27] Letters to Dr. Franklin, II, Part 1, 27. APS.

[28] Penn MSS., Off. Corresp., X, 70.

keep the Anglican Church weak so that they would have less trouble in gaining political control of America and of becoming the principal church in the colonies.[29]

Writers for the Presbyterian interest insisted that the sole object of the Anglicans was to fasten "that yoke of spiritual bondage and jurisdiction" over dissenters "which neither they nor their fathers could bear."[30] Both sides spent much pains picturing the history of the other church as one long succession of intolerance and lust for power.

In historical perspective the dispute over a bishop for America was of relatively little importance mainly because the British ministry, concerned with what seems to be more vital matters, hardly gave passing consideration to the question of an American episcopate. If the ministry had come out strongly for a bishopric, the issue no doubt would have become a major one in all the colonies.[31]

After the turbulent elections of 1764 and 1765, the campaign of 1766 was a mild affair. Both parties to a large extent conducted their appeal to the people largely through newspaper articles, many of which were studded with extracts of letters and essays written during the Stamp Act controversy. By this time, Galloway and Thomas Wharton, finding all the newspapers hostile to the Quaker party, established a new journal called the *Pennsylvania Chronicle* to present their views to the people. William Goddard of Rhode Island was brought to Philadelphia to be editor of the newspaper.[32]

The Quaker party used to good effect Franklin's testimony before the House of Commons. Galloway reported to Franklin that "Our worthy friend, George Ashbridge, has spared no pains to acquaint the country members of every thing, which could tend to rivet their affections for thee," thus "the storm, which was threatened by the [Proprietary party], vanished."[33] In September, Galloway had Franklin's examination published and circulated just before the October election.[34]

Of interest is the manner in which the Quaker party conducted its campaign against Thomas Willing, who had managed to keep his seat in the Assembly in spite of the Quaker landslide of the previous year.

[29] *Pa. Gazette,* Sept. 8, 15, 22, 29, 1768.

[30] *Ibid.,* Nov. 24, 1768; *Pa. Chronicle,* Sept. 25, 1769.

[31] Most of the Episcopalian congregations, especially those in the South, preferred the virtual autonomy of their individual parishes to any benefits which might follow from the establishment of an American episcopate. Smyth, V, 132-134, 404.

[32] *Pa. Mag.,* V, 60, 309-311; *Pa. Gazette,* Sept. 11, 1766; *Six Arguments against J. Galloway, 1766* (A Broadside) HSP; *Pa. Journal,* Sept. 5, 1766. Franklin in January, 1766 sold the *Pennsylvania Gazette* to David Hall who turned against the Quaker party.

[33] Sparks, VII, 314.

[34] Penn MSS., Off. Corresp., X, 84.

John Ross was picked by the party to run against Willing. A few days before the election, the Quaker party held a great political rally at the Brew House. It is not hard to picture John Ross, mug in hand, mounted on a pile of grain sacks, exhorting the multitude. He spoke to a gathering of seven or eight hundred men, it was said, in a way that outdid George Whitefield in eloquence. Ross was followed by Hugh Roberts who asked all who were in favor of turning Thomas Willing out of the Assembly to stand up. They all stood: a few days later Ross was elected.[35]

The election of 1766 proved to be another sweeping victory for the Quaker party. In reporting the event to Franklin, Galloway said that it was generally thought that the Proprietary men were now so thoroughly discouraged that they would not attempt an opposition the next year.[36] Sarah Franklin jubilantly told her father that "We have beat three partys, the Proprietary, the Presbyterians, and the Half and Halfs [Israel Pemberton's followers?]." The Franklin men, she said, had triumphantly turned out at three o'clock in the morning to give several loud huzzas over their victory.[37]

When the Assembly met, it chose Galloway for its Speaker in place of Joseph Fox. Fox from the beginning had been too impartial in his conduct of the speakership to please the Quaker party. For the past year he had greatly irritated the party by questioning the wisdom and policies of Franklin and hearkening to the advice of William Allen.[38]

There were few issues in 1767 to ruffle the waters of Pennsylvania politics. Perhaps the only one which came near provoking a storm was that of the question of establishing circuit courts for the province. Allen said that he had long advocated these courts to save the country people the expense and inconvenience of coming to Philadelphia. The lawyers of the city, however, foreseeing a loss of clients, had successfully put it off. When in the spring of 1767 the Assembly framed a bill for establishing a circuit court, the lawyers in the Assembly again tried to stop it. But the majority remained firm for the bill. Besides the fact that the courts were needed, the Assembly saw in it a chance of getting rid of William Allen as Chief Justice who, it seemed, was too old to undertake circuit duty.

Allen and the Governor tried to make the House amend the bill by providing for the appointment of additional judges for circuit duty, but the Assembly would not yield. When the bill came before the Governor, Benjamin Chew and other lawyers in the Council tried to per-

[35] Sarah to William Franklin, Sept. 30, 1766, Franklin Papers, Bache Coll. APS.
[36] Letters to Dr. Franklin, II, Part 1, 49. APS.
[37] Sarah Franklin to Benjamin Franklin, Oct. 3, 1766, Franklin Coll. Yale U.
[38] Penn MSS., Off. Corresp., X, 80, 140.

suade him not to sign it. Hearing of the pressure being brought to bear, the Quaker party threatened to make an issue of it if the measure failed to become a law. Some members declared that they would use it in making another attempt to get a change of government. Tired of politics and not wishing to see it carried further, Allen advised the Governor to sign the bill. He did so, and Allen, rather than resign, rode the circuit with the others.[39]

When September, 1767, had come, it was apparent that there would be very little opposition to the Quaker party. Pennsylvania politics, it would seem, were back to a state of normalcy. William Allen passively stood aside, partly because opposition was useless, and partly because he hoped to show the moderate Quakers led by Israel Pemberton that the Presbyterians "were not grasping for power" and "were willing to let them order matters to their liking." His forbearance was of no avail, for the Assembly returned was as strong for Franklin and Galloway as the last one. The whole election, Allen said, was conducted without arousing much tension or animosity. "We are at present," he concluded, "in a profound calm."[40] Galloway agreed: "We seem at present very Quiet here," he wrote, "and I am satisfied, that, the watchword Among the P—ns (Presbyterians) is Moderation."[41]

But the calm which had settled over Pennsylvania politics would be of short duration. In June and July Parliament had passed the Townshend Acts and the second great constitutional dispute was already at hand, when Pennsylvanians went to the polls in October, 1767. Again would the Conservatives tremble, for they knew full well that with each rise of the populace the day of a more democratic government for Pennsylvania grew nearer.

[39] *Statutes at Large of Pennsylvania,* VII, 108; Penn MSS., Off. Corresp., X, 94.
[40] Penn MSS., Off. Corresp., X, 94, 102, 116.
[41] Letters to Dr. Franklin, II, Part 1, 101. APS.

XI

THE TOWNSHEND ACTS. 1767-1770

B RITAIN WAS UNFORTUNATE in launching its new taxation and navigation program for America on the eve of an economic slump which
came as the inevitable reaction to wartime inflation and abnormal demand for goods and services. If the program had been undertaken
when business was good, the reaction in the colonies probably would
have been more favorable. Contrary to the opinion of some historians,
the new laws did not cause the depression. Already business had fallen
off before the regulations went into force. In the months to follow,
however, the new laws may have aggravated the distress experienced
in America.[1]

The most harmful part of the Sugar Act of 1764 was that which
related to the importation of molasses from the foreign West Indies,
great quantities of which were consumed by the American distillers.
Although the act reduced the duty by one-half, it was still considered
higher than the industry could afford.[2] This criticism, however, was
largely removed in 1766 when Parliament lowered the duty from three
to one pence per gallon on foreign molasses. Although British West
Indian molasses became subject to the same duty, the fact that most
of this commodity used in the colonies was of foreign origin rendered
the changes more acceptable. James Pemberton no doubt echoed the
sentiment of Philadelphia merchants when he declared that the new
act was proof that Parliament continued to care for the interests of the
American people.[3]

But there were other innovations incorporated in the Navigation
Laws in 1764-1767 which produced new woes for the American colonies.
More products were added to the enumerated list which could be
shipped only to Great Britain. In addition, non-enumerated goods no
longer could be sent to any country north of Cape Finisterre except by
way of the British Isles. A false rumor had it in Philadelphia that the
act also banned the shipment of flaxseed to Ireland. Flaxseed, customarily shipped to Ireland in large quantities, was rendered that year

---

[1] *Pa. Journal,* Aug. 23, 1764; John C. Miller, *Origins of the American Revolution,*
103; Arthur M. Schlesinger, *The Colonial Merchants and the American Revolution,*
1763-1776, 57. Schlesinger attributes the hard times to the acts of 1764. The
Sugar Act, however, did not go into effect until September 29, 1764.

[2] Van Tyne, 126ff; Miller, 103-106; William MacDonald, *Select Charters,* 272-281.

[3] Smith MSS., VII, 34, Ridgway Lib.; Van Tyne, 195-196; 6 Geo. III, c. 52.

almost worthless by the rumor.[4] The law, however, did prohibit the shipment of lumber, iron, and sugar to Ireland. Although Parliament soon modified this restriction by permitting the shipment of lumber and iron to Ireland, the prohibition against sugar remained to irritate the Philadelphia merchants.[5]

As the Navigation and Trade Laws increased, Americans became dismayed at the way these laws were being used to hem them in and restrict colonial industry. William Allen declared in October, 1767, that because the laws had become so confining, his son John was at a loss to know what business to enter. The restrictions placed on the iron industry, said Allen, "has in a manner knocked that branch of business in the head, or, at least, made it unprofitable." In the next year he wrote that the iron regulations had already closed one-half of the iron works in America. America, Allen continued, was being utterly drained of its specie by the new duties and regulations, which would soon have the effect of forcing all the merchants into the contraband trade. He revealed his despair of finding any profitable avenue in business for "poor John" by asking Thomas Penn to get him a public office through his influence at Court.[6]

In October, 1766, and again in October, 1767, a committee of the Pennsylvania Assembly sent Franklin a resumé of the main heads of complaints of the Philadelphia merchants. Especially vexing to them, it was said, were the regulations pertaining to the Irish trade. The Assembly also complained against the rule prohibiting the bringing of Spanish and Portuguese wines, fruit, and olive oil directly from the native port to America. Other restrictions applying to the overseas shipment of sugar and iron were condemned. The regulations pertaining to the Spanish and Portuguese trade, it was well known in America, had been imposed to enable the British merchants to engross the carrying trade between these ports and America. This would also have the effect of destroying the American grain and flour trade to the

---

[4] Penn MSS., Off. Corresp., X, 84; *Pa. Gazette,* Nov. 6, 1766. Parliament granted a bounty on the growth of hemp and raw flax in 1764 in the hope of realizing a lower price of sailcloth and cordage in England. Already Americans, especially the Irish settlers, had made flax-growing a principal industry in Pennsylvania. In March, 1765, it was reported that hemp and flax constituted the best sale crop in the province. *Pa. Gazette,* July 12, 1764, March 21, 1765. See George Beer, *British Colonial Policy,* 217.

[5] John Penn reckoned the entire Irish trade worth £60,000 to Pennsylvania. 4 Geo. III, c. 15, 5 Geo. III, c. 45.

[6] Penn MSS., Off. Corresp., X, 70, 116, 118. See also C. Thomson Papers, *N. Y. Hist. Soc. Coll.,* XI, 7-12. Parliament added pig iron to the list of enumerated articles in 1766.

Iberian countries which was considered a serious competition by British agrarian and commercial interests.[7]

By this time Americans were attempting to assay and weigh the colonial contribution to the economy of Great Britain in order to demonstrate more convincingly the harm which the new laws were inflicting upon all. In 1766 an anonymous writer estimated that in 1762 America bought goods from England valued at four million pounds sterling. Fifty percent of this cost, he believed, could be accounted for in British "taxes, impositions, monopolies, ill-judged laws of trade, and other political blunders." Besides this, the Navigation Laws, by channelizing, restricting, and prohibiting American trade were causing a loss to the colonies of about £500,000 per annum. Quitrents and other levies took another £500,000, so that in all he estimated that America was contributing not less than three million pounds sterling to the British economy and exchequer.[8] Exaggerated as his figures may be, writings like this are proof that Americans were beginning to see that the Navigation Laws and British monopolies constituted in reality no less a tax upon the colonies than the more obvious direct taxation.

So far, except for the defunct Stamp Act and possibly some of the clauses of the Sugar Act, British restrictions and duties could be construed as coming within the scope of the regulatory laws which carried the connotation of constitutionality. But in 1767 Parliament, under the guidance of "Champaigne Charlie" Townshend, Chancellor of the Exchequer, again reverted to outright taxation of America in the form of duties on paper, tea, glass, paint, and lead. The money to be raised was to provide for "the administration of justice, and the support of government" in the colonies. Any residue would be set aside for defraying the cost of protecting and defending America.[9]

It was soon apparent that the Townshend Acts would prove as unpopular as the Stamp Act. Fully as objectionable as the tax was the knowledge that the money would strengthen royal government in the colonies. In the preamble of the Revenue Act, Burke said, the colonial assemblies perceived the death warrant of representative government in America. James Otis no doubt spoke the colonial mind when he remarked that he would sooner see all the money raised by

---

[7] *Votes,* VII, 5946, 6070. As early as 1759, Franklin noted that the landed interest in England had begun to grow jealous of the large American shipments of grain to Europe. Franklin to Norris, March 19, 1759, Franklin Coll. Yale U.; Franklin Papers, Miscel., I, 60. L. of C. The Assembly did not mention the duty on Spanish, Portuguese and Madeira wine. It did stress the great harm caused by the law prohibiting paper money in America. *Ibid.*

[8] *Pa. Gazette,* Jan. 23, 1766.

[9] MacDonald, 324.

the acts go "to the bottom of the sea" than into the pockets of Hutchinson and the other Crown sycophants in America.[10]

Early in December John Dickinson wrote Otis that Massachusetts should take the lead in opposing the Townshend Acts. All the colonies, he said must then "instantly, vigorously and unanimously unite" to maintain their liberties.[11]   Dickinson himself had already touched off the dispute by having published the first number of his *Letters from a Farmer in Pennsylvania*. Relying upon his knowledge of common law, Dickinson furnished arguments for the American cause which to the colonist seemed incontestable.   In reward, Dickinson was toasted throughout the colonies as the American Pitt, and Princeton conferred upon him the degree of LL.D.[12]

Encouraged by the Farmer's letters and spurred on by the Boston Town Meeting, the Boston merchants signed a non-importation agreement in March, 1768, with the proviso that it would become operative when New York and Philadelphia joined.[13]   But the Philadelphia merchants, fearing heavy losses, were not anxious to cut off the trade with England as they had done three years before.   As a body, therefore, they threw their weight against the popular clamor for non-importation.   In March, 1768 a large number of merchants saw fit to meet at the London Coffee House where they resolved that the tax was an unwarranted invasion of American rights.   But they made no move to join in a continental boycott of the British.[14]   The Assembly, led by Galloway, likewise did nothing more than instruct Franklin to seek repeal of the laws.

In May, Galloway reluctantly laid before the Assembly a circular letter from the Massachusetts legislature which concisely set forth the American case against the mother country.   "In all free States the Constitution is fixed," the letter said, and Parliament could not "overleap the Bounds of it without destroying its own Foundation."   Therefore, "the Constitution ascertains and limits both Sovereignty and Allegiance;—and therefore his Majesty's American Subjects,—have an equitable Claim to the full Enjoyment of the fundamental Rules of the British Constitution."   It was an "unalterable Right in Nature, ingrafted into the British Constitution, as a fundamental Law,—that what a Man has honestly acquired, is absolutely his own, which he may

---

[10] Miller, 255.

[11] Van Tyne, 251.

[12] Franklin to Galloway, Aug. 8, 1767, Franklin Coll., William L. Clements Lib., Transcripts, Yale U.; *Pa. Gazette*, April 7, 1768. Galloway tried to prevent Goddard from publishing the Farmer's Letters in the *Pa. Chronicle. Pa. Mag.*, LX, 315.

[13] Van Tyne, 256.

[14] *Pa. Gazette*, March 31, 1768.

freely give, but cannot be taken from him without his Consent." In conclusion, the letter stated that Americans "exclusive of any Consideration of Charter Rights, with a decent Firmness adapted to the Character of Freemen and Subjects, assert this natural Right."[15] Although this strong appeal to fundamental rights stirred America to its very depths, it produced no response from the Pennsylvania Assembly which promptly adjourned until September.

In England the Massachusetts Circular Letter was denounced as positively seditious. Lord Hillsborough, Secretary of State for the Colonies, decided to send out a circular letter of his own. Accordingly letters were dispatched to twelve colonies berating Massachusetts for exciting the colonies to "unwarrantable combinations," and other unlawful acts which denied the authority of the mother country and subverted "the true Principles of the Constitution."[16]

That the British government should attempt to throttle American protest was a great mistake. Governor Penn declared that after Hillsborough's letter was received "even those persons who were the most moderate are now set in a flame and have joined in the General Cry of Liberty."[17] If Americans cannot petition for the removal of their grievances, William Allen said, "we are of all men the most miserable." If the Townshend Acts caused mob violence, England alone was to blame, he thought. It amazed him to think that England was planning on sending more troops to America "to fight windmills" as he called it. Come what may, he would not be over-awed by the might of England. When the Collector of the Customs of Philadelphia applied to him for writs of assistance, he refused to issue them on the grounds that they were unconstitutional.[18]

Fired by Hillsborough's letter, the inaction of the Assembly, and the apathy of the merchants, William Allen and his friends called a great mass meeting at the State House. The principal speakers were John Dickinson and Charles Thomson, who vividly set forth the grievances against the mother country. The meeting closed by resolving that the Assembly should at once petition the King, Lords and Commons.[19] The resolution, reported John Penn, was signed and approved by the great majority of "men of the best understanding among us."[20]

When the Assembly met in September, it would no longer be restrained by Galloway from acting upon the resolution adopted by the

---

[15] *Votes*, VII, 6182.
[16] *Col. Rec.*, IX, 546; Van Tyne, 297.
[17] Miller, 262-263.
[18] Penn MSS., Off. Corresp., X, 170; *William Allen's Letter Book*, 74.
[19] *Pa. Gazette*, Aug. 4, 1768; *Pa. Chronicle*, July 18, 1768.
[20] Penn MSS., Off. Corresp., X, 158.

people at the State House. Petitions were accordingly sent out as directed.[21] By this time Galloway had lost the support of many of his friends, having recently published an article entitled "Pacificus to the Public" in which he defended Hillsborough and attacked the Massachusetts radicals.

Notwithstanding the demands of the mechanics and other radical groups for non-importation, the merchants could not be persuaded to take action against the Townshend duties. Many were for waiting until the British government had a chance to answer the petitions. William Allen said that Pennsylvania waited with the greatest impatience for word from Parliament. "If it should be unfavorable to us, then, and not till then, shall we begin our Constitutional war with our mother country,—we will set up Mfgers & provide for ourselves."[22] Among the merchants willing to act some were for a boycott only on the articles taxed, others insisted on a complete embargo like the ones adopted in Massachusetts and New York.[23] The deadlock in Pennsylvania was finally broken in February, 1769, when about sixty of the more radical merchants, led by Thomson, Mifflin, Clifford, and Reynell, agreed to cut off all British imports until the Townshend Acts were repealed.

A few weeks later, most of the other merchants, perhaps fearing reprisals or even mob violence, gave in and signed the Non-Importation Agreement. According to Thomas Clifford, over three hundred "cooly & with great unanimity resolved to decline ordering any more goods—until those acts of Parliament—are repealed."[24] The Quaker signers were most numerous for the obvious reason that the great majority of Philadelphia merchants were Friends. But more significant was the fact that they owned the largest and strongest business houses in Philadelphia, with long-established reputations and great weight in London commercial circles.

Outstanding among the Quaker signers was John Reynell. A man of great influence in the Society of Friends, Reynell had worked with Israel Pemberton to make peace with the Indians during the wars. Besides directing the Provincial Indian Stores, he performed many acts of public charity and service. As head of a committee for the merchants, Reynell now sent a special petition to the London banker,

---

[21] *Votes*, VII, 6271; Letters to Dr. Franklin, II, Part 2, 143. APS. The Assembly defended its conduct by insisting that it had instructed Franklin as early as February, 1768, to seek the repeal of the Townshend Acts.

[22] Penn MSS., Off. Corresp., X, 186.

[23] Massachusetts and New York began enforcement of non-importation on January 1, 1769. Van Tyne, 258.

[24] Clifford to Walter Franklin, March 11, 1769, Clifford Corresp., XXVIII, Pemberton Papers; *Pa. Mag.*, LIV, 361-366.

David Barclay, and other men prominent in the English business world asking their help in defeating the Townshend Acts.[25]

It was not long before the Non-Importation Association was called upon to enforce the agreement. In July a ship from England containing a cargo of malt consigned to Amos Strettell came to anchor at Philadelphia. At once the whole city was in a great furore. Strettell made no protest at all when the Non-Importation committee, headed by Reynell, ordered the ship captain to return to England with his cargo intact.[26]

After the adoption of non-importation, there followed a long test of endurance between Great Britain and the colonies, a test moreover which sounded the ability of the colonies to act together for the common weal. Since the merchants in general were losing far more than all others by the boycott, they were severely tried. The brunt of non-importation fell especially on the dry goods merchants who suffered great losses. Many others, however, in the West Indian trade were unaffected by the agreement and made handsome profits by smuggling in goods from European sources.

The grievances of the suffering merchants were often matched by consumers who saw the price of goods rising each day. Susanna Greenleaf of Bucks county, complained in July, 1770, that her butter, eggs, cheese, and poultry sold for prices no higher than before Non-Importation. Even so, she was obliged to pay exorbitant prices at the stores for left-over wares which the shopkeepers had had on their shelves for twenty years. She suggested that the farmers should boycott Philadelphia and stay away from the city.[27]

As early as January, 1770, it was rumored that the dry-goods merchants would try to break the Non-Importation Agreement if the Townshend duties were not repealed that year.[28] Agitation on the part of the harassed merchants increased, and by May and June there was much talk of modifying the agreement. Some persons who could

---

[25] Letters to Dr. Franklin, LII, 66. APS; Articles of Agreement, Feb. 6, 1769, Thomson Papers, I. L. of C.; Franklin Papers, Miscel. I, 71. L. of C.; *Pa. Journal,* Aug. 31, 1769. David Barclay, Sr., banker and merchant, died at his home at Bush Hill, near Enfield at the age of eighty-eight in 1769. He was the son of Robert Barclay, author of the famous *Apology* of the Quakers. In the course of the banker's life he entertained three kings at his home when they attended London for the coronation. He was on intimate terms with scores of leading Quakers in America and carried on extended business relations with many American correspondents. The Pennsylvania Quakers relied much upon him in the promotion of their business and political interests in Great Britain. See *Pa. Gazette,* May 4, 1769.

[26] *Pa. Journal,* July 20, 1769; *Pa. Gazette,* July 20, 1769; Pemberton Papers, XXI, 59.

[27] *Pa. Chronicle,* July 23, 1770.

[28] *Pa. Gazette,* Jan. 25, 1770.

appreciate the plight of the merchants talked of taking up a subscription for the hard-pressed merchants on the plea that they were suffering for a common cause. Nothing like this was done and at a meeting of the Non-Importation Association a motion to modify the agreement was voted down.[29] Thomas Clifford thought this was evidence enough that Non-Importation was firmly secured until England bowed to the will of the colonies.

Within a few days, however, Clifford was forced to change his mind. News of the repeal of all the Townshend duties except that on tea made it fairly clear that it would be difficult to continue the embargo with only the one item subject to taxation. Most of the merchants now demanded that the Association lift the boycott on all goods except tea and pointed to the reports that similar action would be presently taken by other colonies.

The Radical merchants, backed by the mechanics and other patriotic groups refused to yield to the clamor against the agreement. Determined to hold the line, the Radicals who controlled the committee took vigorous action against all persons found violating the agreement. In June and July, two Philadelphia merchants were forced to return goods smuggled in from Maryland and to make a public confession of their guilt.[30] Four other violators were soon discovered. All escaped being tarred and feathered after confessing their guilt in Bradford's newspaper.[31] Several others were under investigation by the merchants' committee. If found guilty, they would be turned over to the mechanics' committee for punishment.[32]

When word reached Philadelphia in July that the New York merchants had decided (much against the wishes of the Sons of Liberty) to lift the boycott on all British goods except tea, a wave of excitement swept over the city. A large meeting was held in the State House yard on July 14 for considering the action of the New Yorkers. Joseph Fox was chosen moderator. Charles Thomson, backed by the mechanics and other Radicals made the principal speech. He upbraided the New York merchants for their disloyalty and then introduced a resolution that Philadelphia would abide strictly by the original agreement and boycott New York until that city saw fit to reverse its decision. When

---

[29] *Pa. Gazette,* June 7, 1770. Early reports that Rhode Island merchants were flagrantly violating the agreement caused great agitation among merchants in all the colonies. As a result, Rhode Island ships were for a time refused entrance at neighboring ports. This caused the Rhode Island Association to tighten up and declare its loyalty to Non-Importation. Clifford to L. Cooper, June 14, 1770, Clifford Corresp., XXVIII, Pemberton Papers.

[30] *Pa. Journal,* June 28, 1770.

[31] Franklin Papers, XII, 40, U. of Pa.; *Pa. Journal,* July 12, 1770.

[32] *Pa. Journal,* July 5, 1770.

his motion carried the merchants were disgusted, but they could do nothing in a meeting such as this.[33]

The New York merchants had voted to lift the embargo on British goods not taxed, but to refuse the admittance of all dutiable articles, including tea, wine, rum, sugar, and molasses. Their lumping of the duties under the acts of 1764, 1766, and 1767 was something new and demonstrated that they no longer were attempting to acknowledge a distinction between duties under the Navigation Laws and taxation. Thus they swept away the nice distinctions made by John Dickinson in his *Farmer's Letters*, and adopted instead the clear and safe position that all taxation of the colonies by Parliament was unconstitutional. Franklin always maintained that it was impossible to draw a line between duties for regulation and those for revenue. If it were conceded that there was a distinction as Pitt and Dickinson had done, then Parliament would be the judge of where the boundary lay and the colonies would be constantly threatened by taxation. In essence he believed that there was no middle ground and that Parliament could tax America or not. The latter, he thought, had the best arguments to support it. If this concept were accepted, he admitted that it would make America "So many separate states, only subject to the same King." Herein, he believed, was the only practical solution to the problem.[34]

A Pennsylvania writer pointed out in August that if the Philadelphia merchants adopted the New York policy, not only would the West Indian business be ruined but the economy of the whole province would be crippled by cutting off a large part of its supply of sugar and molasses.[35] It was evident that a consistent policy toward British taxation was fraught with endless difficulties. During the period of non-importation it was well-known that the British West Indies imported large quantities of English merchandise; but for fear of hurting the lucrative trade with the islands, little attempt was made by the patriotic associations to force the West Indies to adopt the Non-Importation Agreement.[36]

The clamor for the repeal of Non-Importation became louder as each week passed during the summer of 1770. The merchants argued that it was grossly unfair for those not harmed by the embargo to brand the merchants as enemies of the people. The sane thing to do, they

---

[33] *Ibid*, July 19, 1770; J. Shippen to E. Shippen, July 14, 1770, Balch Papers, Shippen and Swift, HSP.

[34] Smyth, V, 114-115.

[35] *Pa. Gazette*, Aug. 23, 1770; Sam. Coates to William Logan, Sept. 26, 1770, Sam Coates Letter Book, HSP.

[36] *Pa. Chronicle*, July 30, 1770.

said, was to lift the ban on all goods except tea, and have the people pledge themselves to drink no British tea until the tax was removed.[37]

Up until August, Thomas Clifford had favored continuing Non-Importation, but he now joined the repealers, so glaring had become its infractions throughout the colonies. Everywhere the vendues were well-stocked, he said, and the back country was being furnished with quantities of British merchandise from Maryland.[38] An observer in London noted in August that New York merchants had placed huge orders, especially for woolen goods; indeed, so many orders were pouring in that British exporters were experiencing difficulty in procuring the goods. "Thus the ice being now broke," the writer concluded, "the other Colonies must soon follow their Example."[39]

About the middle of September, a group of leading merchants headed by John Reynell took matters in their own hands and chose a committee to contact all subscribers in order to form a definite appraisal of the sentiment within the Association.[40] Hearing of this, the regular committee protested vigorously but finally consented to a meeting of the merchant associators. The meeting, presided over by Thomas Willing, was held at Davenport's Tavern and attended by one hundred thirty-five of the three hundred subscribers. The question of repeal of the embargo on all goods except tea was put to a vote and carried in the affirmative by a vote of two to one. Thereupon, Thomson and Mifflin, and other merchants of the radical wing, resigned in protest from the committee.[41]

A few days later the Radicals tried to retrieve the lost ground by holding a protest meeting at the State House. Speeches were made and resolutions adopted, but it was soon clear that nothing could be done to persuade the merchants to reconsider.[42]

During Non-Importation the American economy suffered much less than might be imagined. Indeed, some very appreciable benefits from the stoppage of American purchases from Britain were discernable. During the year and a half during which the agreement was in force in Pennsylvania, the people paid off most of their British debts and secured a favorable balance of trade because of the self-imposed frugality and the increased consumption of domestic manufactures.

---

[37] *Pa. Gazette,* July 19, 1770.
[38] Clifford to Cowper, Sept. 15, 1770, Clifford Corresp., XXVIII, Pemberton Papers.
[39] *Pa. Gazette,* Nov. 1, 1770.
[40] *Pa. Journal,* Sept. 20, 1770. Others were Jeremiah Warder, Abel James, John Drinker, Thomas Fisher, Tench Francis, and Philip Benezet.
[41] *Pa. Chronicle,* Sept. 24, 1770. A notice of the intended meeting was posted in the *Pennsylvania Journal* of September 20 but the committee may not have known before hand that the notice was given to the newspaper. Prominent among the Radicals were Andrew Allen, Peter Chevalier, George Clymer, Daniel Roberdeau, William Masters, Daniel Benezet, and James Mease.
[42] *Ibid.*

With all kinds of American-made goods in great demand, the mechanics experienced a heyday of prosperity. No wonder that they were the most zealous advocates of Non-Importation and the most resolute group for continuing the boycott until England removed the tax on tea.[43] Mechanics, of course, were everywhere in great demand. In Bristol, England, Thomas Clifford solicited craftsmen for the shops which he had established in Philadelphia. He tried hard to get nail-makers who would indenture themselves for four years.[44] Activity such as this may explain why merchants such as Clifford were as zealous as any mechanic in support of the embargo. Some there were who predicted in 1770 that if Non-Importation could be continued another year "the vend for British manufacturers will be ruined in the future, as industry, manufacturing, and economy gain ground every hour."[45]

Shortly after Non-Importation ceased in Pennsylvania, the annual elections were held. The Quaker party kept control of the Assembly as usual, but for the first time it lost the support of the powerful mechanic class in Philadelphia, a result directly attributable to the reluctance of the Quaker party to vigorously support Non-Importation. In reporting the situation to Franklin, Galloway wrote: "We are all in Confusion, The White Oaks and Mechanicks or many of them have left the old ticket and 'tis feared will go over to ye Presbyterians."[46]

The vote of the mechanics swelled the votes for the Allen party and resulted in the election of John Dickinson to the Assembly, thus ending an interval of five years since his last service in the House. Traditionally loyal to their brother mechanic, Benjamin Franklin, the change in the allegiance of the mechanics was significant. Although many of them would again vote for the "Old Ticket," that party's hold on them was tenuous. With the next great surge of the revolutionary movement in 1774, they straightway deserted the Quaker for the Presbyterian party which claimed the majority of the revolutionary leaders.

For some time the mechanics had been dissatisfied with their relation with the Quaker party. The mechanics maintained that they were the largest single group of people in Philadelphia and owned approximately one-half the property in the city, and yet, none of their members were ever selected for the Assembly.[47] The prominent part played by the mechanics during the late resistance to the Townshend duties gave them a greater feeling of political importance than ever before. In brief, they were fast becoming politically minded, demanding a place

---

[43] Pa. Gazette, Aug. 23, 1770.
[44] Clifford to Livingston, June 10, 1769, Clifford to Stockham, Nov. 26, 1767, Clifford Corresp., XXVIII, Pemberton Papers.
[45] Pa. Chronicle, June 11, 1770.
[46] Letters to Dr. Franklin, III, Part 1, 28. APS
[47] Pa. Packet, March 18, 1776.

in the council chambers of the province. On the eve of the 1770 election one of their spokesmen asserted:

> Let us step forth like Men sensible of our true Interest, and while we glory in the despicable Name of Mechanic, let us, by our Prudence, Moderation and Unanimity, command Respect, and convince the great Ones that truly wise and honest Men, worthy to represent a free People, can be found amongst us.[48]

About this time the mechanics (together with some of the smaller shopkeepers,) formed an association known as the *Patriotic Society*. The old political leaders rightfully viewed the new organization as a threat to their exclusive control of political affairs in the colony. It was known, that the society stood for an increase in the representation of Philadelphia in the Assembly and for a broader suffrage franchise by way of lowering the property qualification.[49]

The fact that Joseph Galloway was henceforth elected to the Assembly from Bucks County was due, it seems, to his loss of support among the mechanics and artisans. His efforts to regain favor in Philadelphia were without the least success. In September, 1771, he was the subject of a bitter attack by William Goddard, who had formerly been one of his supporters. During the campaign for the election of 1772, a cartoon was circulated picturing Galloway going to Bucks County for his election while trampling under foot the Goddess of Liberty, the Bill of Rights, and the Pennsylvania Charter. He was accompanied by Thomas Wharton, "the Buckram Marquis of New Barrataria" as this grandee and Vandalia promoter was dubbed in Pennsylvania.[50] From England, Franklin endeavored to console his friends in Philadelphia. "It must be very discouraging to our friend, Galloway," he wrote, "to see his long and faithful services repaid with Abuse and Ingratitude."[51] Galloway, who was but forty years old, told Franklin that he was sick of politics and that he planned to retire from the Assembly in the near future.[52]

For the most part, the resentment was directed against the Junto, as Galloway's faction in the Quaker party was called, and not against the party as a whole. The party, in fact, continued to control the

---

[48] *Pa. Gazette*, Sept. 27, 1770. See also *Pa. Packet*, March 18, 1776.

[49] *Pa. Gazette*, Sept. 27, 1770, Sept. 2, 29, 1773, Aug. 26, 1772. Oddly enough, in the face of the fact that Philadelphia complained of being under-represented, the city threw away one of its votes for five consecutive years (1757-1761) by electing Franklin to the Assembly during all the time he was in England. Such again was the case in 1773 when Franklin was elected for the city. See *Votes*, VIII, 7024.

[50] *Votes*, VIII, 6683; Smyth, V, 380; *Pa. Chronicle*, Sept. 19, 1772.

[51] Smyth, V, 380 ,461.

[52] *Ibid.*, VI, 6.

Assembly right down to the Revolution.[53] For one thing, the strength of political parties in colonial days rested squarely upon the popularity of the individual politician. The parties, in no way formal organizations, consisted of a loose association of men drawn together by mutual likes and dislikes.[54] This atomistic state of political affairs called for adroit leadership on the part of those who aspired to provincial control of party politics.

After Franklin left the colony in 1764, neither the Quaker nor the Proprietary party had a man among the older politicians progressive enough or possessed with sufficient political wisdom to capitalize on the popular desires of the people. The older leaders looked upon political power as their birthright and thought that the common people should ask no other privilege than that of delivering them their vote on election day. Out of the revolutionary upheaval, however, men arose to supply the populace with the leadership it desired. Some of them, such as Dickinson, Mifflin, Clymer, and Ross would go part way and join Pennsylvania in the independence movement, but it remained for Cannon, Bryan, Matlack, Rittenhouse, and like-minded leaders to go on and give the people the most democratic constitution framed during the revolutionary era.

---

[53] The strength of the anti-Galloway party in 1772, in Philadelphia County and City is shown by the fact that it elected seven out of ten members to the Assembly. See Broadsides, Box 3, Folder L. HSP; *Votes,* VIII, 6896.

[54] As no tickets were prepared by the slate headed by John Dickinson in 1772, all gentlemen who approved it were asked to write a few tickets to give to his friends at the election. Broadsides, Box E, Folder L. HSP.

CARTOON ON THE REPEAL OF THE STAMP ACT.

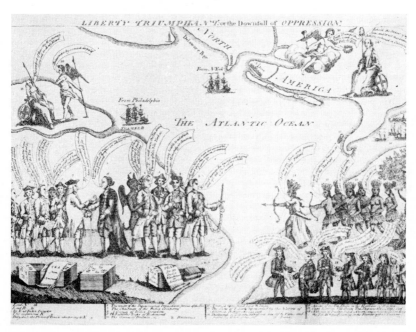

CARTOON REPRESENTING AMERICAN VIEWS IN THE TEA EPISODE, 1774.

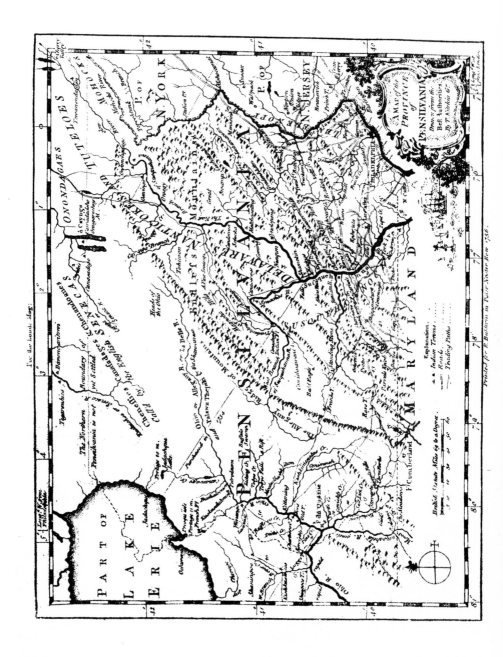

For the hand-map:

A Map of this PROVINCE of PENSILVANIA. Drawn from the Best Authorities By T. Nichols &c.

Printed for R. Baldwin in Pater-Noster Row 1756.

Explanation:
▲▲ Indian Towns ....
Roads ....
Trading Paths ———

British Statute Miles 69 to a Degree
10 20 30 40 50 60

PART OF LAKE ERIE

N YORK

PENNSILVANIA

MARYLAND

N. JERSEY

XII

OUTBREAK OF THE REVOLUTION. 1774-1775

WHEN Great Britain repealed the Townshend duties on everything but tea, the colonies, after remonstrating against the tax, turned and ordered their tea from Holland, and smuggled it into the country. The loss of the American tea market was an important factor contributing to a serious financial crisis for the British East India Company. That Company had misjudged American resourcefulness when, after the repeal of Non-Importation by the colonies, it stocked quantities of tea in anticipation of large orders from America. By 1772 not only was the plight of the East India Company acute, but repercussions throughout the British economy were threatening a general business paralysis.[1]

In the hope of relieving the British East India Company by reopening a market in America for its tea, Parliament in 1773 removed the duty collectable in England on tea, leaving only the tax levied at the American port. This move made it possible for the Company to undersell all other tea in the colonies. The Company was to place its business in the hands of friendly agents in the principal American cities, thus excluding the other merchants from the tea business.[2]

The reaction in America against this clever stratagem of Lord North and the British Parliament was as immediate as it was portentous. This time, however, the first demonstrations were held in New York and Philadelphia, and not in Boston. In Philadelphia the leaders who had fought the Stamp Act and the Townshend Acts called a meeting at the State House, where it was resolved that the consignees for the tea should resign at once.[3] Resentment against the new measures was directed as much against the monopolistic character of the act as against the tax. Yet they saw clearly enough that the principle of taxation was at stake even if they had not heard Lord North's witticism that he would try a "case" in America.[4]

---

[1] Smyth, V, 459-460, VI, 12-13, 22.

[2] *Ibid*, VI, 124-125; Miller, 337-340. New York and Philadelphia were the centers for tea smuggling. Many of the Boston merchants went back to their London dealers for tea. However, Van Tyne estimates that nine-tenths of the tea used during this period was smuggled. Van Tyne, 370.

[3] *Pa. Journal*, Oct. 20, 1773.

[4] *Ibid.*, Dec. 27, 1773. Franklin wrote that the ministry had no idea that people would act from other motives than self-interest and thought that the reduction in price would "overcome all the Patriotism of an American." Smyth, VI, 57.

Upon the arrival of the tea ship *Polly* in December, the city was thrown into the greatest excitement. Tea agents Abel James and Henry Drinker, who had not resigned at the request of the meeting two months before, were now given a few hours to resign as Thomas Wharton already had done. Drinker did so, but James would not comply until a large crowd had collected menacingly before his house.

Meanwhile, about eight thousand citizens had gathered at the State House, shouting their approval of the Boston Tea Party and leaving no doubt that a like fate would attend the tea sent to Philadelphia, unless the vessel returned at once. Handbills were circulated containing threats against Captain Ayres if he attempted to land the cargo. Realizing the futility of landing the tea, Ayres consented to return with his cargo. Not a thing was allowed to be landed: not even Thomas Wharton's new coach which was on shipboard. No sooner had the last scene of the drama closed than Lawyer Joseph Reed candidly informed Lord Dartmouth that "any further attempt to enforce this act—must end in blood." America was "hastening to desperate resolutions, and unless internal peace is speedily settled,— anarchy and confusion" will follow.[5]

When it became known early in 1774 that Great Britain had ordered the port of Boston closed until the city paid for the tea destroyed at its tea party almost everyone in Pennsylvania joined the general cry against the tyranny and cruelty of the British Government. James Tilghman, who, like many others, had frowned upon the extreme action of the Bostonians, now declared that a policy of force would only inflame America and lead to greater trouble.[6]

By this time the people of Pennsylvania were not unprepared for the crisis which confronted them. For several months past, patriotic committees had been formed by town meetings all over the province after the New England fashion. Charles Thomson said that one object of forming the committees was to organize the resistance movement on a provincial basis so that the merchants could not have it in their power to drop the dispute whenever their interest was served in doing so.[7] The principal leadership, nevertheless, continued to come from Philadelphia, the metropolis and nerve center of the province.

It was with deep apprehension that the conservative-minded people of Pennsylvania watched the rise of the democratic town meetings. James Tilghman echoed the feelings of the conservatives when he said that Pennsylvania ought to be above aping New England and en-

---

[5] *N. Y. Gazette*, Jan. 3, 1774; Reed, I, 54-55.
[6] Penn MSS., Off. Corresp., XI, 150.
[7] *Pa. Mag.*, II, 417.

couraging mobocracy.[8] By this time William Allen and many of his friends, who had been the most forward in opposing Great Britain in years past, began to fear that the resistance movement might lead to open rebellion and anarchy.

On May 19 the citizens of Philadelphia received a letter from the Boston Town Meeting delivered by Paul Revere. The Bostonians appealed for help and support in the face of the closure of the port of Boston by order of the British government. To do this effectively, they proposed holding a Continental Congress at which the colonies could adopt measures for protecting themselves and safeguarding their liberties.[9]

The next day, three hundred or more of the principal citizens of Philadelphia collected in the long room of the City Tavern to consider what should be done. The town meeting had been speedily planned and arranged by Charles Thomson, Thomas Mifflin, and Joseph Reed, three of the most fiery Radicals in the city. Reed was a promising young lawyer of thirty-three, who after practicing in Trenton, had recently moved to Philadelphia where his marriage to the daughter of the London merchant, Dennis deBerdt, placed him in the upper circle of Philadelphia society. Thomas Mifflin was three years younger than Reed and thus far in life had shown more adeptness in politics than in his languishing merchant business. From the start it was apparent that the meeting had been well planned. Because of the aversion to town meetings among the Quakers and conservatives, special care had been taken in advance to secure the approval of the leaders of the old Quaker and Proprietary parties. The chairmen of the meeting—Dickinson, Thomas Willing, and Edward Pennington, all known for their moderation—were also chosen in advance and approved by the leading men in the city.[10]

The meeting opened by reading the Boston Port Bill and the correspondence from Boston. This was followed by a speech by Joseph Reed, whose mild and pleasant manner inspired confidence among the fainthearted. According to plan, Mifflin followed Reed with a fiery speech, the violence of which threw the meeting into an uproar. At this juncture Charles Thomson fainted; that was about the only thing that he had not planned. Dickinson was scheduled to speak next, in order that he might quiet the meeting sufficiently to allow Thomson to introduce the resolutions which the Radicals wanted carried. Thomson reasoned that the Conservatives and Moderates would then accept his

[8] *Ibid.*

[9] William Smith, Notes and Papers on the Commencement of the American Revolution, 1-2, HSP.

[10] *Pa. Mag.*, II, 415-416.

resolves for fear of more extreme motions from Mifflin. Thomson recovered in time to carry out his part, and his resolves were accepted. Thus the Radicals succeeded in having the meeting endorse the spirited resistance of the Massachusetts people. Joseph Reed declared that this "was a great point gained" considering the conservatism in Philadelphia.[11] It was a victory, too, for the popular town meeting in which the Conservatives had joined in spite of their dislike for it.

Before the meeting adjourned, a committee of correspondence was chosen to draft the reply to Boston. The committee was to be ten in number, but as both the Radicals and Conservatives prepared a list of nominees, the chairmen resolved the difficulty by taking both lists and had them approved as a committee of twenty.[12]

Pennsylvania's reply to Massachusetts, said to have been written for the committee by the Rev. William Smith, one of its members, was much too mild in tone to please the Radicals. The letter admitted that Massachusetts was "suffering in the General Cause." Pennsylvania hoped that England, it read, would be petitioned and given every opportunity for removing American grievances before more drastic measures of resistance were undertaken. If England did this, America, it was thought, should pay for the tea destroyed at Boston. The committee let Boston's call for a Continental Congress go unanswered as it did not feel authorized to commit Pennsylvania to the proposition.[13]

The Pennsylvania letter, especially the reference to the Boston Tea Party, irked the New England Radicals no end. The whole tone of the Pennsylvania answer, they believed was lukewarm, if not actually cool.[14] Samuel Adams, however, thought his friends were too severe with Pennsylvania. He even admitted that there was merit in their suggestion regarding the tea, and he was highly pleased that the people of Philadelphia had acted in a typical New England fashion in having the whole question discussed and acted upon in an open and democratic town meeting.[15]

On June 1, the day the port of Boston was closed by the British, Charles Thomson and other forward patriots asked everyone to make it a day of mourning and prayer as was being done in other colonies. In Philadelphia the bells were tolled, flags were lowered to half-mast, and services were held in some of the churches. Disconcerting, however, was the fact that the Quakers generally refused to conform and went about their daily pursuits as usual. It was contrary to their

---

[11] "Joseph Reed's Narrative," *N. Y. Hist. Soc. Coll.* (1878), 269-272.

[12] *Ibid.*, William Smith, Notes and Papers, 12. HSP.; *N. Y. Gazetteer,* June 9, 1774.

[13] William Smith, Notes and Papers, 9.

[14] *N. Y. Gazetteer,* June 9, 1774.

[15] William V. Wells, *The Life and Public Services of Samuel Adams,* II, 171-172.

religion, they declared, to set aside "appointed days" of any kind.[16] Despite this explanation, it was clear to the Radicals that the Quakers were becoming daily less inclined to support the resistance movement in Pennsylvania.

Pennsylvania had hardly sent its reply to Massachusetts before a call from Virginia for a Continental Congress was echoed throughout the colonies.[17] Already town meetings in many parts of the country had taken up the cry for a congress to consider what America must do to safeguard its liberties. Such a resolution, the first in Pennsylvania, was adopted at the frontier town of Hanover on June 2.[18] Meanwhile, the Philadelphia Radicals had been busy on the same proposition. By June 7 they had secured the signatures of nearly one thousand Whigs on a petition asking Governor Penn to convene the Assembly for the purpose of naming delegates to a Continental Congress. Penn declined saying that he could see no occasion for a special session of the legislature.[19] Realizing that the full weight of all patriotic elements in the province must be brought to bear if Pennsylvania was to keep abreast of the Revolutionary movement, the Philadelphia Committee led by Dickinson, Thomson, Reed, Mifflin, and Clymer sent out a call for another town meeting for June 18. Everyone knew what the Radicals had in mind. They wanted a new committee more representative of the popular interest which would proceed, with or without the aid of the Assembly, with the business of sending a delegation to Congress.[20]

In response to the call which was addressed to all religious, patriotic, and fraternal societies, meetings and committees of the various organizations mushroomed all over the city. The Mechanics Association, constituting one of the most radical units in Philadelphia, was particularly active. On June 9, this group appointed a committee to cooperate with one recently formed by the merchants. Six days later, twelve hundred mechanics met at the State House and resolved to support a Continental Congress. They then chose a committee of correspondence, of which David Rittenhouse was a member, and instructed it to answer a communication just received from the mechanics of New York.[21]

---

[16] N. Y. Gazetteer, June 30, 1774.

[17] Pa. Journal, June 15, 1774; Edmund C. Burnett, The Continental Congress, 20; Votes, VIII, 7091.

[18] Van Tyne, 429; L. L. Nixon, James Burd, 152.

[19] N. Y. Gazetteer, June 16, 1774; Clifford to Thomas Frank, June 21, 1774, Clifford Corresp., XXIX, Pemberton Papers; Penn MSS., Off. Corresp., XI, 149.

[20] Smith, Notes and Papers.

[21] Pa. Journal, June 15, 1774. In 1773 after the Gaspee affair, Virginia initiated the committee of correspondence by suggesting the need of better inter-colonial communications. Thus the committees of correspondence became the machinery for calling the First Continental Congress. Votes, VIII, 6969; Burnett, Continental Congress, 16-17; Van Tyne, 371-372.

The town meeting of June 18 was attended by nearly eight thousand inhabitants of Philadelphia, almost all the adult males of the city. John Dickinson and Thomas Willing, known for their moderation, were chosen chairmen of the meeting. From the start, however, it was apparent that the Radicals would govern the meeting. Amid shouts and cheers the inhabitants resolved that the people of Boston were suffering for a common cause, that the closure of the port of Boston was unconstitutional, oppressive, and dangerous to the liberties of the colonies. The meeting then resolved that a Continental Congress must be held as soon as possible. A committee of correspondence consisting of forty-four members was thereupon appointed for the purpose of implementing Pennsylvania's participation in the Congress. The new committee which included the twenty members of the former one, was composed of men from all the religious and economic groups in the city. Although it still contained many Moderates and Conservatives, the great majority were prepared to follow the leadership of Charles Thomson and like-minded men.[22]

Without delay the Philadelphia Committee went ahead with plans for the projected Continental Congress. Plans were soon announced for holding a Provincial Convention for choosing delegates and instructing them on what to do in Congress. Letters were therefore sent to all the county committees in the province, asking them to send delegates to the Provincial Convention.[23] In this way it was believed the voice of the people would be heard and their sovereign will registered by their representatives in Convention. The proposal was definitely revolutionary. "The laws and the constitution," declared the conservatives, were being replaced by the "resolves of the people." "It is the Beginning of Republicanism."[24]

Perceiving rather late that their efforts to block the popular movement had miscarried, and in view of the fact that they had secured a promise from the Philadelphia Committee that the Assembly could choose the delegation to Congress, the Conservatives now prevailed upon Speaker Galloway to call the Assembly in a "voluntary" conference.[25] Realizing in his turn that the Radicals could not be stopped, Governor Penn took advantage of reported Indian hostilities in the Ohio region to send out a call for the Assembly to meet on July 18.[26]

Thomson and the Philadelphia Whigs, however, had determined not to trust the liberties of the province to an Assembly dominated by

---

[22] Broadsides, Box 3, Folder, R. HSP.; *Pa. Journal,* June 22, 1774.
[23] *Pa. Journal,* June 22, 29, 1774; *Pa. Gazette,* July 6, 1774.
[24] *N. Y. Gazetteer,* July 28, 1774.
[25] Smith, Notes and Papers, 9.
[26] *Votes,* VIII, 7085-87.

Galloway. The committee therefore resolved that the Convention would be held for the purpose of instructing the Assembly on the will of the people. Election of delegates to the Convention was set for July 15 three days before the convening of the Assembly. The committee recommended to the counties that they allow only qualified voters to choose their delegates at the "town meetings." In open meetings such as these, however, this ruling, pleasing to the Conservatives, must have meant very little.[27]

The enthusiastic way in which the people all over the province responded in chosing delegates to the Convention was indicative of the popularity of the undertaking. The Convention met at the appointed time with about seventy-five members present. Nearly half of them were from the city and county of Philadelphia which sent thirty-four delegates. Nearly all of the delegates from the west were zealous Whigs such as George Ross, William Atlee, Jasper Yeates, James Wilson, Edward Biddle, and James Smith, ready to support the plans of the Philadelphia Radicals.[28] Thomas Willing was made chairman and Charles Thomson, secretary. As chairman of the Philadelphia Committee John Dickinson proceeded to present to the Convention a cogent analysis of the powers of Great Britain and the rights of the colonies under the English constitution. Next he offered proposals for sending a Pennsylvania delegation to the Continental Congress.

After considering Dickinson's recommendations, the Convention resolved "That there is an absolute necessity that a Congress of Deputies from the several Colonies be immediately assembled,—for the Purposes of procuring Relief for our suffering Brethren, obtaining Redress of our Grievances, preventing future Dissentions, firmly establishing our Rights and restoring Harmony between Great Britain and her colonies on a constitutional Foundation." Among other resolves adopted was one which held that all the colonies should be morally bound to abide by the decisions of the Continental Congress in case recourse to non-importation was deemed advisable. A committee was then appointed to wait upon the House with the resolves of the Provincial Convention.[29]

On July 19, the day after the Assembly convened, the committee presented the resolves to the House. Their work done, the delegates swarmed into the State House to follow the debates and actions of the House. On the third day the Assembly accepted the recommendation of the Convention to name a delegation to Congress. It then chose Galloway, Rhoads, Mifflin, Humphreys, Morton, Ross, and Biddle— all members of the House—to represent Pennsylvania at the Con-

[27] *N. Y. Gazetteer,* July 28, 1774.
[28] *Pa. Journal,* July 23, 1774.
[29] *Votes,* VIII, 7092-93; *Pa. Journal,* July 23, 1774; *Pa. Gazette,* July 27, 1774.

tinental Congress. Galloway, as everyone knew was a dangerous enemy
to the popular cause, but with Mifflin, Biddle, Ross, and Morton in the
delegation, the Radicals felt reassured. Thereupon the Convention
which had waited until the Assembly acted, dissolved itself.[30]

There was much criticism, however, in Radical circles of the Assembly's confining the appointments to members of the House. Thomson thought that this was no less than a studied rebuff, inasmuch as it
was known that the Convention wanted Thomson, Dickinson, Wilson,
and Willing in the delegation.[31] The real reason behind the Assembly's
action may have been little more than legislative jealousy, for feeling
was strong against the presumptions of the Convention. In any event,
when Dickinson was elected to the Assembly in October, he was at
once added to the Pennsylvania delegation.[32]

After choosing the Pennsylvania delegation, the Assembly named a
committee for drafting instructions for their use. The majority, which
included Michael Hillegas, Samuel Miles, John Jacobs, and George Ross,
were warm supporters of the Revolutionary movement. The instructions, submitted by the committee and adopted by the House, were
broad and general. Because of the nature of their trust, the instructions
read, it was quite impossible to give the delegates specific instructions.
They were urged, therefore, to exert their "utmost Endeavors to form
and adopt a Plan which shall afford the best Prospect of obtaining a
Redress of American Grievances, ascertaining American Rights, and
establishing that Union and Harmony which is most essential to the
Welfare and Happiness of both Countries."[33] Years afterward, Galloway said that he was the author of these instructions. If such were the
case they were as good a guide for the delegates as anyone could have
devised in 1774.

The Provincial Convention, it is true, had recommended more specific
instructions than those adopted by the Assembly. In considering the
proper basis upon which England and America could come to terms,
the Convention had recommended that Great Britain should renounce
all power over American internal affairs, repeal the duties for taxation
as well as the Quartering Act, reduce the powers of the Admiralty
Courts, and repeal the late acts directed against Massachusetts. In
return, the colonies should guarantee to obey the Navigation Laws,
settle a certain annual revenue for the Crown, and compensate the East

---

[30] *Ibid.*, VIII, 7092-98; *N. Y. Gazette,* July 25, 1774.
[31] These three had long been enemies of the Quaker party.
[32] *Ibid., VIII,* 7167.
[33] *Votes,* VIII, 7100.

India Company for the tea destroyed at Boston.[34] No doubt the colonies would not settle for less than that, but perhaps it was best for the Assembly to adopt general instructions and let Congress decide upon the specific terms for a settlement.

Early in September the Continental Congress met at Philadelphia. From the start Galloway was on the defensive. His first defeat came when Congress turned down his offer to meet in the State House in favor of Carpenters' Hall. The latter belonging to the most powerful guild association was a symbol of radicalism in Pennsylvania. Next, to Galloway's surprise, Congress appointed his bitter enemy, Charles Thomson, to be its secretary. This had been arranged ahead of time in fine retribution for Galloway's having confined the delegation to members of the Assembly.[35]

Soon after Congress assembled, news of the passage of the Quebec Act by Parliament set off a fresh wave of indignation throughout the colonies. The act, which extinguished claims of the colonies to trans-Allegheny territory by incorporating the Ohio Valley with the Province of Quebec, was pictured as a bid to "bring the Canadians and savages upon the English colonies." Joseph Reed told Lord Dartmouth that so great was the change brought by this report that "the people are generally ripe for any plan the Congress advise, should it be war itself." Governor Penn observed that the resentment against the Quebec Act came as much from the "first and best people in all the colonies" as from the populace.[36]

In spite of the mounting resentment against Great Britain, the Conservatives in Congress were able to worry the Radicals for fear that no decisive action would be taken. Until compromises were made in the plan for non-intercourse with Great Britain, Galloway was able to use the violent opposition of South Carolina, which feared the ruin of its rice and indigo business, to obstruct Congress. His plan of union, which was offered when opposition to non-intercourse was very strong, failed of adoption by only the vote of one colony. John Adams considered Galloway's plan to be no more than a red herring by which the Tories hoped to throw Congress into confusion. "Among all the difficulties in the way of effective and united action in 1774" he declared, "this was the most alarming".[37]

---

[34] *Pa. Journal,* July 23, 1774; *Pa. Gazette,* July 27, 1774. One the committee which drafted these instructions were Dickinson, James Reed, William Atlee, James Smith, James Wilson, Rev. Smith, John Kid, Elisha Price, Daniel Broadhead, John Okeley, and William Scull. The majority were radicals. Probably only the Rev. William Smith would be considered a conservative.

[35] Burnett, *Continental Congress,* 33-34.

[36] Penn MSS., Off, Corresp., XI, 173; Reed, I, 78-79.

[37] John Adams, *Works,* II, 387; Chalmers MSS., Phila., II, 64. NYPL. See Julian Boyd, *Joseph Galloway's Plan to Preserve the British Empire.*

The Continental Congress constituted the first great milestone on the road toward federal union. To please the Moderates, Congress sent a petition, drawn by Dickinson, to the British government. But the most important accomplishment was the creation of the Continental Association which put non-importation on a national basis. Signed by all members of Congress, including Galloway who dared not do otherwise, it bound each and everyone in the colonies to obey the articles of the Association.[38] Joseph Reed echoed the sentiment of the majority of Americans when he said that "the cloud which hung over the Colonies —begins to disperse. Instead of divided counsels and feeble measures, which at one time there was too much reason to apprehend, all now is union and firmness."[39]

In obedience to a recommendation of Congress, new committees were chosen in Pennsylvania for the purpose of carrying out the resolves of the Continental Congress. The Revolutionary committees, now clothed with a *raison d'être* by Congress, entered a new phase of their existence. The committees chosen at this time were the largest yet in Pennsylvania. Philadelphia's committee of sixty members was soon surpassed by Cumberland County, which had nearly one hundred on its rolls. In Bucks County, too, a stronghold of the Tories and pacifists, the patriots turned out in great numbers and elected a committee of ninety. "Those who voted were all freeholders, and some of the best property of the county," wrote Joseph Reed, who was there during the election.[40]

The new committees began functioning in late November. They proceeded at once to regulate, as Congress had directed, the use of scarce articles such as wool, and to control the prices of all merchandise likely soon to become scarce under the embargo. All patriotic citizens were asked to cooperate and make the program a success. In order to provide more effectively for the enforcement of the prohibitions on trade, sub-committees, called Committees of Inspection and Observation, were created and assigned specific duties. Thus Philadelphia divided its committee into six divisions of ten men each. Soon the Committees of Inspection were busy checking ships, cargoes, and all reports of infractions of the Association.[41]

The rising tide of the revolutionary movement in Pennsylvania was reflected in the fall elections, the results of which constituted a significant victory for the Whigs. There was little doubt now but that

---

[38] The importation of certain articles from Great Britain would be banned after Dec. 1, 1774, but full non-importation would not start until later and exports to Great Britain were not to be stopped until September, 1775.

[39] Reed, I, 85; Burnett, 33ff.; Van Tyne, 436ff.

[40] Reed, I, 91; *Pa. Gazette,* Nov. 9, 16, 1774; *Pa. Journal,* Nov. 2, 1774.

[41] *Pa. Journal,* Nov. 2, Dec. 7, 1774; *Pa. Packet,* July 3, 1775.

the Assembly could be counted upon to cooperate fully with the patriotic forces in the province. The majority would be correctly classed as moderates, but the leadership was definitely on the revolutionary side. Most prominent among these were Charles Thomson, Thomas Mifflin, John Dickinson, Michael Hillegas, John Jacobs, John Morton, Anthony Wayne, George Ross, and Edward Biddle.[42]

The character of the new Assembly was shown in the choice of its speaker, Edward Biddle, a leader of the revolutionary movement in Berks County. Joseph Galloway's Toryism, so vividly displayed in the sessions of the Continental Congress, made his leadership altogether untenable in the House. Few there were to lament his retirement as speaker. To Radicals like Reed, Galloway was altogether disingenuous; but so evasive and cunning that it was difficult actually to prove much against him.[43]

After choosing its officers, the Assembly unanimously approved the proceedings of the late Congress. Convening as it did in October, right after the meeting of Congress, this sanction constituted the first official approval of the proceedings of the Continental Congress by a provincial legislature. Soon a delegation, consisting of Biddle, Dickinson, Ross, Mifflin, Morton, Humphreys, and Galloway, was appointed to attend a second Continental Congress scheduled to meet in the spring. This was the same delegation as had attended the first Congress, with the exception of Rhoads who had become Mayor of Philadelphia and did not care to serve.[44] No attempt apparently was made to omit Galloway. Throughout the Revolutionary movement, in fact, the Radicals in Pennsylvania did what they could to promote harmony and encourage the more conservative people to go along with the patriotic cause.

In January, 1775, the Philadelphia Committee called a second Provincial Convention of the county committees for the purpose of coordinating the work of the committees and making it more effective. Many Whigs opposed having the Convention for fear of offending the Assembly. However, as was pointed out, the Assembly, which was not then in session, had no authority over the committees which were now the instruments of the Continental Congress.

Although inclined to doubt the wisdom of having the Convention at this time, Joseph Reed consented to serve as President for the sake of promoting harmony. After approving the proceedings of Congress, the Convention turned to a discussion of the problems facing the province. Plans were made for speeding up the manufacture of gunpowder, iron, steel, nails, cloth, and other articles of which the colonies would now

---

[42] Reed, I, 91.
[43] Votes, VIII, 7148.
[44] Votes, VIII, 7162, 7167.

have to depend upon their own production. One new enterprise already
had several hundred employees manufacturing cotton, linen, and woolen
goods, but more were needed if the colonies were to hold out successfully.[45] Everyone was enjoined to give preference to domestic manufactures and to report profiteers to the Committees of Inspection.

About this time, at a meeting of the United Company of Philadelphia
for Promoting American Manufactures, at Carpenters' Hall, a speaker
attacked the physiocratic principle that manufacturing was not a true
source of wealth. Manufacturing, he said, had made England and
France wealthy and powerful. It could do the same for America. He
assailed the argument that labor costs were too high in America to
support manufacturing. There were many women and children ready
to do the work in the textile industry, he said, and machines were being
invented constantly to lessen the work. Furthermore, manufacturing,
he told his listeners, did not of itself impair the health of workers which
was attributable to insufficient food, clothing, and heating.[46] The promotion of manufacturing in Philadelphia made rapid progress. By
September the United Company had four hundred operators employed
in making cloth. At the London Coffee House stock in the enterprise
was on sale for anyone desiring to participate in the endeavor.[47]

The Provincial Convention authorized the Philadelphia Committee
to be a committee of correspondence for the entire province and have
the power to call a Provincial Convention whenever the necessity
arose.[48] The more radical men at the Convention wanted to undertake
organizing military associations and securing arms for the defense of
the province in case of attack. They pointed to the New England
minutemen and similar precautions being taken in other provinces.
But the opposition to doing anything which might be construed as
armed rebellion was too strong in Pennsylvania, and the matter was
laid aside.[49]

Upon the convening of the Assembly in February, 1775, Governor
John Penn sent the House a message advising it to seek redress of
grievances through a petition to the Crown. This action, it was supposed, was instigated by Galloway in an effort to get Pennsylvania to
act independently of Congress as a first step toward breaking off
relations with that body. However, when the motion on Penn's recommendation was acted upon, George Ross and others attacked it with

---

[45] *Ibid.*, VIII, 7390; *Pa. Packet*, Jan. 30, 1775; *Pa. Gazette*, Jan. 25, 1775; *Pa.
Journal*, Feb. 1, 1775. Printers were recommended to use "Germantown type"
in preference to imported type.
[46] *Pa. Packet*, March 20, 1775.
[47] *Ibid.*, Sept. 25, 1775.
[48] *Pa. Gazette*, Jan. 25, 1775.
[49] *Pa. Packet*, Jan. 30, 1775.

great warmth. On the vote it was defeated by a vote of nearly two to one.[50]

Apparently John Penn did not realize how little influence Galloway and the Tories had in the Assembly, for, even after the Battle of Lexington, he sent a message recommending a plan for reconciliation proposed by the House of Commons. When the message was read in the House, it was met with stony silence. In answer, the House emphatically declared that it would in no case act independently of Congress in matters which were of such a vital concern to all. "If no other objection to the Plan proposed, occurred to us," the Assembly declared, "we should esteem it a dishonest Desertion of Sister Colonies, connected by an Union."[51]

By this time, like John Hughes a decade earlier, Galloway had ruined himself politically in Pennsylvania. In February he had James Rivington, the New York Tory, publish a pamphlet entitled *Candid Examination of the Mutual Claims of Great Britain and the Colonies,* in which he scored Dickinson's constitutional opinions and declared that the authority of Parliament was supreme over all the British Empire. This power was the only safeguard to individual freedom and protection against lawless and wilful men. Now becoming desperate, Galloway opened fire on the Radicals right in the Assembly. "I censured & condemned the Measures of the Congress in every Thing," he wrote William Franklin. Everything that Congress did, he told the Assembly, was intended "to incite America to sedition & terminate in Independence." Galloway was now out in the open and the Whigs hammered him unmercifully. Even old William Allen, who had more scores to settle than anyone, joined Dickinson, Thomson, and Mifflin in the attack.[52]

The news of the Battle of Lexington-Concord, fought on April 19, 1775, fanned the flames of revolt throughout the colonies. Even the strictest Quakers were aroused by this event to the point of joining in the general denunciation of the British. Although he had but recently derided the Patriots and called them rebels, James Pemberton now undertook to raise money among the Quakers for relieving Boston. Christopher Marshall noted in his diary on May 7 that the language of the Tories was much softened since the reports of the battle had arrived, and that many of the "stiff Quakers" seemed ashamed of having opposed the Whigs.[53]

---

[50] *Votes,* VIII, 7212; Meeting of the Committee of Observation, March 30, 1775, Yeates Papers, 1762-1780; *Pa. Journal,* April 12, 1775.

[51] *Votes,* VIII, 7224-30.

[52] Boyd, 45-50; *Pa. Packet,* May 15, 1775.

[53] Christopher Marshall's Diary, May 7, 1775.

It was about this time that Philadelphia felt the first shock of the enveloping war when reports came that the British would soon order all ports closed in America. Soon the news was published that the port of New York had been closed, and that the port of Philadelphia would be next. The report caused panic among the merchants of the city. Thomas Clifford described with what haste all ships were dispatched, loaded or not. Cargoes were left lying on the wharves as the ships sought the safety of the open seas.[54]

Prior to the Battle of Lexington-Concord, little had been done in Pennsylvania in way of preparations for defense. But with the news of fighting to the northward, companies of military associators sprung into existence all over the province. On the day following the news of the battle, about eight thousand people gathered at the State House and there resolved "to associate together to defend with arms our property, liberty, and lives." John Adams noted a few weeks later that "the Martial Spirit throughout this Province is astonishing, it arose all of a Sudden, Since the News of the Battle of Lexington."

On June 23, Joseph Reed, in behalf of the Philadelphia Committee, sent the Assembly a memorial requesting the adoption of laws to strengthen the defense of the province. A similar letter was sent by the officers of the newly formed Philadelphia militia. In response, the Assembly officially approved the military associations and made provision for arming and equiping them at provincial expense. In each county a number of strong and hardy "Minute Men" were to be on call to march to the defense of the colony while the older members of the Association remained on guard at home. Five thousand muskets and bayonets were ordered by the Assembly and £35,000 appropriated to meet the expenses incurred in preparing for defense. Finally a Committee of Safety was created with Dickinson, chairman, and with power to call out the militia associations and take other measures necessary to protect the people. All this was done, said Thomson, with only three dissenting voices in an Assembly of which more than half still professed to be Quakers.[55]

The Second Continental Congress met in Philadelphia on May 10, 1775. Important changes were to be noted in the Pennsylvania delegation as Congress convened. Galloway had resigned and his resignation had been accepted without regrets by the Pennsylvania Assembly. Thomas Willing and James Wilson, both of whom had been forward in the Whig cause, had been added to the delegation. But that which was most talked about was the presence of Benjamin Franklin, who

---

[54] Thomas Clifford to Thomas Frank, May 6, 1775, Clifford Corresp., XXIX, Pemberton Papers.

[55] *Votes*, VIII, 7238-7345.

had just returned from England burning with resentment and anger against the British.[56]

If there had been any doubt in Franklin's mind as to where his loyalty lay, it was removed after his encounter with Wedderburn, the solicitor-general, at a meeting of the Privy Council on January 29, 1774. There, in the presence of thirty-five great gentlemen, Wedderburn called Franklin a low thief who had stolen and made public the private letters of Governor Thomas Hutchinson of Massachusetts. For an hour the solicitor-general scorched Franklin before an array of the greatest men in the realm. Friends who were present, such as Shelburne, Priestley, and Burke, were powerless and unable to save him. Right then Franklin realized as never before that England was an alien country and that America was his home. Galloway and the Whartons could go on with their schemes for aggrandizement and riches through the favor of these men, but Franklin was through.[57]

Leadership of the Pennsylvania delegation, notwithstanding Franklin's return, remained with Dickinson. Franklin had been away now over ten years, and there was a great deal for him to learn before he cared to say much. Some there were, too, such as Thomas Bradford, who remembering Franklin's part in the Stamp Act episode, were not sure that he could be trusted. Was Franklin a spy for the British, was a frequent question heard at this time.[58]

Out of regard for Dickinson and the Moderates all over the country, Congress resolved to petition the Crown again before resorting to the more extreme measures desired by the Radicals. The petition itself was drawn up by Dickinson and incorporated his own ideas.[59]

John Adams, the foremost leader of the Radicals, had nothing but scorn for another petition. Franklin shared his sentiments regarding the value of a petition but said little. It was too late, both men felt, to be petitioning. America had a war on its hands, and decisive action must be taken or the results would be disastrous.

Instead of petitioning England, Adams said that Congress should proceed at once to the formation of a central government and to other means of implementing the most effective resistance. With this accomplished, America would demand a new position in the British Empire, if Adams had his way. Adams was thinking that England must adopt what amounted to a commonwealth system, not unlike that which materialized more than one hundred years later. If this could not be

---

[56] *Ibid,* 7234; *Pa. Journal,* May 10, 1775.

[57] Bernard Fay, *Franklin, the Apostle of Modern Times,* 366-367.

[58] Edward Shippen to Jasper Yeates, May 15, 1775. Balch Papers, Shippen II, HSP.

[59] Lincoln, 205.

realized, he already was convinced that independence was the only solution so far as America was concerned.[60]

Each day Adams became more irritated with the note of caution stressed in Congress by the Pennsylvania delegation. He rightly held Dickinson to be most responsible for blocking the path of the Radicals. With characteristic sarcasm he berated Dickinson as "A certain great Fortune & pidling Genious, whose Fame—trumpeted so loudly, has given a silly cast to our whole doing."[61] These were hard words, for, after all, besides his natural mildness, Dickinson was moved by an awareness that if the people were to be brought along without serious division and opposition, they must be convinced that all possible means had been taken to reach an understanding with Great Britain.

With his understanding of Pennsylvania politics, Thomson acknowledged the expediency of sending another petition. Franklin thought that there might be some reason for sending one for its influence on American thinking, but that it would produce no good in England where the government did not have "sense enough" to be reasonable. Already Franklin was certain that England had lost the colonies forever.[62]

By this time it was being whispered that the rebellion would end in independence, unless England saw fit to reverse its policies. None of the leaders of the Pennsylvania Whigs, however, if they thought this, were saying as much in public. But with the common people, especially the Scots Irish Presbyterians, it was different. Many of the latter, by the time Bunker Hill (June, 1775) was fought, were saying that they not only thought that independence was coming, but that they were whole-heartedly for it.

With each new development in the Revolutionary movement the Quakers had grown more cool toward the American cause. If continued unchecked, they saw in it not only the likelihood of war and independence, but also Presbyterian political control of Pennsylvania, the bugaboo which had haunted them for over a quarter of a century. The Quakers, therefore, felt that they must do everything possible to discourage radicalism and restore peace and friendship between the colonies and the mother country.

Before the year 1774 had ended, Israel Pemberton and other Quaker leaders had begun action to hold back the revolutionary movement in Pennsylvania. In their meetings they resolved that all Quakers should disassociate themselves from the Whigs entirely. Christopher Marshall

---

[60] S. E. Morison, ed., *Sources and Documents Illustrating the American Revolution,* 125-136.

[61] Shippen Papers, VII, 127. HSP.

[62] Smyth, VI, 408.

noted in his diary that the Quakers in January, 1775, were meeting daily in order "to defeat the pacific proceedings of the Continental Congress," and were "calling upon their members not to meet the county committees but entirely withdraw from them under penalty of excommunications."[63] Presently the Quakers had the temerity to come out in the open and warn the people of Pennsylvania against the "usurpation of power and authority, in opposition to the laws and government, and against all combinations, insurrections, conspiracies, and illegal assemblies."[64]

The publication of this testimony raised a storm of indignation; so menacing did it become that the Quakers felt compelled to issue another paper which amounted to a retraction of their statement. They sought to assure everyone that Quakers were not condoning the illegal and arbitrary actions of the British ministry and that it was their fervent desire to support all those who were striving to hold fast to the true principles of English liberties.[65] But the Quaker effort to explain away the clear implications of their earlier pronouncement sounded to the Whigs very much like fine-spun sophistry. There was no need, they thought, for over-nice distinctions and subtle interpretations with the British heel already on their necks.

In April, ten days before the Battle of Lexington, Christopher Marshall noted that both Galloway and the Reverend William Smith were conniving with the Quaker leaders, Israel and James Pemberton, to embarrass and discredit the patriotic cause. But after the Battle when the Quakers were less critical of the Whigs, some thought they might even be induced to come back into the associations and committees. This hope, however was soon dispelled. In August, John Pemberton, a Quaker preacher, used his powers of persuasion to convince Quakers that they should not observe August 20 as a day of prayer and fasting, as recommended by Congress. As the weeks wore on and the war assumed more ominous proportions, agitation among the Radicals grew more urgent for a law which would distribute the burdens of defense by taxing the immense wealth of the Quakers and other non-associators.

It was not long before the Assembly was flooded with petitions from patriotic groups requesting it to follow out a recommendation of Congress and provide a law whereby military service would be compulsory for all except conscientious objectors. Up to that date the defense units in Pennsylvania were composed entirely of volunteers. The Whigs felt that this system—which placed the entire burden upon the associa-

---

[63] Christopher Marshall's Diary, Jan. 24, 1775.
[64] Broadsides, Box 3, Folder A. HSP.; Marshall's Diary, Jan. 2, 1775.
[65] *Pa. Journal,* Feb. 1, 1775.

tors—was inadequate, with the colonies menaced by the entire armed might of Great Britain.[66] It was only fair, they thought, that all should bear arms or pay for their exemption inasmuch as everyone would gain from a war fought for the preservation of liberty.

The Quakers, of course, did not at all agree with the reasoning of the patriots. Their leaders insisted that the Society of Friends could not sanction any form of participation in war: Quakers must not serve in the militia or pay for being exempted; neither could they pay any taxes levied for the support of war. So that none could think that they were using their religious scruples to avoid taxation, they pointed to the large sums of money which Quakers had already contributed for relieving distress and suffering in Massachusetts and other places. In the hope of convincing the patriots that they were legally exempt from military obligations, the Quakers sent a petition to the Assembly in October stating that the Provincial Charter exempted them not only from military duties but also from any "Fines, Penalties, or Assessments" in lieu thereof.[67]

The Quaker petition brought down upon their heads a storm of wrath and indignation from all sides. Within a few days, seventy members of the Philadelphia Committee met at Philosophical Hall and prepared a memorial against the Quakers. With this in hand, they marched to the State House and presented it to the Speaker. Their remonstrance declared that the Quakers wished "to withdraw their persons and their fortunes from the service of their country, at a time when their country stands most in need of them." This threw all the burden onto others, while allowing the Quakers to reap benefits from the sacrifices of the patriots. The doctrine of pacifism, the paper said, was an unrealistic ideology in a world in which freedom and happiness had to be safeguarded by force.[68]

Protests against the Quakers also were voiced by the Committee of Privates and the Committee of Officers of the Philadelphia Association. They cited the Royal Charter of 1681 in proof that no one was exempt from either civil or military obligations.[69] The officers of the Association ridiculed the doctrine of passive obedience, which they declared was altogether incompatible with reason in an age of science.[70]

Fearing that they would be classified with the Quakers as Tories, the Mennonites and the German Baptists issued a declaration stating that although they were pacifists they were willing to support the

[66] Votes, VIII, 7259, 7262, 7312, 7337, 7340; Marshall's Diary, Oct. 30, 1775.
[67] Ibid., VIII, 7326-30.
[68] Pa. Gazette, Nov. 8, 1775.
[69] Pa. Gazette, Nov. 13, 1775.
[70] Ibid.

patriotic cause in any manner short of bearing arms.[71] Furthermore, they gave assurance that their churches would not censure any of their members who saw fit to join a military organization. Realizing the difficulty of all conscientious objectors, the Lancaster Committee published in May, 1775, a paper denouncing all those who were insulting and abusing the pacifists.

The release of this paper threw the county into a great uproar. A committee which would undertake to shield suspected Tories was not fit, it was said, to direct the patriotic forces of the county. So intense was the resentment against it that the whole committee decided to resign and let the people chose another. The new committee succeeded in quieting the populace by issuing a schedule of rates which nonassociators should pay for their exemption from military duties.[72]

By this time the Philadelphia Committee had taken steps to curb the Tories. The Committee on Inspection met daily at the Coffee House at noon to receive reports of all incoming cargoes. All captains were required to report to the committee within twenty-four hours of landing.[73] Vendue masters were compelled to take an oath not to buy any smuggled goods. The committee checked all invoices belonging to the vendues. Offenders had their names published in the newspapers. After that, on more than one occasion, the populace took the culprits in hand.[74]

In September several Tories were apprehended in Philadelphia and made to acknowledge the error of their ways, on threat of being tarred and feathered. Lawyer Isaac Hunt was carted through the streets and made to confess his crime of defending a profiteer. Dr. John Kearsely, a well known Tory physician, did not fare so well. When the mob following Hunt was surging by, thinking that they were after him, Kearsley threw open a window and presented a pistol at the throng. Before he could discharge his gun, he was grabbed and pulled through the window and hustled off to Committee headquarters at Bradford's Coffee House. Refusing to admit any wrong doing or ask for pardon, the Committee ordered him paraded through the streets, but would not let the mob tar and feather him.[75] After his release that night, the mob threw stones and bricks through his windows, but did not attempt to enter the house. Soon one of the doctor's letters to

[71] *Ibid.*, Nov. 20, 1775.

[72] Edward Shippen, et al. to committee, June 3, 1775, Yeates Papers, Corresp., 1762-1780. HSP.; Committee of Safety, July 1, 1775, Lancaster Co. L. of C.; Broadsides, Box 3, Folder A. HSP.; Miscel. Papers, 1772-1816, Lancaster Co, 11. HSP.

[73] *Pa. Packet*, June 12, July 3, 1775.

[74] *Ibid.*, Sept. 25, 1775.

[75] Marshall's Diary, Sept. 6, 1775.

England was intercepted and found to contain information innimical to the patriotic cause. Kearsley was forthright jailed. Some time later, while languishing in prison at Carlisle, he died.[76]

The new Assembly, elected on October 1, 1775, was composed of about the same membership as the former one. A noteworthy change, however, was the fact that Galloway was not returned, thus leaving the Tory members of Bucks and Lancaster counties without a leader. In reading over the names of the prominent members such as Mifflin, Thomson, Dickinson, Hillegas, Jacobs, Morton, Wayne, Biddle, and Ross, one notes that they were without exception leaders in the various patriotic committees as well as officers in the military associations. Indeed Charles Thomson, who was now serving as secretary for the Continental Congress, was quite pleased with the election and thought it proof that the people were determined to remain firm.[77]

In November the Assembly adopted a militia law which by its compromising nature was disappointing to many Whigs. Admittedly the law strengthened the Associations by providing rules and regulations by which they were to be governed. But the law was displeasing to many Whigs because it still left recruiting on a voluntary basis and did not tax the non-associators enough. The law provided that all non-associators between the ages of sixteen and fifty must pay an exemption fee of £2 10s.[78] This penalty was deemed too low, but worse still was the fact that non-associators over fifty years of age were not obliged to pay anything. In this category fell some of the wealthiest men in the county.[79] Before long complaints appeared over the lax way in which the law against non-associators was being enforced in the province. Led by Israel Pemberton, the Quakers put on a big campaign to defeat the purpose of the act.

In this session the Assembly resolved that £80,000 in bills of credit should be emitted with provisions for funding them by a property tax.[80] This came in addition to £35,000 raised in June by the same method. The House next appointed a Committee of Safety consisting of thirty-two well-known Whigs and headed by Benjamin Franklin. Significant is the fact that the Assembly now transacted all its important business by way of legislative resolution. Only trivial bills, mostly of a private nature, were still sent to the Governor for his approval. This action in itself signified the revolutionary temper of the Pennsylvania Whigs.

---

[76] *Pa. Packet*, Oct. 30, 1775; Graydon, *Memoirs,* 127.

[77] *Pa. Mag.*, II, 423.

[78] *Pa. Packet*, Dec. 4, 1775; *Votes,* VIII, 7351, 7380, 7382.

[79] *Votes*, VIII, 7486.

[80] *Ibid.*, VIII, 7358.

Now thoroughly aroused, the Quakers, inspired by the resolute Israel Pemberton, defiantly condemned the defense measures of the Assembly as both illegal and arbitrary. Everywhere Quakers were reminded both in and out of the Meetings that the paper money was issued for waging war and that it should not be used by any faithful Friend. Israel Pemberton, whose taxes during the French and Indian War were collected by forced sales upon his property, led off again by declaring that he would not pay the tax.[81]

In November complaints were made to the Assembly that some persons were already refusing to accept paper money. The House answered by resolving that anyone found refusing the money would be pronounced an enemy of the country and dealt with accordingly.[82] As it happened, early in 1776 several Quakers were investigated and brought before the Committee of Inspection on charges of refusing paper money. John Drinker, hatter, and Thomas and Samuel Fisher, merchants, pleaded religious scruples when called to answer charges against them. Others were soon charged with the same offense. All had their names advertised in the newspapers as enemies of the people. Strangely enough, Gaius Dickinson, a Quaker preacher, had not the courage of his convictions and gave promise that he would not refuse any bills in the future. The treatment meted out to Tories and pacifists at this time, however, was but a taste of what lay ahead.

Although powerful in certain sections, the Quaker and Tory opposition in 1775 constituted but a rather small minority in Pennsylvania. The great mass of the people enthusiastically supported the revolutionary movement. Everywhere men flocked into the military associations. The principal leadership of the revolutionary movement came from persons long associated with the Proprietary-Presbyterian party.[83] Joined with them were many of their erstwhile political foes such as Franklin, Thomson, Roberdeau, and Ross. Inside of a few months however, serious division overspread the State when suddenly emerged the question of national independence and the problem of framing a new state constitution.

---

[81] Pemberton Papers, XXVIII, 75; Minutes of the Meeting for Sufferings, II, Nov. 30, 1775; *Pa. Gazette*, Feb. 18, 1768.

[82] *Votes*, VIII, 7365.

[83] The personnel on the committees and at the conventions show this. See *Pa. Packet*, Jan. 16, 23, 30, Feb. 19, Aug. 16, 1775, for lists of members of committees.

XIII

TRIUMPH OF THE RADICALS. 1776

A s THE YEAR 1775 drew to a close, it was apparent to the most observing that the possibilities of ever achieving a reconciliation with Great Britain were indeed small. Every overture of the colonies for working out an understanding was met by the English government with new measures which were considered coercion and oppression. In August, 1775, Britain proclaimed America to be in a state of rebellion and called upon all loyal subjects to aid in quelling it. Before the year was over, American towns had been burned and pitched battles fought. But the leading Whigs in Pennsylvania persisted in the hope that a solution other than independence could yet be found.

When in September, 1775, a report was circulated that the military associators of Chester County were agitating for independence, the Chester Committee of Safety, with Anthony Wayne chairman, declared the rumor to be utterly false.[1] The very thought of independence was abhorrent to the Whigs of Chester County, the Committee maintained. In August, Jasper Yeates, a leading patriot of Lancaster, thought that union with Great Britain was absolutely necessary for the safety and well-being of America. "Our present glorious Struggle," he declared, "is for the Preservation of our Privileges, not for an Independence."[2]

Although the leading Whigs in Pennsylvania denounced the very thought of independence in 1775, many lesser known Radicals were already anxiously awaiting the time when they could start a campaign for it. When the Assembly in November, 1775, instructed the Pennsylvania delegation to work for reconciliation, the disgust of many Whigs was all too apparent. "The Honorable House—seems desperately afraid of independency," wrote one critic who thought that the delegates should have been given the liberty to vote for independence if Britain did not have an immediate change of heart.[3] Another writer bitterly attacked Dickinson, the author of the instructions, who no longer had any standing among the Radicals.[4]

Sentiment for independence mounted rapidly during the early weeks of 1776, as a result of an accumulated hatred engendered by actual war,

---

[1] *Pa. Packet,* Oct. 2, 1775.

[2] Jasper Yeates to Edward Burd, Aug. 2, 1775, Papers of Edward Shippen Burd. HSP.

[3] *Pa. Journal,* Nov. 29, 1775.

[4] *Ibid.,* Dec. 6, 1775.

175

and a realization of the advantages which a declaration of independence would offer America in the diplomatic field. Early in January, Thomas Paine's *Common Sense* was published. In plain words he told the American people that it behooved them to sever their political ties with Great Britain and to establish an independent nation. Franklin's observation that Paine's pamphlet "made a great impression in Pennsylvania" was a masterful understatement. Within a few weeks nearly one hundred thousand copies were sold in the colonies, and Paine's words were on everyone's lips. Many who had hitherto hesitated to espouse independence now became enthusiastic for it. Others reacted as violently in the opposite direction. One of these called it "the most artful, insidious, and pernicious pamphlet" he had ever read.[5] Joseph Shippen was shocked by the boldness of Paine's essay. He admitted, however, that if the British hired foreign troops to fight the Americans, Congress would have no choice but to embrace independence.[6] Edward Shippen agreed. "It is in everybody's mouth," he wrote, "as a thing absolutely necessary in case foreign Troops should be landed."[7]

The sudden outburst for independence was frightening to the Quakers. Only a few days after the release of *Common Sense*, the Quakers boldly published an address signed by John Pemberton, clerk for the Monthly Meeting of Philadelphia. The paper read:

> The benefits, advantages, and favor we have experienced by our dependence on, and connection with, the kings and government, under which we have enjoyed this happy state, appear to demand from us the greatest circumstances, care and constant endeavours, to guard against every attempt to alter, or subvert that dependence and connection. . . . May we therefore firmly unite in the abhorrence of all writings, and measures as evidence a desire and design to break off that happy connection we have heretofore enjoyed, with the kingdom of Great Britain.[8]

The addresses and speeches of the Quaker leaders, both in and out of their meetings, kept most of the members of the Society of Friends from advocating independence. Some, especially among the younger generation, acted otherwise and paid little attention to the biddings of the Meetings. Quite a number of the errant Quakers actually left the Meeting and formed themselves into a body known as the Free Quakers.

In answer to the Address of the Philadelphia Monthly Meeting, the patriots turned ridicule, sarcasm, and abuse upon the Quakers. By

---

[5] Lincoln, 236.
[6] Shippen Papers, VII, 149. HSP.
[7] *Ibid.*, VII, 190.
[8] Pemberton Papers, XXVIII, 161.

affording comfort to the enemy, the Quakers, they declared, were sabotaging the cause of liberty and aiding the forces of evil in the world. Thomas Paine bitingly alluded to the Quakers as "ye fallen, cringing, priest, and Pemberton ridden people."[9]

With rebellion rapidly shifting from a mere resistance movement to a war for indepence, many Whigs who had hitherto kept abreast of the Revolution now began to waver and show definite signs of hesitation.[10] Those who held back came mainly from the gentlemen class which had made up the Proprietary party of former days and had been the heart of the early resistance movement. Prominent in this group were the Allens, Shippens, and Burds, together with Dickinson, Thomas Willing, Robert Morris, and many others. The shades of opinion among the Moderates varied all the way from an unalterable opposition to independence, to a reluctant acceptance of its premature imposition. To the aid of the Moderates came the Quakers and the Tories and all elements in the State opposed to independence. Arrayed in this coalition was by far the greater number of men of wealth and social prominence in the State.

The division in the ranks of the Whigs at least had the advantage of relieving the Radicals of the necessity of compromising any further. Moreover, the leadership of the Radicals was daily improving as new leaders were thrust forward by the exigencies of the hour. Besides Thomson, Mifflin, and Reed, the independence movement was supported by George Clymer, John Bayard, Daniel Roberdeau, Thomas McKean, George Bryan, Timothy Matlack, George Ross, Benjamin Franklin, John Morton, and David Rittenhouse. Certainly the Radicals had no want of respectability on their side.

Sentiment in Congress reflected the growing feeling that reconciliation was no longer possible. All were aware, however, that independence could not be undertaken without the support of Pennsylvania. But the Pennsylvania Assembly was held by the Moderates, who would not admit that the hope of reconciliation was gone. At their head was Dickinson, who refused to have the House consider a change in the instructions and who, as a delegate in Congress, headed the anti-independence bloc.

Confronted by the intransigence of the Moderates, the Radicals resolved to use all the power at their command to bring Pennsylvania into line with the revolutionary movement. The Assembly, argued the Radicals, had no right to bind the delegates with instructions con-

---

[9] M. D. Conway, ed., *The Writing of Thomas Paine*, I, 208.

[10] Edward Burd, a major in the Flying Camp, said that he was willing to fight and die for English liberties, but that he would not take an oath to support independence. E. Burd to J. Yeates, July 2, 1776, Yeates Papers, Corresp., 1762-1780.

trary to the wishes of the people. "The right of instructing lies with the constituents and them only" declared one of their spokesmen; in other words, the people, he thought, should summon a provincial convention to direct the Pennsylvania interest in Congress.[11]

Already there had been much agitation in Radical circles for more representatives in the Assembly for Philadelphia and the western counties. On taking counsel, the Radicals decided that their purposes could be best served by making renewed demands for additional representatives. If their demand was granted, they felt confident of electing most of the new members, and thereby gaining control of the Assembly. If the Assembly refused to give the under-represented districts more seats in the House, they could at once appeal to the people and have a provincial convention assembled to carry out their wishes.

As the Assembly made no positive answer to the petitions for more representatives, the Philadelphia Committee announced that a provincial convention would be speedily called.[12] Confronted by this unequivocal threat to its very existence, the anti-independence coalition voted with the Radicals to create seventeen new seats in the Assembly. By so doing, the Moderates were not without hope of winning some of the seats and perhaps by a small margin maintaining control of the Assembly. In the event of such good fortune, they could with more plausibility insist that they represented the sentiment on independence of the majority in Pennsylvania.

The passage of the resolution on March 14 creating seventeen new seats in the Assembly, and scheduling May 1 for the election, stepped up the battle over independence in Pennsylvania. Prominent among the writers for the Anti-Independence party was the Rev. William Smith. Writing under the pseudonym *Cato,* he vigorously attacked the Radicals, insisting that they were but a minority in thirst for power. When he quoted earlier declarations of well-known Radicals to the effect that independence was neither practical nor desirable, he was answered by "The Forester" James Cannon that the past year had entirely changed the character of the struggle and had made former views untenable.[13] The column-space given to polemics of this kind in the newspapers attests the truth of Joseph Reed's observation that it was all "a terrible wordy war."

On May 1 the two sides turned to the polls to test their respective strength in the districts where representatives were to be chosen. The Radicals slated George Clymer, Col. Daniel Roberdeau, Owen Biddle,

---

[11] *Pa. Evening Post,* March 5, 1776.
[12] *Votes,* VIII, 7428, 7436; *Pa. Packet,* March 11, 1776; Shippen Papers, VII, 156-157.
[13] *Pa. Packet,* March 18, 25, April 1, 8, 15, 22, 29, 1776.

and Frederick Kuhl for the four seats allotted the city.[14] The Anti-Independence party put up Thomas Willing, Samuel Howell, and Alexander Wilcox and boldly headed the ticket with Andrew Allen, the most outspoken critic of the Radicals.

Both sides worked feverishly to influence electors and to get as many as possible to the polls. Records are conflicting in regard to the Quakers. Some accounts insist that, to prove their neutrality, they stayed at home. Other reports have it that they were extremely active. Many, it seems, actually refrained from voting, but others could not resist the temptation of casting votes against the Radicals.

To the disappointment and confusion of the Radicals, the Moderates elected enough candidates out of the seventeen to keep control of the Assembly by a slim margin. In Philadelphia the Moderates elected three of their candidates including Andrew Allen.[15] The last time would this be that any of the Allens were elected to public office in Pennsylvania. Within a year Andrew Allen was with General Howe who in 1777 named him Lieutenant Governor of Pennsylvania: a reminder of how the Tories would have fared had the British won the war.

Although George Clymer was the only Radical elected in Philadelphia, the contest was very close. The Radicals found a ready explanation for their defeat by the fact that so many of their supporters were away with the army. Independence sentiment, to be sure, was strong among all ranks and grades in the military associations.

In the western counties the Radicals succeeded in electing nearly all of their candidates, but only after a stronger opposition than was expected. In Northampton County, an old stronghold of the Allen party, the opposition was so strong that James Allen was swept into office by a vote of over eight hundred to fourteen. Quite clearly, not all the people on the frontiers were ready for independence either.

Failing to gain control of the Assembly, the Radicals at once turned their invective against the old property qualifications for voting, which they declared had operated to the advantage of the Moderates. Here was reason enough, they declared, for abolishing the Charter and substituting it with a new and up to date constitution. They began again, therefore, to talk of holding a provincial convention which, in the name of the people, would establish a government capable of carrying out their will.

Meanwhile, John Adams, seeking a way to solve the Pennsylvania dilemma, offered a resolution in Congress, requesting those states which

---

[14] *Ibid.*, May 6, 1776; Marshall's Diary, April 18, May 1, 1776.

[15] Many Germans being upset by something one of the Radicals said voted for the Moderates. William Bradford's Register, May-June, 1776. HSP.

had bound their delegates with instructions to repeal them, thus leaving
the delegates free to do as they thought best. After much debate the
motion was rejected.

This setback did not dampen the spirit of the Radicals. On learning
that the Pennsylvania Radicals had decided to launch an attack upon
the Charter itself, John Adams brought Congress to their aid by getting
through a motion on May 15 for all states to establish a government
capable of safeguarding the general welfare. By denying the duty of
allegiance to governments which derived their authority from the
Crown, both the Charter and the Assembly of Pennsylvania were effectively undermined.[16] John Adams was confident that Congress had now
sealed the fate of British authority in the United Colonies.

After the announcement of this resolution, the Pennsylvania Assembly, convening on May 20, was showered with a barrage of petitions
and addresses from county committees and military associations asking
for an immediate change in the instructions to the Pennsylvania delegation in accordance with the Congressional recommendation. But the
Radicals did not wait for the Assembly to act.

On the very day that the Assembly met, the Philadelphia Committee
called a town meeting, which was attended by more than seven thousand inhabitants. The meeting as usual was held in the State House
yard where the people stood in a soaking rain. Major John Bayard,
chairman of the Philadelphia Committee of Inspection, called the meeting to order. Franklin's old friend, Colonel Daniel Roberdeau, a very
popular man with the people for his out-spoken democratic views, was
chosen chairman.[17]

The people listened in silence when the Assembly's instructions to
the Pennsylvania delegates were read. This was immediately followed
by a reading of the resolution of Congress, whereupon the crowd burst
into loud applause. After that Col. Thomas McKean, who was serving
in the Continental Congress for Delaware, addressed the meeting.
Since the Assembly, he said, was no longer a suitable government for
the State, the people must call into being a new government by means
of a constitutional convention.

The meeting thereupon resolved that the instructions given the
Pennsylvania delegation were prejudicial to the liberties of the people
and must be forthwith changed; that the Assembly, having ignored the
will of the citizens, had forfeited its right to be recognized as the government of the State; and that the Assembly, therefore, which owed
its existence to the Crown, should be superseded by a government

---

[16] Paul Selsam, *The Pennsylvania Constitution of 1776*, 113; *Votes*, VIII, 7525.
[17] *Pa. Packet*, May 27, 1776.

emanating from the people. For this purpose a constitutional convention should be called, arrangements for which would be made by a
conference of representatives of the city and county committees.[18]
Like hundreds of others, William Bradford, Jr., rejoiced in the thought
that the town meeting had given the "coup de Grace to the King's
authority" in Pennsylvania.[19]

The Assembly was at once notified of the resolves of the town meeting. A few days later, the Philadelphia Committee sent Congress an
address highly critical of the Assembly, in which it stated that the
people of the province had lost all faith in it.[20] Thus beset on all sides
by hostile forces, but still hoping to save itself, the Assembly chose a
committee to study the recommendation of Congress of May 15.

A fortnight later, realizing that the Revolutionary pressure was too
great to be withstood, Dickinson and the Moderate majority in the
Assembly bowed to the inevitable, and on June 5 appointed a committee to draft new instructions for the Pennsylvania delegation.[21]
James Allen's only comment was that he had done all in his power to
oppose independence, "but the tide was too strong."

That same day the Assembly received notification from Virginia that
her delegates had been instructed to "declare the United Colonies free
and independent."[22] Two days later, Richard Henry Lee moved in
Congress "That these United Colonies are, and of right ought to be,
free and independent States." But action upon the motion was postponed when it was learned that only Franklin and Morton of the
Pennsylvania delegation would support the measure.

When the motion on independence came up again on July 2, the
Pennsylvania delegation had instructions which permitted them, but
did not compel them, to vote for it.[23] This time, however, the Pennsylvania vote was delivered for independence. The action was made
possible only by Wilson's joining Franklin and Morton in favor of the
resolution and by the absence of Dickinson, Morris, and Andrew Allen.
Two of the delegates, Humphreys and Willing, actually voted against
independence.

The animosity of the Radicals toward John Dickinson, the arch-foe
of independence, had gathered momentum daily during the long dispute
over the issue. While attending a meeting of the officers of the First
Battalion, of which he was colonel, he was openly berated for being

[18] Lincoln, 255.
[19] William Bradford's Register, May-June, 1776. HSP.
[20] *Pa. Packet*, May 27, 1776; *Votes*, VIII, 7514-16.
[22] *Votes*, VIII, 7534.
[23] *Ibid.*, VIII, 7542.

chiefly responsible for delaying independence. In attempting to defend himself, Dickinson did not deny the part he had played, but tried to explain why he considered independence unwise or at least premature. But Dickinson must have been aware, as he dwelt on his reasons for opposing independence, that there was nothing he could do or say which would rehabilitate him in the eyes of his fellow countrymen.[24]

In June when the Moderates and Tories gave up their struggle to block independence, they realized that their defeat also spelled the doom of the Pennsylvania Charter. The corporate colonies of Connecticut and Rhode Island could make the change to independency with no appreciable inconvenience, while retaining their charters, but this was hardly possible in either the Royal or Proprietary colonies. Therefore, in spite of the fact that the Philadelphia town meeting had decided to have a constitutional convention called by a provincial conference, the Moderates in the Assembly took immediate counsel as to ways and means of foiling the Radicals. Plans were presently under way for conducting an election for delegates and holding a constitutional convention under the direction of the Assembly.

But the Radicals were not to be thwarted in this manner. When the question of holding a convention came to the floor of the House, they adopted the stratagem of blocking all discussions and action by absenting themselves from the meetings. Without a quorum, the Speaker was compelled to adjourn the House after calling the roll. After repeated attempts to get a quorum, the Assembly finally, about the middle of June, gave up and adjourned until August. Everyone realized that as a functioning legislative body the Pennsylvania Assembly was at an end.

A contemporary obituary on the demise of the Assembly concluded that by deserting the public trust at a time of supreme danger it had forfeited its right to existence. "Like James the Second," it said, "they have abdicated the government, and by their act of desertion and cowardice have laid the Provincial Conference under the necessity of taking instant charge of affairs."[25] It made no difference that the Assembly had emitted bills of credit for arming the State, commissioned ships to fight the English, instituted a Court of Admiralty for condemning English ships, and absolved the people of the necessity of taking oaths of allegiance to the Crown.[26] It had failed in the hour of supreme test and its doom was sealed. Had the Assembly, admitted one writer, kept pace with the revolutionary movement in America

---

[24] William Bradford's Register, May-June, 1776.
[25] Pa. Packet, June 24, 1776.
[26] Ibid., June 3, 1776; Votes, VIII, 7457-60.

and not tried to prevent independence, it might have been allowed to direct the making of a constitution for the State.[27]

While plans for a convention were coming to naught in the Assembly, the Philadelphia Committee went swiftly forward with preparations for a provincial conference. A circular letter was sent to all the county committee containing the resolutions of the Philadelphia town meeting and naming June 18 for convening the conference. James Cannon, Timothy Matlack, and Dr. James Young, three spirited revolutionary leaders, were named to go to the counties to give advice in carrying out the radical program. Edward Shippen warned Jasper Yeates a few days later that "a certain bawling New England Man" [Doctor Young] would soon be in Lancaster "to persuade the people there to join in the late attempt to dissolve our Assembly and put everything into the Hands of a Convention."[28]

Every possible means was taken to generate enthusiasm for the radical program. A few days before the Provincial Conference convened, Col. Timothy Matlack issued a call for the officers of the Fifth Philadelphia Battalion to meet for considering the questions confronting the State. Not to be excluded from this important work, James Cannon, secretary for the privates, signified that the opinions of the whole battalion should be gathered. Thereupon the entire battalion, officers and men, met together and voted to support the measures of Congress and to give all possible encouragement to the framing of a constitution for the State. This action was followed by similar resolutions by the other Philadelphia battalions. Over fourteen hundred men voted in the affirmative, it was said, while only twenty-six dared to voice their disapproval.[29]

In commenting upon this event, Dr. James Clitherall declared "that before the meeting of the Conference every method was taken to force men into Independency." "They put the question to the City Battalion under arms," he said, "and any man who dared oppose their opinion was insulted and hushed by their interruptions, cheers, and hissing." The doctor, however, admitted that only a small percentage of the men were opposed to the resolutions.[30]

When the Provincial Conference met on June 18, at Carpenters' Hall, Col. Thomas McKean, chairman of the Philadelphia Committee, was named President. The Conference was attended by one hundred and eight representatives of the committees. The revolutionary character

---

[27] *Pa. Packet*, June 10, 1776. This article signed "A Watchman" was probably written by Thomas Paine.

[28] Edward Shippen to Jasper Yeates, May 23, 1776, Balch Papers, Shippen II.

[29] *Pa. Packet*, June 17, 1776.

[30] *Pa. Mag.*, XXII, 471.

of the meeting was revealed in the scores of unknown and somewhat bewildered men who packed the Hall. As might be imagined, the direction of the meeting fell into the hands of the more experienced persons such as Franklin, McKean, Jonathan B. Smith, John Bayard, Benjamin Rush, William Atlee, Timothy Matlack, and Christopher Marshall.

After approving the resolution of Congress of May 15, the Conference resolved that the government of Pennsylvania was "not competent to the exigencies of our affairs," that Great Britain by her cruel and illegal actions had forfeited the allegiance of the colonies, and that the people of Pennsylvania were ready to support a declaration of independence. Therefore, it was concluded to be imperative for Pennsylvania to hold a convention and frame a new constitution. July 18 was accordingly chosen as the date for the meeting of the Constitutional Convention.[31] The election of delegates was set for July 8.

The most far-reaching rule adopted by the Conference was that one fixing the voting qualifications for the election of delegates to the Convention. It was decided that no one would be allowed to participate in the election who would not abjure any and all allegiance to Great Britain. All associators, on the other hand, who were twenty-one, who had lived in the State one year, and who had at some time paid taxes, could vote.[32] The new ruling on the suffrage, therefore, cut off hundreds of Moderates and Tories, while enfranchising a host of formerly voteless persons. In no way could the Conference more clearly display its revolutionary character.

Only a few days before the suffrage resolution was adopted, the Committee for the Privates of the city battalion had addressed a protest to the Assembly, deploring the fact that so many associators were without the ballot. A similar petition from the German associators was sent directly to the Conference, asking that the ballot be given to all men rendering military service.[33] Fully realizing the need for all the votes possible, the Conference complied without the least hesitation.

Thus an extra-legal body effectively bridled the Moderates and Tories, and made sure that none but Radicals would control the Convention. The county committees and the military associations saw to it that the rules laid down by the Conference were followed at the elections of delegates to the Convention.

That the Convention would be dominated by the republican-minded people of the State, of whom the Presbyterians were most numerous,

---

[31] *Pa. Packet,* July 1, 1776; *Proceedings Relative to Calling the Conventions of 1776 1790* (Harrisburg, 1825), 37-38. The Conference also adopted measures for increasing the militia strength of the State and other urgent measures for defense.

[32] Broadsides, Box 3, Folder A. HSP.

[33] *Votes,* VIII, 7546; Proceedings, *op. cit.*

was now certain. Jonathan D. Sergeant, a member of Congress from New Jersey, was sure that the Scots Irish Presbyterians were the main pillar supporting the Revolution in Pennsylvania.[34] James Allen thought likewise: victory for the Radicals, he said, spelled the complete triumph of the "new light Presbyterian Party."[35] James Tilghman went even farther and said that they were the backbone of the Revolution in all the middle colonies.[36] So prominent was their part in the Revolution that a Hessian officer expressed the conviction that the American Revolution was "nothing more than an Irish-Scotch Presbyterian Rebellion."[37] A few years later, Franklin observed that the Irish immigrants and their children are now in possession of the government of Pennsylvania by their majority in the Assembly, as well as of a great part of the territory."[38] These Scots Irish were with few exceptions, declared a New England traveler, "the most God-provoking Democrats on this side of Hell."[39]

Many Whigs who had thus far been associated with the Radicals and who had supported independence, refused any longer to follow when the extremists insisted upon changing the constitution of the State. Others who did not oppose having a new constitution with moderate changes did not perceive until too late that the Convention was altogether in the hands of the most radical men in the State, men who were determined to make a truly democratic government. When this became apparent there developed in the Convention itself strong opposition to the constitution in the process of being drafted. Thus the leadership of the Radical party was continually narrowing, and as it narrowed, the power of the Scots Irish grew with each successive advance of the revolutionary movement.

The Moderates and Tories who had dominated Pennsylvania politics down to the Revolution had nothing complimentary to say of the membership of the Constitutional Convention. They charged that it was an incompetent body, unversed either in political affairs or in the theory of government. No good could come from such a body they were sure. Such an appraisal of the Convention has been generally accepted by historians, who have not paused to consider fully the source of their information. The Convention was condemned by excited men who, having lost their political leadership, feared the advent of political innovations and the rule of the democratic elements in the State.

---

[34] John Adams, *Works,* II, 426.
[35] James Allen's Diary, Feb. 17, 1777. HSP.
[36] Penn MSS., Off. Corresp., XI, 153.
[37] *Pa. Mag.,* XXII, 137.
[38] Sparks, X, 131.
[39] Vernon L. Parrington, *Main Currents of American Thought,* I, 359.

As a body, the members of the Convention were, in reality, fully as capable as those who had filled the seats of the Assembly in the era before the Revolution. If the historian goes back over the names of the men who sat in the Assembly before the Revolution, he will discover that—as is the way with legislatures, or of constitutional conventions for that matter—there were comparatively few persons of outstanding ability. The great majority were ordinary individuals from the countryside, led by a few prominent men such as Franklin, Kinsey, Allen, and Galloway. When the Rev. Francis Alison said that the members of the Convention were "honest, well-meaning Country men," hardly equal to the task before them, his remark could have been applied to the Assembly at any time during the Colonial period.

Still another critic of the Convention declared that not one-sixth of the members had ever read a word on the subject of politics and government. His statement may have been true, but one can not help thinking that perhaps this lack of learning in the political theory of the times was more of an asset than a liability. Their minds were free at least to experiment in government, without being fettered by traditional concepts concerning the proper form of civil government.

But to dwell on the educational shortcomings of many of the delegates was entirely misleading. Most of these men, although they heartily approved of the kind of work being done, contributed very little to the actual drafting of the constitution. The principal persons who framed the constitution, namely James Cannon, Owen Biddle, Timothy Matlack, David Rittenhouse, George Bryan, and John Jacobs, were well within the brackets of upper-class respectability and possessed the education and culture of their kind. About the only noticeable difference was their tendency to approve the democratic aspirations of the common man. Their enemies, quite naturally, attributed their political apostasy to an inordinate desire for power, to which ends they were willing to fan the flames of social unrest.

Although the lesser known figures at the Convention are not without their importance—and one wishes that he could learn more about them —they are more significant as a group than as individuals. It was they who expressed the new place of the common man in the political life of America.

Out of the West there appeared a motley throng of backwoods farmers and country politicians to take their seats at the Convention.[40] Not all, however, were obscure frontiersmen. Among the Scots Irish, who were the most numerous, was John Harris, a wealthy slave-holder and operator of the principal ferry across the Susquehanna. Also to be noticed

---

[40] Short biographical sketches of the members of the Convention are found in *Pa. Mag.*, III, IV.

were John Grier, Jonathan Hoge, John Burd, Robert M'Pherson, James M'Clean, and John Mackey, all of whom were men of education and good social connections.

More representative of the western element, however, was James Smith. He had helped blaze the road through the wilderness to get supplies to Braddock's army in 1755. Later he was captured by the Indians, but made his escape near Montreal in 1759. Next he appeared as a leader of the Black Boys, who waylaid the wagon trains of Baynton, Wharton and Morgan, laden with goods for trading with the Indians. A few years later he explored unknown parts of Kentucky and Tennessee. During the Revolution he served as a colonel fighting the Indians. After the war he settled in Kentucky, where he died in 1814. With such a background this soft-spoken frontiersman must have been keenly pleased to see the Convention in the hands of those who, for most of their lives, had fought both the Indians and the Quakers.

The large German element in the Convention (there were about twenty-five in all) is indicated by such names as Slaymaker, Sherrer, Slagle, Lesher, Eckert, Dresback, Arndt, Stroud, Weitzell, and Buckholder. For the first time in Pennsylvania history, the Germans found an occasion to take an active part in an important political undertaking. The great German population (with the exception of the sectarians), having cast off the Quakers, now generally went along with the Presbyterians and added their weight in favor of republicanism.[41] The presence of such a large number of Germans with their heavy accents and unsophisticated ways was proof enough to the conservatives that incompetence reigned in the Convention.

The most eminent man in the Constitutional Convention was the seventy-year-old philosopher and statesman, Benjamin Franklin. Although chosen President he was too preoccupied with Congressional and Continental affairs to give the question of a state constitution as much attention as it deserved. Franklin's liberal turn of mind, however, prepared him to go along with the radical majority.

Next to Franklin the most eminent men in the Convention so far as political experience was concerned were those who were presently in violent opposition to the constitution, namely George Ross, the Vice-President, George Clymer, James Smith, the lawyer, and John Bayard.

Lawyer George Ross, formerly a supporter of the Quaker party, was a colonel in one of the Philadelphia battalions. A popular man with good humor and wit, Ross made an excellent presiding officer for the Convention. Chosen by the Convention to be one of Pennsylvania's delegates in Congress, he became a signer of the Declaration of Independence. After Ross became identified with the Anti-Constitutional-

---

[41] Graeff, 251.

ists, he was not returned to Congress. Two years later, at the age of forty-nine he died, just after having been named by Congress as a judge of the Admiralty Court.

George Clymer like Ross had vigorously supported independence, only to draw back when the Radicals refused to provide a government with a system of checks and balances. A shy, modest man of forty-four, Clymer was the scion of one of the first families of Philadelphia. Ever since the Stamp Act, he had been as forward as any man in the province in resisting the measures of the British. In 1773 he was chairman of the committee that sent the tea back to England, and in the turbulent years which immediately followed, he was constantly at the front of the revolutionary movement. As one of the new appointees to Congress, he signed the Declaration of Independence. Although no orator or flashy politician, he was much sought after for his sound advice and close reasoning.

Perhaps the equal in ability to either Ross or Clymer was Col. James Smith, a lawyer of York County. Smith had been educated by Rev. Francis Alison in his school at the New London Crossroads. He prac- ticed law for awhile in York, but, as the legal profession did not pay well on the frontier, he turned to surveying. Although a Scots Irish Presbyterian, he feared an unrestrained democracy. The Radicals, he thought, were making Pennsylvania the laughing stock of the world. The men who framed the constitution, he believed, were craving for popularity and for political power to attain which they had "embraced leveling principles" as the surest road to success. The end product of it all, he concluded, was a forcing upon Pennsylvania of a thorough- going democratic "Agrarian constitution."[42]

John Bayard was the son of the owner of Bohemia Manor in Mary- land, once the pride of Augustine Herman. Like the other three, Bayard had gone along with the Radicals until confronted with a democratic constitution.

Among the Radical leaders in the Convention were Frederick Kuhl, a director of the newly-organized American Manufacturing Company, William Van Horn, a Baptist minister with an M.A. from the College of Rhode Island, Col. John Bull, scion of a substantial Quaker family, John Hubley, a lawyer who had studied under Edward Shippen, Robert Loller, a classical scholar and teacher, Robert Whitehall, one of Alison's students at the College of Philadelphia, John Jacobs, a prominent citizen of Chester County, Owen Biddle, a scientist, merchant, and landholder, William Henry, an inventor, scientist, and gun manu- facturer, as well as such other prominent men as George Schlosser, Col.

---

[42] Harold D. Eberlein and Cortland Van Dyke Hubbard, *Diary of Independence Hall*, 189.

Jacob Stroud, Jonathan Hoge, and Thomas Porter. But the three principal leaders of the Radicals in the Convention were James Cannon, David Rittenhouse, and Timothy Matlack.

David Rittenhouse, a Presbyterian of German and Welsh extraction, was second only to Franklin in his scientific achievements. It was he, who in 1769, had made such accurate calculations on the transit of Venus as to acquire world-wide recognition. During the Revolution, among other things, he superintended the manufacture of gunpowder in Pennsylvania. Many years after the Revolution, when the constitution he had helped to make had been superseded by another, he was one of those who rallied to the support of Jefferson and carried the fight for democracy into the national arena.

Col. Timothy Matlack, whose Quaker upbringing had not at all cramped his fondness for horse racing, cock fighting, and conviviality once sold "the Best Bottled Beer at the old Brew House in Sixth Street." His extravagance had already cost him his membership in the Society of Friends, besides some time in the debtor's prison. This background was, however, in no wise a hindrance to success in revolutionary politics. As secretary for the Committee for the Officers of the Philadelphia battalions, he rose rapidly in political circles. In 1775 he was named assistant secretary of the Continental Congress. Shortly afterwards, Congress appointed him a storekeeper for military supplies. In 1776 after the adoption of the Pennsylvania constitution, he became secretary for the Council of Safety. Few men during the Revolution exercised more power in Pennsylvania than did Timothy Matlack.

Of interest is a letter from Timothy Matlack to James Pemberton in 1778 which throws light on his political philosophy. It reads: "I have ever considered personal liberty and safety as the first object of civil government, and the possession and security of property the next."[43] Putting property second to personal liberty places Matlack far in advance of the general thinking of the time on the theory and practice of government. Having men like him in the Convention inspired confidence among the American liberals. To the conservatives, on the other hand, it was frightening.

The chief architect of the Pennsylvania constitution, however, was James Cannon, an Episcopalian of Scottish birth and education, who taught mathematics at the College of Philadelphia. In the capacity of secretary for the Committee for Privates, Cannon exercised great power, and indeed, was one of those chiefly responsible for the constant radical pressure in Pennsylvania during the Revolution. A disciple of Turgot, Cannon had an abiding faith in the people and in the principles of democracy. Keenly aware of the conservative temper of the mer-

---

[43] Matlack to Pemberton, March 7, 1778, Quaker Material, Franklin Coll. Yale U.

chants and their allies, the lawyers, he advised the people not to choose persons from the old governing class to represent them in the Convention, but to elect men with "unsophisticated understanding" from among themselves. Cannon's answer to the charge that the Convention was packed with men who were strangers to higher education was to scoff at the pretensions of the intellectuals. "All learning," he told the people, is "an artifical restraint on human understanding." When George Clymer, Bayard or Ross cited Montesquieu in favor of a two-house legislature with checks and balances, Cannon answered that these were but shackles with which the élite fettered the will of the people. A man like Cannon, backed by like-minded men such as Rittenhouse, Paine, and Franklin, was capable of overturning the smug composure of Eighteenth Century society.

Although not a member of the Convention, George Bryan exercised great influence on the kind of constitution which was made. Above all, Bryan wanted to keep the unicameral legislature as the principal requirement for a popular government.

Born in Dublin in 1731, Bryan came to America at the age of twenty-one. He had not been in Pennsylvania long before he was recognized as one of the principal leaders on the Presbyterian wing of the Proprietary party, a fact which accounted for his appointment as judge in 1765. Not much is heard of Bryan after he attended the Stamp Act Congress in New York, except for occasional reports that his merchant business was failing. In 1772 the easy-going Bryan closed out his business before the sheriff did so for him. Probably nothing more would have been heard of George Bryan, had not the Revolution come along to thrust him right into the center of Pennsylvania politics.[44]

Perhaps no man in Pennsylvania had more influence upon the proceedings in the Convention than did Thomas Paine. Although it is well-known that his advice was sought after by Radicals everywhere in America, it is impossible to present any of the details of what went on between Paine and the members of the Convention. In any event Paine's popularity at this time was at its height, and he made no secret that his philosophy was that of a physiocratic agrarian who favored a thorough-going democratic form of government.

Many prominent Radicals like Bryan were not at the Convention. Preoccupation with military duties, committee work and other things accounted for the absence of many of them such as Thomas Wharton, Jr., Charles Willson Peale, William Bradford, William Shippen, Dr. James Young, Samuel J. Atlee, Christopher Marshall, Daniel Roberdeau, Joseph Reed, John Armstrong, and Jonathan B. Smith.

---

[44] Burton A. Konkle, *George Bryan and the Constitution of Pennsylvania, 1731-1791,* 121.

JOSEPH REED   GEORGE BRYAN
TIMOTHY MATLACK   DAVID RITTENHOUSE

THOMAS MIFFLIN   THOMAS McKEAN
CHARLES THOMSON   GEORGE CLYMER

Acting upon the advice of the Provincial Conference, the Convention proceeded to take over the governing of the State. It assumed the direction of military affairs, disarmed non-associators, and made laws for regulating currency and prices.[45] It reappointed Franklin, Wilson, Morton, and Morris to Congress and added Ross, Clymer, Smith, Rush and Taylor, all of whom signed the Declaration of Independence in August.

Much opposition was naturally encountered in executing the directives of the Convention. In September, when the old Assembly met for a few days to close its books before dissolving, it took a parting shot at the Radicals by resolving that the Convention had brazenly usurped authority and made dangerous attacks upon "the Liberties of the good people of Pennsylvania."[46]

When one considers the composition of the Constitutional Convention, it becomes apparent that almost any procedure adopted in choosing a drafting committee would have given it a radical majority. Those named for the Committee were Vice-President George Ross, Col. James Smith, Col. John Bull, Col. Jacob Stroud, the Rev. William Van Horn, John Jacobs, Owen Biddle, Jonathan Hoge, Robert Martin, and Col. Thomas Smith. Within a few days the radical representation was greatly strengthened by the addition of Cannon, Rittenhouse, Matlack, Thomas Porter, Col. Galbreath, and Robert Whitehill.[47]

The Convention sat from July 15 until September 28. Balked by the triumphant Radicals on every proposal to restrain the power to be vested in the Assembly, the opposition led by Ross and Clymer could do little more than register its protest. Upon the adoption of the final draft, Cannon, Rittenhouse, and Jacobs were chosen to write a preamble. When the constitution was ready for signing, twenty-three of the ninety-six members signified their dissatisfaction by refusing to affix their names to it.

In his book entitled *The Revolutionary Movement in Pennsylvania,* Charles Lincoln, like so many other writers before and after him, depreciated the fact that political power fell into the hands of the Radicals by the failure of so many of the Moderates to support independence. Their refusal, he said, "to accept the inevitable in 1776 assured the control of the State to the advocates of unrestricted democracy." But in his earlier chapters, he was at pains to applaud the growth of democracy and castigate what he called the Quaker oligarchy. Nevertheless, when the Revolution opened the door to democracy and held

[45] Lincoln, 274.
[46] *Votes,* VIII, 7586.
[47] Selsam, 159-168; Proceedings, 49.

the Conservatives in check, surprisingly enough, he thought it an unfortunate development.[48]

General elections under the new constitution were scheduled for November 5, after which date the new government was to take over. No provision was made for submitting the constitution to the people for ratification. With the war coming ominously closer to Pennsylvania and the Patriotic army in retreat before the victorious Howe, the Radicals could argue that there was not time for ratification.

The preamble of the constitution, penned by schoolmaster James Cannon, contained the familiar natural rights and social contract theories of the origin of government. The opening sentence reads:

> WHEREAS all Government ought to be Instituted and supported for the Security and Protection of the Community as such and to enable the Individuals who compose it to enjoy their Natural rights, and the other Blessings which the Author of Existence has bestowed upon Man; And whenever these great Ends of Government are not obtained, the people have a right by common Consent to change it, and take such Measures as to them may appear necessary to promote their Safety and happiness.[49]

In the Declaration of Rights which follows, the framers adhered closely to the Virginia Bill of Rights, written by George Mason. All power, declare both constitutions, is vested in, and consequently derived from the people. The fundamental rights of the people—freedom of religion, freedom of speech, freedom of the press, and the freedom of the people to assemble—were declared to be inviolable in the Pennsylvania constitution. Pacifists were not to be compelled to bear arms, but they were expected to pay a stipend for their exemption.

The most controversial feature of the new constitution was the retention of a unicameral legislature. Alexander Graydon declared that the constitution was "severely reprobated by those, who thought checks and balances necessary to a legitimate distribution of the powers of government."[50] The framers were familiar with Montesquieu's theory of checks and balances but, unlike the constitution makers in the other states, except in Georgia, they rejected it for the more democratic system which Pennsylvania had enjoyed since 1701. Little need was there for Cannon or Bryan to remind the people that, ever since the founding of the colony, Pennsylvania conservatives had sought for an upper house to act as a restraint upon popular government. When

---

[48] Lincoln, 277.
[49] Appendix II: Preamble.
[50] Alexander Graydon, *Memoirs of His Times*, 286.

called upon to voice his opinion, Franklin declared himself "to be clearly and fully in favor of a legislature to consist of a single branch, as being much the safest and best." A two-house system, he said, was like putting one horse in front of the cart and another behind it, each pulling in opposite directions.[51]

Having in mind the long conflict with the colonial governors, the framers proceeded to weaken the executive branch of the government by placing it in the hands of a Supreme Executive Council consisting of twelve members. Each of the eleven counties and the city of Philadelphia elected one councillor for a term of three years. Abuse of executive power was further guarded against by a system of rotation in office whereby one-third of the members were elected each year in a manner similar to that later adopted for the United States Senate. The constitution made clear the democratic objective of this procedure,

> By this mode of Election and Continual rotation more Men will be trained to public Business, there will in every subsequent year be found in the Council a Number of persons acquainted with the proceedings of the foregoing years, whereby the Business will be more consistantly Conducted and moreover the danger of Establishing an inconvenient Aristocracy will be effectually prevented.[52]

Remembering the vetoes of the Proprietary governors, the framers allowed the Council no power over the acts of the legislature. Its function was purely administrative. A president and vice-president of the Commonwealth were chosen by the Assembly and the Supreme Executive Council. These offices, however, were largely honorary, having little power other than what the incumbent might bestow by virtue of his qualifications for leadership.

In order to further safeguard the constitution against reactionary interests and to strengthen the hold of the Radicals upon the State, a Council of Censors was established. This body was to be composed of two members from each county and the city who were to meet once in every seven years.

> And whose duty it shall be to Enquire whether the Constitution has been preserved Inviolate in every part? and whether the Legislative and Executive Branches of Government have performed their duty as Guardians of the People or assumed to themselves, or exercised other or greater powers than they are Intitled to by the Constitution. They are also to enquire whether the public Taxes have been Justly laid and collected in all parts of this Common Wealth, in what Manner the

---

[51] Selsam, 185-186.

[52] Appendix II: *Constitution*, Sec. 19.

Public Monies have been disposed of, and whether the Laws
have been duly Executed.[53]

The Council of Censors was also empowered to call a convention
within two years after its sitting (1783) for the purpose of amending
the constitution. All changes proposed in the constitution were to be
"promulgated at least Six Months before the day appointed for the
Election of such Convention, for the previous Consideration of the
People, that they may have an Oppertunity of Instructing their
Delegates on the Subject."[54] The duties placed upon the Council of
Censors were a large order for any body of men and if an attempt had
been made to carry them out, much confusion might have resulted.
However, although the Council of Censors proved abortive in Penn-
sylvania, a similar system in Vermont and New York functioned with
considerable success.[55]

Perhaps the most democratic feature of the constitution was the
removal of most of the property qualifications for voting and for holding public office in the State. The constitution reads:

Every Freeman of the full age of Twenty one years, having
resided in this State for the Space of one whole year next
before the day of Election for Representatives, and paid public
Taxes during that time, shall enjoy the right of an Elector:
Provided always, That Sons of Freeholders of the Age of
Twenty one years, shall be Intitled to Vote, altho' they have
not paid Taxes.[56]

The principle contained in this provision was supported by a clause
in the Declaration of Rights which said that all men having sufficient
evidence of a permanent common interest with, and attachment to
the community, have a right of suffrage.

Instead of high property qualifications for holding office, a provision
found in so many of the state constitutions, Pennsylvania asked only
for men "noted for wisdom and virtue." That no persons, however,
would get a monopoly on office-holding, as had been the case during
the colonial period, it was provided that no one could serve in the
Assembly for more than four out of every seven years.[57]

To equalize the uneven distribution of representatives which had
existed for so long, it specifically provided that representation would

---

[53] *Ibid.*, Sec. 47.

[54] *Ibid.*

[55] Selsam, 200-201.

[56] Appendix II: *Constitution*, Sec. 6.

[57] *Ibid.*, Sec. 7-8. The Constitution abolished imprisonment for debts, an act which
gave Pennsylvania the distinction of being the first body politic in modern times
to do so. Not until well within the Nineteenth Century did the movement to
abolish imprisonment for debts become common in Europe and America.

be apportioned among the counties and cities on the basis of taxable inhabitants. For the first two years, however, after the constitution went into force, each county and the city of Philadelphia would have six representatives in the Assembly. In either case the Radicals were almost certain to control the government under the provisions of the constitution.

As the principal organ of the government the Assembly conferred upon itself all the powers of government, for the carrying out of which it was accountable only to the Council of Censors and to the people. The Constitution in this particular reads:

> THE GENERAL ASSEMBLY . . . shall have power to choose their Speaker; The Treasurer of the State and their other Officers; Sit on their own Adjournments; Prepare Bills and Enact them into Laws; Judge of the Elections and Qualifications of their own Members; . . . They may Administer Oaths or Affirmations on Examination of Witnesses: Redress Grievances . . . Impeach State Criminals, Grant Charters of Incorporation: Constitute Towns Burroughs, Cities, and Counties: And shall have all other Powers necessary for the Legislature of a Free State or Common Wealth; But they shall have no power to add to, Alter, Abolish or Infringe any part of this Constitution.[58]

These broad powers were condemned by the Anti-Constitutionalists, who cited Montesquieu to prove that the constitution was politically unsound. Nevertheless, nearly all of these powers were contained in William Penn's Frame of Government, or had been acquired or assumed by the Assembly during the long conflict with the Proprietors. In reality, therefore, they were not so concerned with the character of the constitution as they were with the fact that they no longer would be the ones exercising its powers and holding offices of state.

The whole democratic tone of the constitution made it in fact immensely popular among the common people throughout the State Thomas Paine once said that the constitution "was the political Bible of the State. Scarce a family was without it."[59]

Elections under the new constitution were set for November 5. By October, mass meetings were being held all over the State by both Radicals and Conservatives. The Anti-Constitutionalists hoped to elect enough members to have it in their power to prevent a quorum (two thirds of the members) in the Assembly. They would try to compel the Radicals to agree to the amendments they wanted in the constitution.

---

[58] *Ibid.*, Sec. 9.
[59] Selsam, 208.

They also would try to persuade the voters not to elect members of the Supreme Executive Council at this time, but to wait until they had secured the desired changes in the constitution.

Last-minute plans were made by the Anti-Constitutionalists at a meeting at Philosophical Hall a few days before the election. George Clymer, James Parker, Robert Morris, Michael Schubert, John Bayard, and Samuel Morris, the Anti-Constitution candidates for the Assembly, were named a committee to prepare amendments for the constitution in case their party was successful at the polls.[60]

Strangely enough, despite the lowering of the suffrage requirements, the Anti-Constitutionalists elected all of their candidates in the city and county of Philadelphia. This surprising turn of events may have been due to the fact that so many of the newly enfranchised were with the army in the field of battle endeavoring to stop the steady advance of the victorious enemy. However, there was a widespread dislike of the test oath requiring all voters to support the constitution. If friends of the constitution stayed away from the polls, so likewise did many of its enemies, notwithstanding the fact that the oath was not administered in Philadelphia. Among the latter, the Quakers in particular were absent from the polls, having since independence renounced all participation in politics. The voting, therefore, in spite of the bitterness evident on all sides, was very light.[61]

Outside of the Philadelphia area, except for Bedford County, the Radicals were triumphant. It is a blot upon their record, however, that they did not offer their opponents a fair or free election in the districts they controlled. It was a "khaki" election with the associators patrolling the towns with fife and drum. Hundreds of Anti-Constitutionalists were intimidated—others were barred from voting by their refusal to take the oath supporting the new order.

Since the Conservatives had won enough seats in the Assembly to prevent a quorum, they proceeded to bargain with the Radicals in favor of a convention to revise the constitution, in return for which they would agree to the necessary moves in organizing the House and passing urgent legislation. So critical was the military plight of America, however, that the agreement, although made, was ignored by the Radicals.[62] The constitution of 1776 stood until 1790, when its enemies at last succeeded in gaining control of the State and in framing a constitution more in accord with the political theory of that age.

---

[60] Instructions to the Philadelphia Representatives to the Assembly, Nov. 8, 1776, Hazard Family Papers. HSP.

[61] Selsam, 228-229.

[62] Robert L. Brunhouse, *The Counter-Revolution in Pennsylvania, 1776-1790*, 12-22.

The Pennsylvania constitution of 1776, the most liberal constitution adopted during the Revolutionary period, was the culmination of the growth of democratic thought in Pennsylvania during the Eighteenth Century. The upheavals attending the Revolution provided an opportunity for the spread of leveling principles and the establishment of popular government. Parallel developments were to be found in other states, but in Pennsylvania alone did the democratic forces become dominant.

It is no doubt true that a less radical constitution would have saved Pennsylvania from a prolonged and bitter political struggle and afforded the state greater unity during the war with England. It seems unfortunate that the prosecution of the war had to suffer from internecine conflict, but it would have been a far greater misfortune if the democratic revolution had failed in Pennsylvania. A counter-revolution was sure to roll back some of the gains made during the war, but the triumph of the Radicals during the Revolution prepared the way for the victories of Jeffersonian democracy at a later date.

The Pennsylvania Radicals brought forth and put into operation a constitution dedicated to the principles that all men are free and equal; that public officers are the servants of the people. Although this constitution was soon replaced by another, the essential principles of the original Declaration of Rights have remained a part of the Pennsylvania constitution to this day. The authors of the constitution— James Cannon, George Bryan, David Rittenhouse, Timothy Matlack, John Jacobs, and their mentor, Thomas Paine—had a vision of the world of their tomorrow. Certainly the authors deserve much praise for defying the traditional theories of government and for framing a constitution which breathed the spirit of Eighteenth Century Enlightenment and of the principles of the Declaration of Independence.

BIBLIOGRAPHY

MANUSCRIPTS

I. Historical Society of Pennsylvania: Etting Collections; Norris Papers and Letter Books; Pemberton Papers; Pemberton Papers, Clifford Correspondence; Penn Manuscripts (Official Correspondence, Indian Affairs, Additional Miscellaneous Letters, Penn-Hamilton Correspondence, Correspondence of Thomas Penn, Richard Penn and James Hamilton); Peters Manuscripts and Letter Books; Shippen Papers; Weiser Manuscripts.

II. Other manuscripts used at the Historical Society of Pennsylvania: James Allen's Diary, 1777; Autograph Collection (Selected Manuscripts); Balch Papers (Shippen and Swift); Balch Papers (Shippen); Berks and Montgomery counties, Miscellaneous Manuscripts; Board of Trade Transcripts: Papers and Journals of the Board of Trade and Plantations; Bradford's Register, 1776; Chester County, Miscellaneous Papers; Samuel Coates Letter Book; Franklin Papers, Hazard Family Papers; Hughes Manuscripts (Miscellaneous Papers); Lamberton Scotch Irish Collection; Thomas Lawrence Letter Book; Logan Papers; McKean Papers; Christopher Marshall's Letter Book and Diaries; Daniel Roberdeau's Letter Book; John Smith Correspondence; Wayne Manuscripts; Thomas Wharton's Letter Book.

III. Library of Congress: Franklin Papers; Minutes of the Committee of Safety, Lancaster County; Pennsylvania Miscellany; Charles Thomson Papers; Letters of Thomas and Richard Penn; Photostats of Franklin Papers in J. P. Morgan Library; George Bryan, Memoranda of Events, 1764.

IV. Collections in other libraries: American Philosophical Society: Bache Collection (Franklin Papers); Franklin Papers; Horsefield Papers.
Friends Book Store, Phila.: Minutes of the Meeting for Sufferings, 1763-1775.
New York Historical Society: Charles Thomson Papers.
New York Public Library: Chalmers Collection (Pennsylvania and Philadelphia).
Public Records Division, Pennsylvania Historical and Museum Commission, Harrisburg: Provincial Papers; Revolutionary Papers; Baynton, Wharton, and Morgan Letter Book, 1763-1775.
Ridgway Library: Smith Manuscripts.
University of Pennsylvania: Early American Manuscripts; Franklin Papers; University Manuscripts.
Yale University: Franklin Collection: Photostats of Franklin Papers in the William L. Clements Library.

NEWSPAPERS

The Pennsylvania Gazette, Franklin, Hall, Sellers, editors.
The Pennsylvania Chronicle, William Goddard, editor.
The Pennsylvania Packet, John Dunlap, editor.
The Pennsylvania Evening Post, Benjamin Towne, editor.
The Pennsylvania Journal, William and Thomas Bradford, editors.
The New York Gazetteer, James Rivington, editor.
The New York Gazette and the Weekly Mercury, Hugh Gaine, editor.

PRINTED SOURCES

Acts of the Privy Council (Colonial). 6 vols. London, 1908-1911.

Adams, Charles F., ed. *John Adams: Letters Addressed to His Wife*. 2 vols. Boston, 1841.

Adams, Charles F., ed. *The Works of John Adams with a Life of the Author. Notes and Illustrations*. 10 vols. Boston, 1850-1856.

Balch, Thomas W., ed. *Letters and Papers Relating Chiefly to the Provincial History of Pennsylvania (Shippen Family)*. Philadelphia, 1855.

Bigelow, John, ed. *The Complete Works of Benjamin Franklin*. 10 vols. New York, 1887-1888.

Boyd, Julian P., ed. *Indian Treaties, Printed by Benjamin Franklin, 1736-1762*. Philadelphia, 1938.

Brock, Robert A., ed., *The Official Records of Robert Dinwiddie*. Virginia Historical Society Collections. 2 vols. Richmond, 1883-84.

Burnett, Edmund C., ed., *Letters of the Members of the Continental Congress*. Washington, 1921-1936.

Butterfield, L. H., ed. *Letters of Benjamin Rush*. 2 vols. Princeton, 1951.

Conway, Moncure D., ed. *The Writings of Thomas Paine*. 4 vols. New York, 1894-1896.

Corner, George W., ed. *The Autobiography of Benjamin Rush*. Princeton, 1948.

Crane, Verner W., ed. *Benjamin Franklin's Letters to the Press, 1758-1775*. Chapel Hill, 1950.

Graydon, Alexander, *Memoirs of His Times with Reminiscences of the Men and Events of the Revolution*. J. S. Littell, ed. Philadelphia, 1846.

Hazard, Samuel. *Register of Pennsylvania: Devoted to the Preservation of Information Respecting Pennsylvania*. 16 vols. Philadelphia, 1828-1836.

Labaree, Leonard W., ed., *Royal Instructions to British Colonial Governors, 1670-1776*. 2 vols. New York, 1935.

MacDonald, William, ed. *Select Charters and other Documents Illustrative of American History, 1606-1775*. New York, 1904.

Morison, Samuel E., ed. *Sources and Documents Illustrating the American Revolution, 1764-1788*. London, 1929.

New York Historical Society Collections. 75 vols. New York, 1868-1843.

O'Callaghan, E. B., ed. *Documents Relative to the Colonial History of the State of New York*. 15 vols. Albany, 1856-1887.

Pargellis, Stanley M., ed. *Military Affairs in North America, 1748-1765*. New York, 1936.

Pennsylvania Archives, First Series, 1664-1790. 12 vols. Samuel Hazard, ed. Philadelphia, 1852-1856.

Pennsylvania Archives, Third Series, 1682-1801. 30 vols. W. H. Egle and G. E. Reed, editors. Harrisburg, 1894-1899.

Pennsylvania Archives, Eighth Series. 8 vols. Gertrude MacKinney, ed. Harrisburg, 1931-1935.

Pennsylvania Colonial Records: Minutes of the Provincial Council, 1683-1776, vols. I-X; Minutes of the Supreme Executive Council, 1776-1790, vols. XI-XVI. Samuel Hazard, ed. Philadelphia, 1852-1853.

Pennsylvania Historical Commission, *The Papers of Colonel Henry Bouquet*. Harrisburg, 1940-1943.

(Pennsylvania) *Journals of the House of Representatives of the Commonwealth of Pennsylvania, 1776-1781, with the Proceedings of the several Committees & Conventions before & at the Commencement of the American Revolution*. Michael Hillegas, ed. Philadelphia, 1782.

(Pennsylvania) *Proceedings Relative to Calling the Conventions of 1776 and 1790.* Harrisburg, 1825.

(Pennsylvania) *Statutes at Large, 1682-1801.* Compiled by James T. Mitchell and Henry Flanders. Harrisburg, 1897.

Smith, William. *Brief State of the Province of Pennsylvania.* London, 1755.

Smyth, Albert H., ed. *The Writings of Benjamin Franklin.* 10 vols. New York, 1905-1907.

Sparks, Jared, ed. *The Works of Benjamin Franklin.* 10 vols. Boston, 1836-1840.

Statutes at Large of Great Britain, 4-7, George III. Cambridge, 1762-1807.

Sullivan, James et al., editors. *The Papers of Sir William Johnson.* 9 vols. Albany, 1921-1939.

Tappert, Theodore and Doberstein, John W., editors. *The Journals of Henry Melchoir Muhlenberg.* 2 vols. Philadelphia, 1942-1945.

Thorpe, F. N., ed. *Federal and State Constitutions, Colonial Charters, and other Organic Laws.* 7 vols. Washington, 1909.

Van Dorne, Carl, ed. *Letters and Papers of Benjamin Franklin and Richard Jackson, 1753-1785.* Philadelphia, 1947.

Walker, Lewis B., ed. *The Burd Papers: Extracts from Chief Justice Allen's Letter Book.* Pottsville, Pa., 1897.

SECONDARY WORKS

Abernethy, Thomas P. *Western Lands and the American Revolution.* New York, 1937.

Andrews, Charles M. *The Colonial Period of American History.* 4 vols. London, 1934-1938.

Bailey, Kenneth P. *The Ohio Company of Virginia and the Westward Movement of 1748-1792.* Glendale, Calif., 1939.

Barton, William. *Memoirs of the Life of David Rittenhouse.* Philadelphia, 1813.

Beer, George L. *British Colonial Policy, 1754-1765.* New York, 1907.

Beer, George L. *The Old Colonial System, 1660-1754.* New York, 1912.

Bond, Beverly W. *The Quitrent System in the American Colonies.* New Haven, 1919.

Boyd, Julian P. *Anglo-American Union: J. Galloway's Plans to Preserve the British Empire, 1774-1788.* Philadelphia, 1941.

Brunhouse, Robert L. *The Counter-Revolution in Pennsylvania, 1776-1790.* Harrisburg, 1942.

Burnett, Edmond C. *The Continental Congress.* New York, 1941.

Burt, Struthers. *Philadelphia, Holy Experiment.* New York, 1945.

Crane, Verner W. "Benjamin Franklin and the Stamp Act." *Col. Soc. of Mass.,* XXXII (1937), 56-77.

Cribbs, George A. *The Frontier Policy of Pennsylvania.* Pittsburgh, 1919.

Cummings, Hubertis M. *Richard Peters: Provincial Secretary and Cleric.* Philadelphia, 1944.

Davidson, Philip. *Propaganda and the American Revolution, 1763-1783.* Chapel Hill, 1941.

Dickerson, Oliver M. *American Colonial Government.* Cleveland, 1912.

Dunaway, Wayland F. *The Scotch Irish in Colonial Pennsylvania.* Chapel Hill, 1944.

Eberlein, Harold D. and Hubbard, Cortlandt Van Dyke. *Diary of Independence Hall.* Philadelphia, 1948.

Faust, Albert B. *The German Element in the United States.* 2 vols. Boston, 1909.

Fay, Bernard. *Franklin, the Apostle of Modern Times.* Boston, 1929.

Fisher, Sydney G. *The Making of Pennsylvania.* Philadelphia, 1932.

Ford, H. J. *The Scotch-Irish in America.* Princeton, 1915.

Gegenheimer, Albert F. *William Smith: Educator and Churchman.* Philadelphia, 1943.

Geiser, Karl F. *Redemptioners and Indentured Servants in the Colony and Commonwealth of Pennsylvania.* New Haven, 1901.

Gipson, Lawrence. *The British Empire Before the American Revolution.* Vols. 4-7. New York, 1939-1949.

Gordon, Thomas F. *A History of Pennsylvania from its Discovery by Europeans to the Declaration of Independence in 1776.* Philadelphia, 1829.

Graeff, Arthur D. *The Relations Between the Pennsylvania Germans and the British Authorities (1750-1776).* Norristown, Pa., 1939.

Greene, Evarts B. and Harrington, Virginia D. *American Population before the Federal Census of 1790.* New York, 1932.

Harding, Samuel B. "Party Struggles over the First Pennsylvania Constitution," *Annual Report of the American Historical Association for 1894.* Washington, 1895.

Harley, L. R. *Life of Charles Thomson.* Philadelphia, 1900.

Jackson, Joseph, *Encyclopedia of Philadelphia.* 4 vols. Harrisburg, 1931-1933.

Kistler, Ruth M. "William Allen, Provincial Man of Affairs," *Pennsylvania History,* I, No. 3 (July, 1934).

Klett, Guy S. *Presbyterians in Colonial Pennsylvania.* Pennsylvania, 1937.

Konkle, Burton A. *George Bryan and the Constitution of Pennsylvania, 1731-1791.* Philadelphia, 1922.

Kuhns, Oscar. *The German and Swiss Settlements of Colonial Pennsylvania: A Study of the So-Called Pennsylvania Dutch.* New York, 1901.

Kuntzelman, Oliver C. *Joseph Galloway, Loyalist.* Philadelphia, 1941.

Lincoln, Charles H. *The Revolutionary Movement in Pennsylvania, 1760-1776.* Philadelphia, 1901.

McKinley, Albert E. *The Suffrage Franchise in the Thirteen English Colonies in America.* Boston, 1905.

Mereness, Newton D. *Maryland as a Proprietary Province.* New York, 1901.

Nevins, Allen. *The American States During and After the Revolution.* New York, 1927.

Nixon, Lily L. *James Burd: Frontier Defender, 1726-1793.* Philadelphia, 1941.

Nolan, J. Bennett. *Early Narratives of Berks County.* Reading, Pa., 1927.

Nolan, J. Bennett. *The Foundation of the Town of Reading in Pennsylvania.* Reading, Pa., 1929.

Osgood, Herbert L. *The American Colonies in the Eighteenth Century.* 4 vols. New York, 1924.

Pargellis, Stanley M. *Lord Loudoun in North America.* New Haven, 1933.

Parrington, Vernon L. *The Colonial Mind.* New York, 1927.

Pennsylvania Magazine of History and Biography. Vols. 1-71. Philadelphia, 1877-1947.

Pound, Arthur. *The Penns of Pennsylvania and England.* New York, 1932.

Reed, William B. *Life and Correspondence of Joseph Reed.* 2 vols. Philadelphia, 1847.

Root, Winfred T. *The Relations of Pennsylvania with the British Government, 1696-1765.* Philadelphia, 1912.

Savelle, Max. *George Morgan, Colony Builder.* New York, 1932.

Scharf, J. T. and Wescott, T. *A History of Pennsylvania.* 3 vols. Philadelphia, 1884.

Schlesinger, Arthur M. *The Colonial Merchants and the American Revolution, 1763-1776.* New York, 1918.

Schutz, John A. *Thomas Pownall, the British Defender of American Liberty: A Study of Anglo-American Relations in the Eighteenth Century.* Glendale, Calif., 1951.

Selsam, Paul P. *The Pennsylvania Constitution of 1776; A Study in Revolutionary Democracy.* Philadelphia, 1936.

Sharpless, Isaac. *A Quaker Experiment in Government.* Philadelphia, 1898.

Sharpless, Isaac. *Political Leaders of Provincial Pennsylvania.* New York, 1919.

Shepherd, William R. *History of Proprietary Government in Pennsylvania.* New York, 1896.

Siebert, Wilbur H. *The Loyalists of Pennsylvania.* Columbus, O., 1920.

Stackhouse, A. M. *Colonel Timothy Matlack—Patriot and Soldier.* Privately printed, 1910.

Stillé, Charles J. *The Life and Times of John Dickinson.* Philadelphia, 1891.

Van Doren, Carl. *Benjamin Franklin.* New York, 1938.

Volwiler, Albert T. *George Croghan and the Westward Movement, 1741-1782.* Cleveland, 1926.

Thayer, Theodore. *Israel Pemberton: King of the Quakers.* Philadelphia, 1943.

Tolles, Frederick. *Meeting House and Counting House: The Quaker Merchants of Colonial Philadelphia, 1682-1763.* Chapel Hill, 1948.

Wallace, Anthony F. C. *King of the Delawares: Teedyuscung, 1700-1763.* Philadelphia, 1949.

Wallace, Paul A. W. *Conrad Weiser, 1696-1760: Friend of Colonist and Mohawk.* Philadelphia, 1945.

Watson, John T. *Annals of Philadelphia and Pennsylvania in the Olden Times.* Philadelphia, 1857.

Wells, William V. *The Life and Public Services of Samuel Adams.* 3 vols. Boston, 1865.

Werner, Raymond C. "Joseph Galloway (1731-1803), Politician and Statesman," *University of Iowa Studies in the Social Sciences,* X, no. 3 (1934).

Wolff, Mabel P. *The Colonial Agency of Pennsylvania, 1712-1757.* Philadelphia, 1933.

APPENDIX I

THE CHARTER OF PRIVILEGES.* 1701

The CHARTER of PRIVILEGES *granted by* WILLIAM PENN, *Esq.;*
to the Inhabitants of Pennsylvania *and Territories.*

WILLIAM PENN Proprietary and Governour [sic] of the Province
of Pennsilvania [sic] and Territories thereunto belonging To all to
whom these presents shall come Sendeth Greeting WHEREAS King
Charles the Second by his Letters Patents under the Great Seale [sic]
of England bearring [sic] Date the fourth day of March in the yeare
[sic] one thousand Six hundred and Eighty was Graciously pleased
to Give and Grant unto me my heires [sic] and Assignes for ever this
Province of Pennsilvania, with divers great powers and Jurisdictions
for the well Governement [sic] thereof AND WHEREAS the King's
dearest Brother James Duke of York and Albany &c: by his Deeds
of ffeofment [sic] under his hand and Seale duely perfected bearring
date the twenty fourth day of August one thousand Six hundred
Eighty and two Did Grant unto me my heires and Assignes All that
Tract of Land now called the Territories of Pensilvania [sic] togather
[sic] with powers and Jurisdictions for the good Governement thereof
AND WHEREAS for the Encouragement of all the ffreemen and
Planters that might be concerned in the said Province and Territories
and for the good Governement thereof, I the said William Penn in the
yeare one thousand Six hundred Eighty and three for me my heires
and Assignes Did Grant and Confirme [sic] unto all the ffreemen
Planters and Adventurers therein Divers Liberties ffranchises and
properties as by the said Grant Entituled[sic] the FFRAME OF THE
GOVERNMENT OF THE PROVINCE OF PENSILVANIA AND
TERRITORIES THEREUNTO BELONGING IN AMERICA may
Appeare [sic] which Charter or frame being found in Some parts of
it not soe [sic] Suitable to the present Circumstances of the Inhabitants,
was in the third Month in the yeare One thousand Seven hundred
Delivered up to me by Six parts of Seaven [sic] of the ffreemen of
this Province and Territories in Generall [sic] Assembly mett [sic],
provision being made in the said Charter for that End and purpose
AND WHEREAS I was then pleased to promise that I would restore
the said Charter to them again, with necessary Alterations or in lieu

205

[sic] thereof Give them another better Adapted to Answer the present
Circumstances and Conditions of the said Inhabitants which they have
now by theire [sic] Representatives in a Generall Assembly mett at
Philadelphia requested me to Grant KNOW YE therefore that for the
the [sic] further well being and good Governement of the said Province
and Territories and in pursuance of the Rights and Powers before
mentioned [sic] I the said WILLIAM PENN doe [sic] Declare Grant
and Confirme unto all the ffreemen Planters and Adventurers and other
Inhabitants in this Province and Territories these following Liberties
ffranchises and Priviledges [sic] soe far as in me lyeth [sic] to be
held Enjoyed and kept by the ffreemen Planters and Adventurers and
other Inhabitants of and in the said Province and Territories thereunto
Annexed for ever . . . FIRST . . . Because noe [sic] people can be
truly happy though under the Greatest Enjoyments of Civill [sic]
Liberties if Abridged of the ffreedom of theire Consciences as to theire
Religious Profession and Worship. And Almighty God being the only
Lord of Conscience ffather of Lights and Spirits and the Author as
well as Object of all divine knowledge ffaith and Worship who only
Enlighten the mind and perswade [sic] and Convince the under-
standings of people I DOE HEREBY Grant and Declare that noe
person or persons Inhabiting in this Province or Territories who shall
Confesse [sic] and Acknowledge one Almighty God the Creator up-
holder and Ruler of the world and professe [sic] him or themselves
Obliged to live quietly under the Civill Governement shall be in any
case molested or prejudiced in his or theire person or Estate because
of his or theire Consciencious perswasion [sic] or practice nor be
compelled to frequent or mentaine [sic] any Religious Worship place
or Ministry contrary to his or theire mind or to doe or Suffer any other
Act or thing contrary to theire Religious perswasion AND that all
persons who alsoe professe to beleive [sic] in JESUS CHRIST the
SAVIOUR of the world, shall be capable (nothwithstanding theire
other perswasions and practices in point of Conscience and Religion)
to Serve this Governement in any capacity both Legislatively and
Executively he or they Solemnly promiseing [sic] when lawfully re-
quired Allegiance to the King as Soveraigne [sic] and fidelity to the
Proprietary and Governour And takeing the Attests as now Establisht
[sic] by the law made at Newcastle in the yeare One thousand and
Seven hundred Intituled an Act directing the Attests of Severall [sic]
Officers and Ministers as now amended and Confirmed this present
Assembly . . . SECONDLY . . . ffor the well Governeing of this
Province and Territories there shall be an Assembly yearly [sic]
Chosen by the ffreemen thereof to Consist of foure persons out of each
County, of most note for Virtue wisdome and Ability (Or of a greater

number at any time as the Governour and Assembly shall Agree) upon the first day of October for ever And shall Sitt [sic] on the ffourteenth day of the said Month in Philadelphia unless the Governour and Councell [sic] for the time being shall See cause to appoint another place within the said Province or Territories Which Assembly shall have power to choose a Speaker and other theire [sic] Officers and shall be Judges of the Qualifications and Elections of theire owne Members Sitt upon theire owne Adjournments, Appoint Committees prepare Bills in or[der] to pass into Laws Impeach Crimnnalls [sic] and Redress Greivances [sic] and shall have all other Powers and Priviledges of an Assembly according to the Rights of the ffreeborne Subjects of England and as is usuall [sic] in any of the Kings Plantations in America AND if any County or Counties shall refuse or neglect to choose theire respective Representatives as aforesaid or if chosen doe not meet to Serve in Assembly those who are soe chosen and mett shall have the full power of an Assembly in as ample manner as if all the representatives had beene [sic] chosen and mett Provided they are not less then [sic] two thirds of the whole number that ought to meet AND that the Qualifications of Electors and Elected and all other matters and things Relateing [sic] to Elections of Representatives to Serve in Assemblies though not herein perticulerly [sic] Exprest shall be and remains as by a Law of this Government made at New-castle in the yeare One thousand [Seven] hundred Intituled AN ACT TO ASCERTAINE THE NUMBER OF MEMBERS OF ASSEMBLY AND TO REGULATE THE ELECTIONS . . . THIRDLY . . . That the ffreemen [in each] respective County at the time and place of meeting for Electing theire Representatives to serve in Assembly may as often as there shall be Occasion choose a Double number of persons to present to the Governour for Sheriffes [sic] and Coroners to Serve for three yeares if they Soe long behave themselves well out of which respective Elections and Presentments the Governour shall nominate and Comissionate one for each of the said Officers the third day after Such Presentment or else the first named in Such Presentment for each Office as aforesaid shall Stand and Serve in that Office for the time before respectively Limitted And in case of Death and Default Such Vacancies shall be Supplyed [sic] by the Governour to serve to the End of the said Terme PROVIDED allways [sic] that if the said ffreemen shall at any time neglect or decline to choose A person or persons for either or both the aforesaid Offices then and in Such case the persons that are or shall be in the respective Offices of Sheriffes or Coroner at the time of Election shall remaine therein untill they shall be removed by another Election as aforesaid AND that the Justices of the respective Counties shall or may nominate and present to the

Governour three persons to Serve for Clerke of the Peace for the said
County when there is a vacancy, one of which the Governour shall
Commissionate within Tenn [sic] dayes [sic] after Such Presentment
or else the first Nominated shall Serve in the said Office during good
behaviour . . . FOURTHLY . . . That the Laws of this Government
shall be in this Stile [sic] Viz^t [By the Governour with the Consent
and Approbation of the ffreemen in Generall Assembly mett] And shall
be after Confirmation by the Governour forthwith Recorded in the
Rolls Office and kept at Philadelphia unless the Governour and Assembly shall Agree to appoint another place . . . FIFTHLY . . . that
all Criminalls shall have the same Priviledges of Wittnesses [sic]
and Councill [sic] as theire Prosecutors . . . SIXTHLY . . . That
noe person or persons shall or may at any time hereafter be obliged
to answer any Complaint matter or thing whatsoever relateing to
Property before the Governour and Councill or in any other place
but in the Ordinary courts of Justice unless appeales [sic] thereunto
shall be hereafter by law appointed . . . SEVENTHLY . . . That noe
person within this Governement shall be Licensed by the Governour
to keep Ordinary Taverne [sic] or house of publick entertainment but
Such who are first recommended to him under the hands of the Justices
of the respective Counties Signed in open Court which Justices are
and shall be hereby Impowred [sic] to Suppress and forbid any
person keeping Such publick house as aforesaid upon theire Mis-
behaviour on Such penalties as the law doth or shall Direct and to
recommend others from time to time as they shall see occasion . . .
EIGHTHLY . . . If any person through Temptation or Melancholly
[sic] shall Destroy himselfe [sic] his Estate Reall [sic] and personall
shall notwithstanding Descend to his wife and Children, or Relations
as if he had dyed [sic] a Naturall Death And if any person shall be
Destroyed or kill'd by casualty or Accident there shall be noe forfeiture
to the Governour by reason thereof AND noe Act Law or Ordinance
whatsoever shall at any time hereafter be made or done to Alter
Change or Diminish the forme or Effect of this Charter or of any part
or Clause therein Contrary to the True intent and meaning thereof
without the Consent of the Governour for the [Time being and Six
parts] of Seven of the Assembly [mett]. BUT because the happiness
of Mankind depends So [sic] much upon the Enjoying of Libertie
[sic] of theire Consciences as aforesaid I Doe hereby Solemnly Declare
Promise and Grant for me my heires and Assignes that the first
Article of this Charter Relating to Liberty of Conscience and every
part and Clause therein according to the True Intent and meaning
thereof shall be kept and remaine without any Alteration Inviolably
for ever AND LASTLY I the said William Penn Proprietary and

Governour of the Province of Pensilvania and Territories thereunto belonging for my Selfe my heires and Assignes Have Solemnly Declared Granted and Confirmed And doe hereby Solemnly Declare Grant and Confirme that neither I my heires or Assignes shall procure or doe any thing or things whereby the Liberties in this Charter contained and expressed nor any part thereof shall be Infringed or broken And if any thing shall be procured or done by any person or persons contrary to these presents it shall be held of noe force or Effect IN WITTNES [sic] whereof I the said WILLIAM PENN at PHILADELPHIA in PENSILVANIA have unto this present Charter of Liberties Sett my hand and Broad Seale this twenty Eighth day of October in the yeare of our Lord one thousand Seven hundred and one being the thirteenth yeare of the Reigne of KING WILLIAM the Third over England Holland ffrance and Ireland &c And in the Twenty first yeare of my Government. AND notwithstanding the closure and Test of this present Charter as aforesaid I think fitt [sic] to add this following Provisoe thereunto as part of the same That is to say that notwithstanding any Clause or Clauses in the above mentioned [sic] Charter obligeing the Province and Territories to Joyne [sic] Togather in Legislation I am Content and doe hereby Declare That if the representatives of the Province and Territories shall not hereafter Agree to Joyne togather in Legislation and that the same shall be Signifyed [sic] to me or my Deputy In open assembly or otherwise from under the hands and Seales of the Representatives (for the time being) of the Province or Territories or the Major part of either of them any time within three yeares from the Date hereof That in Such case the Inhabitants of each of the three Counties of this Province shall not have less than [sic] Eight persons to represent them in Assembly for the Province and the Inhabitants of the Towne [sic] of Philadelphia (when the said Towne is Incorporated) Two persons to represent them in Assembly and the Inhabitants of each County in the Territories shall have as many persons to represent them in a Distinct Assembly for the Territories as shall be requested by them as aforesaid Notwithstanding which Seperation [sic] of of [sic] the Province and Territories in Respect of Legislation I doe hereby promise Grant and Declare that the Inhabitants of both Province and Territories shall Seperately Injoy [sic] all other Liberties Priviledges and Benefitts [sic] granted Joyntly to them in this Charter Any law usage or Custome of this Governement heretofore made and Practised or any law made and Passed by this Generall Assembly to the contrary hereof Notwithstanding.

                                                      WM PENN

This Charter of priviledges being Distinctly
read in Assembly & the whole & Every part
thereof being Approved of and Agreed to
by us, Wee [sic] do Thankfully receive the
Same from our Proprietary & Governour at
Philadelphia this Twenty Eighth day of
October 1701.

Signed on behalf and by order of the
Assembly

p JOS: GROWDON *Speaker:*

EDWD: SHIPPEN ....⎫
PHINEAS PEMBERTON .⎪
SAM: CARPENTER .....⎬ Prop^ty and Govern^g Councill
GRIFFITH OWEN ....⎪
CALEB PUSEY ....⎪
THO: STORY ....⎭

RECORDED in the Rolls Office at Philadelphia
in Patent Book A. vol. 2. page 125 to 129
the 31st 8mo 1701.
By me THO: STORY Mr Ibim

---

* From Original Document in American Philosophical Society, Philadelphia.

APPENDIX II
THE CONSTITUTION OF PENNSYLVANIA.* 1776

WHEREAS all Government ought to be Instituted and supported
for the Security and Protection of the Community as such and to
enable the Individuals who compose it to enjoy their Natural rights,
and the other Blessings which the Author of Existence has bestowed
upon Man; And whenever these great Ends of Government are not
obtained, the people have a right by common Consent to change it,
and take such Measures as to them may appear necessary to promote
their Safety and happiness, AND WHEREAS, The Inhabitants of this
Common Wealth have in Consideration of Protection only heretofore
acknowledged Allegiance to the King of Great Britain, and the said
King has not only withdrawn that protection but commenced and still
Continues to carry on with unabated Vengeance a most cruel and
Unjust War against them, employing therein not only the Troops of
Great Britain, but foreign Mercenaries, Savages and Slaves for the
avowed purpose of reducing them to a Total and abject Submission
to the despotic Domination of the British Parliament (with many
other Acts of Tyranny more fully set forth in the Declaration of
Congress) whereby all Allegiance and Fealty to the said King and his
successors are dissolved and at an End, and all power and Authority
derived from him ceased in these Colonies, and Whereas it is absolutely necessary for the welfare and Safety of the Inhabitants of
said Colonies that they be henceforth Free and Independant [sic]
States and that Just permanent and proper forms of Government
[exist in every part of] them, derived from, and founded on the Authority of the people only, agreeable to the Directions of the Honourable
American Congress.

WE THE REPRESENTATIVES of the FREEMEN of PENN-
SYLVANIA in GENERAL CONVENTION MET for the Express
purpose of framing such a Government, confessing the goodness of the
great Governor of the Universe (who alone knows to what degree of
Earthly happiness mankind may attain by perfecting the Arts of Government) in permitting the People of this State by common Consent,
and without Voilence [sic] deliberately to form for themselves such Just
rules as they shall think best for Governing their future Society and
being fully Convinced that it is our Indispensable duty to establish
such Original Principles of Government as will best promote the
General Happiness of the People of this State and their posterity, and
provide for future improvements without partiallity [sic] for or
prejudice against any particular class, sect or denomination of Men

whatever. DO by Virtue of the Authority vested in us by our Constituents ORDAIN, DECLARE and ESTABLISH the following Declaration of Rights, and frame of Government to be the Constitution of this Common Wealth, and to remain in force therein forever, Unaltered, except in such Articles as shall hereafter on Experience be found to require Improvement, and which shall by the same Authority of the People fairly delegated as this frame of Government directs be amended or improved for the more Effectual obtaining and Securing the Great End and Design of all Government herein before Mentioned.

A DECLARATION of the Rights of the Inhabitants of the Common Wealth or State of PENNSYLVANIA.

First.

That all Men are born equally free and Independant [sic], and have Certain Natural inherent and unalienable rights, among which are the enjoying and defending Life and Liberty, Acquiring, Possessing and Protecting Property and pursuing and obtaining happiness and Safety.

Second.

That all Men have a Natural and unalienable right to Worship Almighty God according to the dictates of their own Consciences and Understanding. And that no Man ought or of right can be compelled to attend any Religious Worship or Erect or support any place of Worship, or Maintain any Ministry, contrary to, or against his own free Will and Consent Nor can any Man who acknowledges the being of a God be justly deprived or abridged of any Civil right as a Citizen, on Account of his Religious Sentiments, or peculiar Mode of Religious Worship. And that no Authority can or ought to be vested in, or assumed by any power whatever that shall in any Case interfere with or in any Manner Controul [sic] the right of Conscience in the free Exercise of Religious Worship.

Third.

That the People of this State have the sole exclusive and Inherent right of Governing and regulating the Internal Police [sic] of the same.

Fourth.

That all power being originally Inherent in and consequently derived from the People: therefore all Officers or Government whether Legislative or Executive are their Trustees and Servants, and at all times accountable to them.

Fifth.

That Government is or ought to be Instituted for the Common Benefit Protection and Security of the People, Nation or Community, and not for the particular Emolument or advantage of any Single man, Family or set of Men, who are a part only of that Community, And that the Community hath an Indubitable, Unalienable and Indefeasible right to reform Alter, or Abolish Government in such Manner as shall be by that Community, Judged most conducive to the public Weal.

Sixth.

That those who are Employed in the Legislative and Executive Business of the State may be restrained from oppression, the people have a right at such Periods as they may think proper to reduce their public Officers to a private Station and supply the Vacancies by certain and regular Elections.

Seventh.

That all Elections ought to be free, and that all Free Men, having a sufficient evident Common Interest with and Attachment to the Community have a right to elect Officers, or to be elected into Office.

Eighth.

That every Member of Society hath a right to be protected in the Enjoyment of Life, Liberty and property and therefore is bound to Contribute his proportion towards the Expence [sic] of that protection and yeild [sic] his personal Service when necessary or an equivalent thereto But no part of a Mans [sic] property can be justly taken from him or applied to public Uses without his own Consent, or that of his Legal Representatives. Nor can any Man who is conscientiously scrupulous of bearing Arms be justly compelled thereto if he will pay such equivalent, Nor are the people bound by any Laws but such as they have in like manner assented to for their common good.

Ninth.

That in all prosecution for Criminal Offences a Man hath a right to be heard, by himself and his Council, to demand the Cause and Nature of his Accusation, to be confronted with the Witnesses, to call for Evidence in his favour and a speedy public Tryal [sic] by an Impartial Jury of the County, without the Unanimous consent of which Jury he cannot be found guilty, nor can he be compelled to give Evidence against himself, nor can any Man be Justly deprived of his Liberty except by the Laws of the Land or the Judgment of his Peers.

Tenth.

That the People have a right to hold themselves, their Houses, Papers, and possessions free from Search and Seizure, And therefore Warrants without Oaths or Affirmations first made, affording a sufficient foundation for them, and whereby any Officer or Messenger may be Commanded or required to Search suspected places or to seize any person or persons, his or their property not particularly described are Contrary to that right and ought not to be Granted.

Eleventh.

That in Controversies respecting property and in suits between Man and Man the parties have a right to Tryal [sic] by Jury which ought to be held Sacred.

Twelfth.

That the People have a right to Freedom of Speech and of Writing and publishing their Sentiments therefore the Freedom of the press ought not to be restrained.

Thirteenth.

That the People have a right to bear Arms for the defence of themselves, and the State: And as standing Armies in the time of Peace, are dangerous to Liberty they ought not to be kept up: And that the Military should be kept under strict subordination to, and Governed by the Civil power.

Fourteenth.

That a frequent recurrence to fundamental principles and a firm Adherence to Justice, Moderation, Temperance, Industry and Frugality, are absolutely necessary to preserve the Blessings of Liberty and keep a Government free. The people ought therefore to pay particular Attention to these points in the choice of Officers and Representatives, and have a right to Exact a due and Constant regard to them from their Legislators and Magistrates in the making and Executing such Laws as are necessary for the Good Government of the State.

Fifteenth.

That all Men have a Natural Inherent right to Emigrate from one State to another that will receive them, or to form a New State in Vacant Countries, or in such Countries as they can purchase, whenever they think that thereby they may promote their own Happiness.

Sixteenth.

That the People have a right to Assemble together to consult for their Common good, to instruct their representatives, and to apply to the Legislature for Redress of Grievances by Address Petition or Remonstrance.

PLAN OR FRAME OF GOVERNMENT FOR THE COMMON WEALTH OR STATE OF PENNSYLVANIA

Section the First.

The Common Wealth or State of Pennsylvania shall be Governed hereafter by an Assembly of the Representatives of the Freemen of the same, and a President and Council in Manner and Form following.

Section the Second.

The Supreme Legislative power shall be vested in a House of Representatives of the Freemen of the Common Wealth or State of Pennsylvania.

Section the Third.

The Supreme Executive Power shall be vested in a President and Council.

Section the Fourth.

Courts of Justice shall be Established in the City of Philadelphia and in every County of this State.

Section the Fifth.

The Freemen of this Common Wealth and their Sons, shall be trained and Armed for its Defence under such Regulations, Restrictions and Exceptions, as the General Assembly shall by Law direct; preserving always to the People the right of choosing their Colonels, and all Commissioned Officers under that rank, in such Manner and as often as by the said Laws shall be directed.

Section the Sixth

Every Freeman of the full age of Twenty one years, having resided in this State for the Space of one whole year next before the day of Election for Representatives, and paid public Taxes during that time shall enjoy the right of an Elector: Provided always, That Sons of Freeholders of the Age of Twenty one years, shall be Intitled to Vote, altho' they have not paid Taxes.

Section the Seventh.

The House of Representatives of the Freemen of this Common Wealth shall consist of Persons most noted for Wisdom and Virtue, to be chosen by the Freemen of every City and County of this Common Wealth respectively, and no person shall be Elected unless he has resided in the City or County for which he shall be chosen two years immediately before the said Election. Nor shall any Member while he continues such, hold any other Office, except in the Militia.

Section the Eighth.

No person shall be capable of being Elected a Member to serve in the House of Representatives of the Freemen of this Common Wealth more than four Years in Seven.

Section the Ninth.

The Members of the House of Representatives shall be chosen Annually by Ballot by the Freemen of the Common Wealth on the second Tuesday in October forever (except this present Year) and shall meet on the fourth Monday of the same Month and shall be stiled [sic], THE GENERAL ASSEMBLY OF THE REPRESENTATIVES OF THE FREEMEN OF PENNSYLVANIA and shall have power to choose their Speaker; The Treasurer of the State and their other Officers; Sit on their own Adjournments; Prepare Bills and Enact them into Laws; Judge of the Elections and Qualifications of their own Members; They may Expel a Member, but not a second time for the same cause, They may Administer Oaths or Affirmations on Examination of Witnesses: Redress Grievances, Impeach State Criminals, Grant Charters of Incorporation: Constitute Towns Burroughs, Cities and Counties: And shall have all other Powers necessary for the Legislature of a Free State or Common Wealth; But they shall have no power to add to, Alter, Abolish or Infringe any part of this Constitution.

Section the Tenth.

A Quorum of the House of Representatives shall consist of two thirds of the whole Number of Members Elected. And having met and chosen their Speaker, shall each of them before they proceed to Business take and subscribe as well the Oath or Affirmation of Fidelity, and Allegiance herein after directed as the following Oath or Affirmation Viz[t]

I   do swear (or Affirm) that as a Member
of this Assembly, I will not propose or assent to any Bill, Vote or
Resolution, which shall appear to me injurious to the people nor do
or consent to any Act or thing whatever that shall have a tendency
to lesson [sic] or abridge their rights and Priviledges [sic] as declared
in the Constitution of this State. But will in all things conduct myself
as a faithfull [sic] honest Representative and Guardian of the People
according to the best of my Judgment and Abilities.

And each Member before he takes his Seat shall make and subscribe
the following Declaration Viz^t

I do beleive [sic] in one God the Creator and Governor of the
Universe the Rewarder of the Good and Punisher of the Wicked. And
I do acknowledge the Scriptures of the Old and New Testament to be
given by Divine Inspiration.

And no further or other Religious Test shall ever hereafter be required of any Civil Officer or Magistrate in this State.

Section the Eleventh.

Delegates to represent this State in Congress, shall be chosen by
Ballot by the future General Assembly at their first Meeting, and Annually for ever afterwards as long as such Representation shall be
necessary. Any Delegate may be superceded at any time, by the
General Assembly appointing another in his Stead. No man shall sit
in Congress longer than two years successively, nor be capable of Re-
Election for three Years afterwards; And no person who holds any
office in the Gift of the Congress, shall hereafter be Elected to
Represent this Common Wealth in Congress.

Section the Twelfth.

If any City or Cities, County or Counties shall neglect or refuse to
elect and send representatives to the General Assembly, Two thirds
of the Members from the Cities or Counties that do elect and send
Representatives, provided they be a Majority of the Cities and Counties
of the whole State when met, shall have all the powers of the General
Assembly as fully and amply as if the whole were present.

Section the Thirteenth.

The Doors of the House in which the Representatives of the Freemen
of this State shall sit in General Assembly, shall be and remain open
for the Admission of all persons, who behave decently except only
when the welfare of this State may require the doors to be shut.

Section the Fourteenth.

The Votes and Proceedings of the General Assembly shall be printed Weekly, during their Sitting with the Yeas and Nays on any Question, Vote, or Resolution, where any two Members require it except when the Vote is taken by Ballot. And when the Yeas and Nays are so taken; Every Member shall have a right to Insert the Reasons of his Vote upon the Minutes if he desires it.

Section the Fifteenth.

To the End that Laws before they are Enacted may be more maturely considered and the Inconvenience of hasty Determinations, as much as possible prevented, all Bills of a public Nature, shall be printed for the Consideration of the people, before they are read in General Assembly the last time for debate and Amendment: And except on occasions of Sudden necessity shall not be passed into Laws until the next Session of Assembly, and for the more perfect Satisfaction of the Public, the reasons and Motives for making such Laws shall be fully and clearly Expressed in the Preambles.

Section the Sixteenth.

The Stile [sic] of the Laws of this Common Wealth shall be "Be it Enacted and it is hereby Enacted by the Representatives of the "Free-"men of the Common Wealth of Pennsylvania in General Assembly "met, and by the Authority of the same." And the General Assembly shall affix their Seal to every Bill, as soon as it is Enacted into a Law, which Seal shall be kept by the Assembly and shall be called, THE SEAL OF THE LAWS OF PENNSYLVANIA: and shall not be used for any other purpose.

Section the Seventeenth.

The City of Philadelphia and each County in this Common Wealth respectively shall on the first Tuesday of November in this present year, and on the Second Tuesday in October Annually for the two next succeeding Years to wit, The year One Thousand Seven hundred and Seventy Seven and the year One Thousand seven hundred and Seventy Eight choose six persons to represent them in General Assembly. But a Representation in proportion to the Number of Taxable Inhabitants is the only principle which can at all times secure Liberty and make the Voice of a Majority of the people the Law of the Land; Therefore the General Assembly shall cause compleat [sic] Lists of the Taxable Inhabitants in the City and each County in the Common Wealth respectively to be taken and returned to them on or before the last meeting of the Assembly elected in the year One Thousand Seven hundred and seventy Eight, who shall appoint a Representation to each in proportion to the Number of Taxables in such returns, which Representation shall continue for the next seven years afterwards, at the End of which a new return of the Taxable Inhabitants shall be made, and a Representation agreeable thereto appointed by the said Assembly and so on Septennially for ever. The Wages of the Representatives in General Assembly and all other State Charges shall be paid out of the State Treasury.

Section the Eighteenth.

In Order that the Freemen of this Common Wealth may enjoy the Benifit [sic] of Elections as equally as may be until the Representation shall commence, as directed in the foregoing Section; Each County, at its own choice, may be divided into Districts, Hold Elections therein, and elect their Representatives in the County and their other elective Officers, as shall be hereafter regulated by the General Assembly of this State. And no Inhabitant of this State shall have more than one Annual Vote at the General Election for Representatives in Assembly.

Section the Nineteenth.

For the present the Supreme Executive Council of this State shall consist of twelve persons chosen in the following Manner. The Freemen of the City of Philadelphia, and of the County's [sic] of Philadelphia, Chester and Bucks respectively shall choose by ballot one person for the City and one for each County aforesaid to serve for three years and no longer at the time and place for electing representatives in General Assembly. The Freemen of the Counties of Lancaster, York, Cumberland and Berks shall in like manner elect one person for each County respectively to serve as Councellors for two years and no longer. And the Counties of Northampton, Bedford Northumberland and Westmoreland, respectively shall in like Manner Elect one person for each County to serve as Councellors for one year and no longer. And at the Expiration of the time for which each Councellor was chosen to serve, The freemen of the City of Philadelphia and of the several Counties in this State respectively shall elect one person to serve as Councellor for three years and no longer and so on every third year forever, by this mode of Election and Continual rotation more Men will be trained to public Business, there will in every subsequent year be found in the Council a Number of persons acquainted with the proceedings of the foregoing years, whereby the Business will be more consistantly [sic] Conducted and moreover the danger of Establishing an inconvenient Aristocracy will be effectually prevented. All Vacancies in the Council that may happen by Death, Resignation or otherwise shall be filled at the next General Election for Representatives in General Assembly, unless a particular Election for that purpose shall be sooner appointed by the President and Council. No Member of the General Assembly or Delegate in Congress shall be chosen a Member of Council. The President and Vice President shall be chosen Annually by the joint Ballot of the General Assembly and Council of the Members of the Council, any person having served as a Councellor for three successive years shall be incapable of holding that office for four years afterwards. Every Member of the Council shall be a Justice of the Peace for the whole Common Wealth by Virtue of his Office. In case new Additional Counties shall hereafter be Erected in this State such County or Counties shall Elect a Councellor, and such County or Counties shall be annexed to the next Neighbouring Counties, and shall take rotation with such Counties. The Council shall meet Annually at the same time and place with the General Assembly.

The Treasurer of the State, Trustees of the Loan Office, Naval Officers, Collectors of Customs or Excise, Judge of the Admiralty, Attornies [sic] General, Sheriffs and Prothonotaries shall not be capable of a Seat in the General Assembly, Executive Council or Continental Congress.

Section the Twentieth.

The President and in his Absence the Vice President with the Council, five of whom shall be a quorum shall have power to appoint and Commissionate Judges, Naval Officers Judge of the Admiralty, Attorney General and all other Officers Civil and Military, Except such as are chosen by the General Assembly or the People agreeable to this Frame of Government and the Laws that may be made hereafter, and shall supply every Vacancy in any office occassioned [sic] by Death, Resignation, Removal or Disqualification until the office can be filled in the time and manner directed by Law or this Constitution. They are to correspond with other States, and transact Business with the Officers of Government Civil and Military, and to prepare such Business as may appear to them necessary to lay before the General Assembly. They shall sit as Judges to hear and determine on Impeachments, taking to their Assistance for Advice only the Justices of the Supreme Court—and shall have power to grant pardons and remit fines, in all cases whatsoever except in cases of Impeachments; and in cases of Treason, and Murder, shall have power to grant Reprieves, but not to pardon, until the End of the next Sessions of Assembly. But there shall be no remission or Mitigation of Punishment on Impeachments except by Act of the Legislature; They are also to take Care that the

Laws be faithfully executed. They are to expedite the Execution of such Measures as may be Resolved upon by the General Assembly; And they may draw upon the Treasury for such Sums as shall be appropriated by the House. They may also lay Embargoes or prohibit the Exportation of any Commodity for any time not exceeding thirty days in the recess of the House only. They may grant such Licences [sic] as shall be directed by Law, And shall have power to call together the General Assembly when necessary, before the day to which they shall stand adjourned. The President shall be commander in Chief of the Forces of the State, but shall not Command in person, except advised thereto by the Council, and then only so long as they shall approve thereof. The President and Council shall have a Secretary and keep fair Books of their proceedings, wherein any Counsellor [sic] may enter his Dissent with his reasons in support of it.

Section the Twenty first.

All Commissions shall be in the Name and by the Authority of the Freemen of the Common Wealth of Pennsylvania, Sealed with the State Seal, Signed by the President or Vice President and attested by the Secretary, which Seal shall be kept by the Council.

Section the Twenty Second.

Every Officer of State whether Judicial or Executive shall be liable to be Impeached by the General Assembly either when in office or after his Resignation or Removal for Mal-Administration. All Impeachments shall be before the President or Vice President and Council who shall hear and determine the same.

Section the Twenty third.

The Judges of the Supreme Court of Judicature shall have fixed Salaries, be Commissioned for Seven years only, tho' capable of Reappointment at the End of that term, but removeable [sic] for misbehavour [sic] at any time by the General Assembly. They shall not be allowed to sit as Members in the Continental Congress, Executive Council or General Assembly, nor to hold any other office Civil or Military, nor to take or receive Fees or Perquisites of any kind.

Section the Twenty fourth.

The Supreme Court and the Several Courts of Common Pleas of this Common Wealth shall besides the powers usually excercised [sic] by such Courts, have the powers of a Court of Chancery, so far as relates to the perpetuating Testimony, Obtaining Evidence from places not within this State, and the Care of the Persons and Estates of those who are Non Compotes [sic] Mentis, and such other powers as may be found necessary by future General Assemblies, not inconsistant [sic] with this Constitution.

Section the Twenty fifth.

Trials shall be by Jury as heretofore, And it is recommended to the Legislature of this State to provide by Law against every Corruption or Partiallity [sic] in the Choice, Return or Appointment of Juries.

Section the Twenty Sixth.

Courts of Sessions, Common Pleas, and Orphans Courts shall be held Quarterly in each City and County. And the Legislature shall have power to Establish all such other Courts as they may Judge for the good of the Inhabitants of the State, All Courts shall be opened and Justice shall be impartially administered without Corruption or unnecessary delay: All their Officers shall be paid an Adequate but moderate compensation for their Services, And if any Officer shall take greater or other Fees than the Laws allow him, either directly or indirectly it shall ever after disqualify him from holding any office in this State.

Section the Twenty Seventh.

All Prosecutions shall commence in the Name and by the Authority of the Freemen of the Common Wealth of Pennsylvania, and all Inditements shall conclude with these Words "against the Peace and dignity of the same." The Stile [sic] of all process hereafter in this State shall be the Common Wealth of Pennsylvania.

Section the Twenty Eighth.

The person of a Debtor where there is not a strong presumption of Fraud, shall not be continued in prison after delivering up bona fide all his Estate real and personal for the Use of his Creditors in such manner as shall be hereafter regulated by Law. All Prisoners shall be Bailable by sufficient Sureties unless for Capital Offences, when the proof is Evident or presumption great.

Section the Twenty Ninth.

Excessive Bail shall not be Exacted for Bailable Offences: and all fines shall be Moderate.

Section the Thirtieth.

Justices of the Peace shall be elected by the Freeholders of each City and County respectively, that is to say, two or more persons may be chosen for each Ward Township or District as the Laws shall hereafter direct: And their Names shall be returned to the President in Council, who shall Commissionate one or more of them for each Ward, Township or District so returning for seven years, removeable [sic] for Misconduct, by the General Assembly, But if any City or County, Ward, Township, or District in this Common Wealth shall hereafter Incline to change the manner of appointing their Justices of the Peace as settled in this Article, the General Assembly may make Laws to regulate the same agreeable to the desire of a Majority of the Freeholders of the City or County, Ward, Township or District so applying. No Justice of the Peace shall sit in the General Assembly unless he first resigns his Commission, nor shall he be allowed to take any Fees, nor any Salary or allowance except such as the future Legislature may grant.

Section the Thirty first.

Sheriffs and Coroners shall be elected annually in each City and County by the Freemen, that is to say, two persons for each office, one of whom for each is to be Commissioned by the President in Council. No person shall continue in the office of Sheriff more than three successive years; or be capable of being Elected again during four years afterwards. The Election shall be held at the same time and place appointed for the Election of Representatives, And the Commissioners and Assessors and other officers chosen by the People, shall also be then and there Elected as has been Usual heretofore until altered or otherwise regulated by the future Legislature of this State.

Section the Thirty Second.

All Elections whether by the People or in General Assembly shall be by Ballot, free and Voluntary; And any Elector, who shall receive any Gift or Reward for his Vote in Meat, Drink, Monies or otherwise, shall forfeit his right to Elect for that time, and suffer such other Penalty as future Laws shall direct. And any person who shall directly or indirectly give promise or bestow any such Rewards to be Elected, shall be thereby rendered incapable to serve for the ensuing year.

Section the Thirty Third.

All Fees, Licence [sic] Money, Fines and Forfeitures heretofore granted or paid to the Governor or his Deputies for the support of Government, shall hereafter be paid into the public Treasury, unless altered or abolished by the future Legislature.

Section the Thirty Fourth.

A Register's Office for the Probate of Wills and granting Letters of Administration, and an Office for the Recording of Deeds, shall be kept in each City and County; The Officers to be appointed by the General Assembly removeable [sic] at their pleasure and to be Commissioned by the President in Council.

Section the Thirty Fifth.

The Printing presses shall be free to every person who undertakes to Examine the Proceedings of the Legislature or any part of Government.

Section the Thirty Sixth.

As every Freeman to preserve his Independance [sic] (if without a sufficient Estate) ought to have some Profession, Calling, Trade or Farm, whereby he may honestly Subsist, there can be no necessity for nor Use in Establishing Offices of Profit, the Usual Effects of which are Dependance [sic] and Servility, unbecoming Freemen in the Possessors and Expectants, Faction Contention, Corruption and Disorder among the People: But if any Man is called into public Service to the prejudice of his private Affairs, he has a right to a reasonable Compensation; And whenever an Office thro' Increase of Fees or otherwise becomes so profitable as to Occassion [sic] many to apply for it the Profits ought to be lessened by the Legislature.

Section the Thirty Seventh.

The future Legislature of this State shall regulate Intails in such Manner as to prevent Perpetuities.

Section the Thirty Eighth.

The Penal Laws as heretofore Used, shall be reformed by the future Legislature of this State as soon as may be, and Punishments made in some Cases less Sanguinary and in general more proportionate to the Crimes.

Section the Thirty Ninth.

To deter more effectually from the Commission of Crimes, by continued visible Punishment or long Duration, and to make Sanguinary Punishments less necessary: Houses ought to be provided for punishing by hard Labour, those who shall be Convicted of Crimes not Capital wherein the Criminals shall be employed for the Benefit of the Public; or for Reparation of Injuries done to private persons. And all persons at proper times shall be admitted to see the Prisoners at their Labour.

Section the Fortieth.

Every Officer, whether Judicial, Executive or Military in Authority under this Common Wealth shall take the following Oath or Affirmation of Allegiance, and General Oath of Office before he Enters on the Execution of his Office.

The Oath or Affirmation of Allegiance.

I do swear or Affirm: That I will be true and faithfull [sic] to the Common Wealth of Pennsylvania, And that I will not directly or Indirectly do any any [sic] Act or Thing prejudicial or Injurious to the Constitution or Government thereof as established by the Convention.

The Oath or Affirmation of Office.

I do swear or Affirm that I will faithfully execute the Office of _____ for the _____ of _____ And I will do equal right and Justice to all Men to the best of my Judgement [sic] and Abilities according to Law.

Section the Forty first.

No public Tax, Custom or Contribution shall be imposed upon or paid by the People of this State except by a Law for that purpose, And before any Law be made for raising it the purpose for which any Tax is to be raised ought to appear clearly to the Legislature to be of more Service to the Community than the Money would be, if not collected, which being well observed, Taxes can never be Burthens [sic].

Section the Forty Second.

Every Foreigner of good Character, who comes to settle in this State, having first taken an Oath or Affirmation of Allegiance to the same may purchase, or by other Just Means Acquire hold and transfer Land or other real Estate, And after one years [sic] Residence, shall be deemed a free Denizen thereof, and Intitled to all the rights of a Natural born Subject of this State, except that he shall not be capable of being Elected a Representative until after two years [sic] residence.

Section the Forty Third.

The Inhabitants of this State shall have Liberty to Fowl and Hunt in seasonable times on the Lands they hold, and on all other Lands therein not Inclosed, and in like manner to fish in all boatable Waters and others not private property.

Section the Forty Fourth.

A School or Schools shall be established in each County by the Legislature for the Convenient Instruction of Youth, with such Salaries to the Masters paid by the public as may Enable them to Instruct youth at low prices: And all Usefull [sic] Learning shall be duly Encouraged and promoted in one or more Universities.

Section the Forty Fifth.

Laws for the Encouragement of Virtue and prevention of Vice and Immorality shall be made and constantly kept in force, and Provision shall be made for their due Execution: And all Religious Societies or Bodies of Men heretofore United or Incorporated for the Advancement of Religion and Learning or for other pious and charitable purposes, shall be encouraged and protected in the Enjoyment of the Priviledges [sic], Immunities and Estates which they were accustomed to Enjoy or could of right have Enjoyed under the Laws and former Constitution of this State.

Section the Forty Sixth.

The Declaration of Rights is hereby declared to be a part of the Constitution of this Common Wealth and ought never to be Violated on any pretence [sic] whatever.

Section the Forty Seventh.

In Order that the Freedom of this Common Wealth may be preserved inviolate for ever, there shall be chosen by Ballot by the Freemen in each City and County respectively on the Second Tuesday in October in the year One Thousand Seven hundred and Eighty three, and on the Second Tuesday in October in every seventh year thereafter two persons in each City and County of this State, to be called the Council of Censors, who shall meet together on the Second Monday of November next ensuing their Election; the Majority of whom shall be a Quorum in every Case except as to calling a Convention in which two thirds of the whole Number elected shall agree, and whose duty it shall be to Enquire whether the Constitution has been preserved Inviolate in every part? and whether the Legislative and Executive Branches of Government have performed their duty as Guardians of the People or assumed to themselves or exercised other or greater powers than they are Intitled to by the Constitution. They are also to enquire whether the public Taxes have been Justly laid and collected in all parts of this Common Wealth, in what Manner the Public Monies have been disposed of, and whether the Laws have been duly Executed. For these purposes they shall have power to send for Persons, Papers and Records, they shall have Authority to pass public Censures, to Order Impeachments and to recommend to the Legislature the repealing such Laws as appear to them to have been Enacted contrary to the principles of the Constitution. These powers they shall Continue to have for and during the space of one year from the day of their Election and no longer. The said Council of Censors shall also have power to call a Convention to meet within two years after their Sitting, if there appear to them an absolute Necessity of amending any Article of the Constitution which may be defective, explaining such as may be thought not clearly Expressed, and of adding such as are necessary for the preservation of the rights and Happiness of the people. But the Articles to be amended, and the Amendments proposed and such Articles as are proposed to be added or abolished shall be promulgated at least Six Months before the day appointed for the Election of such Convention, for the previous Consideration of the People, that they may have an Oppertunity [sic] of Instructing their Delegates on the Subject.

Passed in Convention the 28th Day of September 1776, and signed by their Order

B. FRANKLIN, *President*

Assist.

JOHN MORRIS Jun[r]

Secretary.

---

* From original Document in Public Records Division, Pennsylvania Historical and Museum Commission.

INDEX

Acrelius, Rev. Israel, 2
Adams, John, 161, 166-168, 179-180
———————, Samuel, 156
Albany, Convention, 49; purchase, 50-51
Alison, Rev. Francis, 15, 97, 100, 104, 106, 121, 186, 188
Allen, Andrew, 92, 121, 148n, 179, 181
———————, Ann, 14
———————, James, 118, 121, 179, 181, 185
———————, John, 92, 121, 140
———————, Margaret, nee Hamilton, 14
———————, William, leader of aristocracy, 13-15; political power, 15, 92; critic of British policies, 15, 116-117; opposes Franklin's Association, 22-23; heads opposition to the Quaker Assembly, 54; Smith-Moore case, 69-70; investments, 78-79; opposes Stamp Act, 166ff; 16-18, 27, 29, 36, 47, 59, 64, 72-73, 75, 77n, 79, 87, 90-91, 93, 95-96, 99, 100-103, 105-110, 112-113, 115, 118, 120-122, 125, 133-134, 136-137, 140, 143-144, 154, 165, 186
———————, William, Jr., 121
Americanus, 117
Amherst, Gen. Jeffrey, 72, 75, 80-83
Answer (to *Brief State*), 40-41
Anti-Constitutionalists, 195ff
Arctic Expedition, 15
Armstrong, Col. John, 53, 74, 86, 88, 190
Ashbridge, George, 106, 118, 135
Assembly, Pennsylvania, powers, 5; representatives, 7, 172, 195; King William's War, 9; Queen Anne's War, 10; servant controversy, 12-13, 16; charges against, 17, 40; defended, 18; Riot of 1742, 19; King George's War, 20-21; paper money, 27-30, 37-38, 46, 58, 133; Proprietary instructions, 30, 38; defense appropriations, 31, 38, 42, 44-46, 58-60, 67, 74-75, 82-85, 172; taxation of Proprietors, 42-46, 57-60, 67, 72-74, 83-85; and Indians, 31-32, 44, 51, 60-61, 79-80, 86-88; militia, 46, 85; Smith-Moore case, 63, 68-70; Paxton Riot, 86-88; removal of Proprietors, 90ff; election (1764), 100-104, (1766), 135-136, (1767), 136-137; opposes Independence, 177ff; demise of, 182; 4, 81, 118, 128, 131, 133, 140-143, 157-161, 163, 165-166, 170, 172, 177-178, 180-182, 186, 191, 195
Association, of Continental Congress, 162
———————, military, 21, 23, 46, 55; Revolutionary military, 166, 170, 172-173, 180, 183-184, 189, 196
Atlee, Samuel, J., 190
———————, William, 159, 161n, 184

Aughwick, Pa., 50
Ayres, Captain, 154

Baltimore 129-130
Baptists, 119, 170-171
Barclay, David, 78-79, 145
Barnsley, Captain Thomas, 113
Barre, Isaac, 14
Barton, Rev. Thomas, 77, 129
Bartram, John, 3
Bayard, John, 177, 180, 184, 187-188, 190, 196
Bedford County, 196
Benezet, Daniel, 148n
Berks County, 80, 103, 163
Biddle, Edward, 159-160, 163, 172
———————, James, 105
———————, Owen, 178, 186, 188, 191
Blackwell, Gov. John, 9
Blunston, Samuel, 13
Board of Trade, 5, 16, 26-27, 38, 49, 51, 54, 62, 73, 89, 107
Bond, Phineas, 58n
Boston, Town meetings, 142; Tea Party, 154; Port Bill 155ff
Bouquet, Col. Henry, 60, 67-68, 80-82, 83n, 90
Broadhead, Daniel, 161n
Braddock, Gen. Edward, 38-39
Bradford, Thomas, 114, 121-122, 167
———————, William, 121
———————, William, Jr., 181, 190
Brief State, 39-41, 40n
Bryan, George, Revolutionary leader, 190ff; 86, 92, 101, 104-105, 118, 120, 151, 177, 186, 192, 197
Bucks County, 103, 119, 121, 131, 150, 162, 172
Bull, Col. John, 188, 191
Burd, Edward, 177n
———————, Col. James, 81n, 92, 100-101, 119-120
———————, John, 187
Burke, Edmund, 141, 167
Burlington, N. J., 16
Bushy Run, 82
Bute, Earl of, 14

Candid Examination of the Mutual Claims of Great Britain and the Colonies, 165
Cannon, James, Revolutionary leader, 189ff; 151, 178, 183, 186, 191-192, 197
Carlisle, Pa., 32, 36, 109, 172
Carolina, North, 32, 49, 67
———————, South, 161
Carpenter, Emanuel, 92
Catholics, Roman, 37

Chester County, 6n, 42, 63, 103, 119, 131, 175
Chevalier, Peter, 148n
Chew, Benjamin, 92, 105, 116, 136
Clifford, Thomas, 124-125, 133, 144, 146, 148-149, 166
Clitherall, Dr. James, 183
Clymer, George, 92, 148n, 151, 157, 177-179, 187-188, 190-191, 196
Coleman, William, 58n
College of Philadelphia (University of Pennsylvania), 14, 39, 69, 97, 189
Collinson, Peter, 56
Committee of Inspection and Observation, 162, 164, 171, 173, 180
Committee of Safety, 172, 189
Committees of Correspondence, 100, 157n, 158, 164
Conestoga Massacre, 85, 95
Congregationalists, 134
Connecticut, 5, 182
Constitutional Convention, membership, 186ff; 182, 184-185
Continental Congress, called, 155ff; Second, 166ff; and Independence, 177ff
Council of Censors, 193-194
Courts, circuit, 136-137; admiralty, 160, 182
Cox, John, 121
Coxe, William, 105, 114
Croghan, George, 50, 61n
Cumberland County, 64, 72, 74, 88, 95, 103, 162
Currency, paper, Royal order regarding, 26, 29n, 37, 38n; war issues, 46, 58; post war period, 78, 133; 25-27, 26n, 132n

Democracy in Pa., 46-47, 55-56, 62-63, 65, 85, 91, 93, 126, 154, 181, 185-186 192ff, 197
Denny, Gov. William, characteristics, 57-58, 64-65; on tax bills, 59-60, 67, 72-73; criticizes Assembly, 62; 53, 55, 60-61
Dickinson, Gaius, 173
————, John, defends Proprietary government, 94-95, 99-100; leader of Whigs, 155ff; 97, 103, 105-106, 116, 118, 120-121, 142-143, 147, 149, 157-160, 161n, 162-163, 165-166, 172, 175, 177, 181-182
Dinwiddie, Gov. Robert, 32
Dove, David James, 97
Drinker, Henry, 25, 154
————, James, 125
————, John, 173
Duche, Rev. Jacob, 58n, 59, 62-63, 92, 97, 105

East India Co. (British), 153, 160
Easton, Pa., 52-53, 80, 95

Egremont, Earl of, 75
Episcopalians, bishopric question, 134-135, 135n; 97-98, 102
Evans, Gov. John, 5
Ewing, John, 97, 104, 106

Fauquier, Gov. Francis, 85
Fisher, Samuel and Thomas, 173
Fletcher, Gov. Benjamin, 4, 9
Forbes, Gen. John, 67-68, 80
Fort Augusta, 61
Fort Duquesne, 67-68, 80
Forts, attacked by Indians, 81
Fothergill, Dr. John, 40, 56, 105, 115
Fox, Joseph, 45n, 58n, 86, 96, 106, 118, 136, 146
France, forces invade the Ohio, 30; incites Indians, 50-53, abandons Ft. Duquesne, 67-68
Franklin, Benjamin, defense plan, 21-22; politician, 22-23, 65; German problem, 35-36; aids Braddock, 38-39, taxing Proprietors, 42, 45, 67, 73, 83-84; militia law, 46, 85; Indian trade, 61-62, removal of Proprietors, 63, 89ff; Paxton Boys, 86-88; Vandalia, 94; Stamp Act, 112ff; paper money, 133-134; 32, 40, 45n, 47, 54, 56-59, 58n, 60, 70-71, 76, 79, 85, 95, 97, 99, 101-109, 105n, 128, 135-137, 140, 141n, 142, 147, 149-151, 153n, 166-168, 172-173, 175, 177, 181, 184-187, 190-191, 193
————, Deborah, 119
————, Sarah, 90, 136
————, William, 40, 71n, 72, 79, 93, 105, 114, 117n, 123, 165
Frontier, Pennsylvania, demands protection, 45-46; massacre of Indians, 85-87, 127-128; petition for representatives, 103-104; 77, 85ff, 109, 129

Gadsden, Christopher, 118n
Galbreath, Col. Bartram, 191
Galloway, Joseph, leader of Quaker Party, 79; attacks proprietors, 98-99; defends Stamp Act, 117; opposes Revolutionary movement, 158ff; 40, 58, 63, 71, 93, 96, 102, 108-109, 114, 118, 120, 122n, 123-126, 133, 135-137, 142-144, 149-150, 159-166, 169, 172, 186
Georgia, 192
Germans, emigration, 35; political power, 17-19, 37, 41, 187-188; English schools for, 14, 36; Moravians, 36-37, 47, 58n, 64, 86, 94-95, 101-103, 119-121, 170, 184
Gibson, James, 86
Goddard, William, 135, 142n, 150
Gordon, Gov. Patrick, 26
Granville, Lord, 56
Graydon, Alexander, 192

Great Britain, views on Proprietary government, 89, 108; colonial policy, 111ff; 109-110
Greenleaf, Susanna, 145
Grenville, George, 109, 112, 115, 134
Grier, John, 187

Hamilton, Gov. Andrew, 10
——————, Andrew (Speaker), 14, 25
——————, James, attainments, 25; on paper money, 25-30; Proprietary instructions, 28-30; Indian question, 30-37; second term as governor, 73ff; tax bills, 74-75; Pontiac's War, 81-83; 14, 17, 23, 29, 36, 45n, 55, 58, 70, 71n, 79, 105, 109
Hanbury, John, 31
Hanover, Pa., 157
Harris, John, 186
Harrison, Henry, 105
Heads of Complaints, 71
Henry, William, 188
Herman, Augustine, 188
Hillegas, Michael, 160, 163, 172
Hillsborough, Lord, 108, 143-144
Historical Review of the Constitution of Pennsylvania, An, 72
Hockley, Richard, 69
Hoge, Jonathan, 187, 189, 191
Holland tea trade, 153
Howe, Sir William, 192
Howell, Samuel, 179
Hubley, John, 188
Hughes, John, Stamp Collector, 118ff; 45n, 58n, 93, 96, 106-107, 113-115, 165
Humphreys, Charles, 159, 163, 181
——————, William, 105
Hunt, Isaac, 171
——————, John, 101
Huston, Alexander, 105
Hutchinson, Gov. Thomas, 142, 167
Hyde, Lord, 100

Independence, movement for, 168, 173ff
Indians, Conestoga, 85, 88, 96; Delawares, 49, 50, 52-53; Minisinks, 53-54; Mohawks, 49, 52; on the Ohio, 44, 47, 52, 68, 80-83; Senecas, 54; Shawnees, 49-50; Six Nations, 49-52, 68, 85; on the Susquehanna, 51, 109; trade with, 60-62, 80, 144
Internal Improvements in Pennsylvania, 127-130
Ireland, 128, 140

Jackson, Richard, 63, 72-73, 94, 96, 105, 107
Jacobs, John, 160, 163, 172, 186, 188, 191, 197
James, Abel, 93, 154
Jefferson, Thomas, 189, 197
Johnson, Samuel, 107

——————, Sir William, 43, 50-52, 79
Joncaire de Chabert, 30

Kearsely, Dr. John, 171-172
Kenny, James, 81
Kepple, Henry, 103
Kid, John, 161n
Kinsey, John, 13, 15-16, 19-20, 23, 186
Kittanning, 53
Kuhl, Frederick, 179, 188
Kuhn, Dr. Adam, 92, 120

Lancaster County, 7, 41, 77, 85, 92, 101, 103, 120-121, 129, 170, 172, 183; Borough of, 77, 81, 125, 128, 132, 175
Lawrence, Thomas, 69, 105
Lee, Richard Henry, 181
Leech, Thomas, 56
Lincoln, Charles, 191
Lloyd, David, 4-5
Loan Office, 27, 38, 43, 77-78, 112n, 134
Logan, James, 12, 17, 20
——————, James, Jr., 113
——————, William, 84, 91, 102, 104
Loller, Robert, 188
Loudoun, Lord, 60

Mackey, John, 187
Manufacturing in Pennsylvania, 116, 140, 144, 148-149, 164, 188
Marshall, Christopher, 165, 168-169, 184, 190
Martin, Robert, 191
Maryland, 10, 39, 67, 75, 82, 107, 129-131, 148
Mason, George, 192
Massachusetts, Circular Letter, 143; 98
Masters, Col. William, 56, 148n
Matlack, Timothy, 151, 177, 183-184, 186, 189, 191, 197
McCall, Archibald, 121
M'Clean, James, 187
McConnaughy, David, 118
McKean, Thomas, 177, 180, 183-184
M'Pherson, Robert, 187
Mease, James, 148n
Mechanics of Phila., political power, 149-150, 157; 58n, 102, 132, 146
Mennonites, 100, 170-171
Mercer, Col. Hugh, 61, 81n
Merchants, of Boston, 111n, 142; British, 25-27, 78, 114, 133n, 140; New York, 39n, 111n, 146-147; Pennsylvania, 27, 39n, 78, 80, 111n, 114, 123-128, 131-133, 139-140, 142ff, 154
Mifflin, John, 45n
——————, Samuel, 92
——————, Thomas, 44, 148, 151, 155-157, 159-160, 163, 165, 172, 177
Mildred, Daniel, 78
Miles, Samuel, 160
Militia, 40, 46, 54-56, 85

Monckton, Gen. Robert, 75, 84
Montesquieu, Charles Louis de Secondat, 190, 192, 195
Montgomery, Col. Archibald, 67
————, John, 95, 100
Moore, Rebecca, 69
————, William, 63, 68-71, 105
Morgan, Evan, 45n
————, Dr. John, 14
Morris, Gov. Robert Hunter, characteristics, 35, 57; paper money, 37-38; taxation of Proprietary Estates, 42-46; 30, 33, 41, 43-46, 50-52, 60-61, 63, 73, 75
————, Robert, 121, 181, 191, 196
————, Samuel, 196
Morton, John, 105, 118, 159-160, 163, 172, 177, 181, 191
Muhlenberg, Henry M., 121
Murray, John, 13

Navigation Laws, 3-4, 139-141, 147, 160
Neil, Rev. Hugh, 91
Newcastle, Del., 21, 106
New Jersey, 99, 114
New York, 134, 146, 153, 157
Non-Importation Agreement (1768), 144ff
Norris, Isaac, supports defense, 32, 43; 11, 41, 43, 45n, 58n, 59, 64, 72, 79, 94, 101, 106
North, Lord, 153
Northampton County, 63-64, 103, 130, 179

Ohio Company of Virginia, 30-32
Okeley, John, 161n
Otis, James, 15, 118n, 141-142

Pacifism, 9-10, 12, 21, 23, 31, 32 44, 47, 51, 54, 56, 87-88, 170, 173, 192
Paine, Thomas, 176-177, 190, 195, 197
Palmer, Anthony, 20
Paris, Ferdinand, 55, 71
Parker, James, 196
Parliament (G. B.), paper money, 27, 132, taxing America, 111ff; 70, 77-78, 114, 147, 153
Partridge, Richard, 16, 18, 27
Patriotic Society, 150
Pawling, Henry, 58n, 105
Paxton Boys, 86-88, 95, 99
Peale, Charles Willson, 15, 190
Pemberton, Israel, pacifist leader, 31; defends Indians, 52-54; slandered, 96-97; 13, 17-19, 23, 56n, 86, 88, 94, 101-102, 105, 113, 116, 121, 125, 136-137, 144, 168-169, 172-173
————, James, 19, 56, 91, 104, 108, 118, 120, 125, 139, 165, 169, 189
————, John, 169, 176
Penn, Gov. John, 50, 71n, 83, 85-88, 90, 92-93, 95, 99, 105, 107, 120, 122, 125-126, 143, 157-158, 161, 164-165

————, John (son of William), 11, 14
————, Richard (son of William), 11
————, Springett, 108n
————, Thomas, aids defense, 31, 45; concedes on taxation, 84; 11-12, 15, 22-23, 27-30, 33, 36, 50-51, 55, 58n, 59, 62, 65, 71, 73-74, 83, 90, 92, 101, 108, 132n, 140
————, William, 3-4, 10-11, 74, 83, 89
Pennington, Edward, 155
Pennsylvania, Charter, 3-4; 10, 74, 170; Frame of Government, 4-10, 94, 170; 179-181; Constitution, 192ff; Council, 4-5, 58, 78, 84-85; population, 1; society of, 42n, 54-55, 59
Pennsylvania Hospital, 14, 60, 106
Peters, Rev. Richard, 11, 13, 17, 19-23, 29, 31-32, 36, 43-44, 46, 49-50, 53-58, 60, 65
————, William, 69, 84, 97
Philadelphia, Town Meetings, 154-158, 180, 182; Committee, 162-163, 166, 170-171, 178, 180-181, 183; 2-3, 6-7, 11-12, 21, 85-86, 103-104, 116, 120, 127, 129, 131-132, 150, 153, 161, 164, 196
Pitt, William, 113, 147
Pittsburgh, 77, 81-82
Pleasants, Samuel, 125
Plumsted, William, 63-64
Pontiac's War, 79, 81-82, 112n
Porter, Thomas, 189, 191
Potts, John, 105
Powell, Samuel, 92
Pownall, Thomas, 56-57
Presbyterians, 42, 88, 91, 94, 97, 99, 100, 102, 104-105, 110, 119, 122, 126, 134-137, 149, 168, 173, 184-185, 190
Price, Elisha, 161n
Priestley, Joseph, 167
Privy Council (G. B.), 54-56, 59, 70, 73, 77, 80, 84, 108, 167
Proclamation, Royal (1763), 80
Proprietary Party, and elections, 16-19, 58, 63-64, 100-104; opposes Stamp Act, 116ff; 8, 13, 37, 41, 45, 54-55, 76, 79, 88, 92, 97, 101, 105, 107, 110, 136, 151, 155, 177
Proprietors of Pennsylvania, taxation of their estates, 42-46, 57-59, 71-74, 83-85; charged with fraud, 53-54; instructions to governors, 28-30, 38, 42-45, 57, 59-60, 71, 73-74; movement to remove them, 89ff; 7, 11, 25-26, 31, 45, 49
Provincial Conference, 182-184, 191
Provincial Convention, 158-161, 163-164, 178-179

Purviance, Samuel, Jr., 100-101, 119, 120-121
Quaker Party, and elections, 17, 19, 41, 58-59, 63-64, 100-104; popularity of, 23, 33, 65, 75; and Stamp Act, 112ff; 8, 17, 23, 33, 39, 47, 56, 79, 88, 91, 93, 97, 101, 105, 110, 116, 125, 135, 137, 149, 150-151
Quakers, and the Indians, 52-54, 68, 79; resist Revolutionary movement, 168ff; 8-9, 11-17, 21, 23, 32, 36, 39-42, 56, 58, 61, 63, 86-87, 91, 99-100, 102, 104, 108, 116, 119, 137, 144, 155-157, 165, 166, 168-170, 172-173, 175-176, 179, 196
Quartering in Philadelphia, 60; in America, 112; Act, 77n, 160
Quary, Robert, 5
Quebec Act, 161

Radicals, of Revolutionary movement, 156ff; Party in 1776, 177ff
Reading, Pa., 46, 120
Redman, Dr. John, 14
Reed, John, 134
————, James, 161n
————, Joseph, 154-157, 161-163, 166, 177-178, 190
Revere, Paul, 155
Reynell, John, 125, 144-145, 148
Rhoads, Samuel, 159, 163
Rhode Island, 5, 26, 146, 182
Richards, William, 121
Rittenhouse, David, 3, 151, 157, 186, 189-191, 197
Rivington, James, 165
Roberdeau, Daniel, 56, 58n, 133, 148n, 173, 177-178, 180, 190
Roberts, Hugh, 69, 136
Ross, George, President of Constitutional Convention, 187-188; 101, 109n, 120, 125, 151, 159-161, 163-164, 172-173, 177, 190-191
————, John, 109, 124, 136
Ruggles, Timothy, 118n
Rush, Benjamin, 125, 184, 191
Ryder, Sir Dudley, 37

St. Clair, Sir John, 39
Sauer, Christopher, 36-37, 94, 120
Saunders, Isaac, 92, 95, 100-101, 103, 118, 121
Scarroyady, 51
Schlosser, George, 188
Schubert, Michael, 196
Scots Irish, 1, 35, 47, 86, 91, 94, 101, 103, 168, 184, 186
Scull, William, 161n
Serjeant, Jonathan B., 185
Servants, enlistment of, 12-13, 15
Sharpe, Gov. Horatio, 75, 85
Shelburne, Earl of, 14, 108, 167
Shippen, Edward, 50, 92, 106, 176, 183

————, Joseph, 77n, 103 115n, 116, 176
————, William, 190
Shirley, Gov. William, 30, 38, 71
Shoemaker, Samuel, 105, 121
Smith, James (frontiersman), 187
————, James (lawyer), 86, 159, 161n, 187-188, 191
————, Jonathan B., 184, 190
————, John, 59
————, Matthew, 86
————, Col. Thomas, 191
————, Rev. William, fears Germans, 35-37; Brief State, 39-40; libel case, 68-71; bishopric question, 134-135; 97, 106, 116, 156, 161n, 169, 178
————, William (lawyer), 13
Stamp Act, 108, 110, 111ff, 134
Stamp Act Congress, 118
Stanwix, Gen. John, 64, 72
Stedman, Alexander, 92
Strettell, Amos, 145
Stroud, Col. Jacob, 189, 191
Sugar Act, 111-112, 139
Supreme Executive Council, 193

Taxation, Proprietary estates, 42-45, 57-59, 67, 72-74, 82-85, 93; Pennsylvania taxation, 42n, 72, 74-75, 97, 103-104n; British duties, 141
Taylor, George, 118, 191
Tea Act, 153ff
Teedyuscung, 51-54, 121-122
Tennent, Gilbert, 104
Thomas, Gov. George, 12-13, 16, 19-20, 26
Thomson, Charles, Revolutionary leader, 155ff; 92, 114-115, 119, 121-124, 143-144, 146, 148, 154, 156-163, 165-168, 172-173, 177
Tilghman, James, 92, 121, 154, 185
Tories (Loyalists), 161ff
Townshend Acts, 109, 137, 141ff
Townshend, Charles, 111-112, 141
Turgot, Anne Robert Jaques, 189

Vandalia, 93-94, 150
Van Horn, William, 188, 191
Vendues, 131-132, 148
Virginia, 10, 29, 32-33, 39, 49, 67, 82, 85, 157, 181

Walking Purchase 49, 53-54, 68, 79
Washington, George, 33
Warren, Admiral Peter, 21
Watts, John, 84
Wayne, Anthony, 163, 172, 175
————, Isaac, 63, 68
Webb, James, 120
Wedderburn, Alexander, Solicitor General, 167
Weiser, Conrad, 30-32, 36, 50

West, Benjamin, 14
West Indies, 139, 145, 147
Wharton, Samuel, 94, 125
————————, Thomas, 104, 113, 116, 125, 135, 150, 154
————————, Thomas, Jr., 190
Whitefield, George, 136
Whitehall, Robert, 188, 191
White Oaks, 119, 149
Wilcox, Alexander, 179
Williams, Roger, 5
Williamson, Hugh, 97, 122

Willing, Thomas, 69, 92, 101, 105, 120, 135-136, 148, 155, 158-160, 166, 179, 181
Wilson, James, 159-160, 161n, 166, 181, 191
Wrangle, Provost Charles Magnus, 86
Wraxall, Peter, 50
Wyoming Valley, 49-50, 122

Yeates, Jasper, 159, 175, 183
York, Pa., 36, 67, 129
York County, 103, 188
Young, Dr. James, 183, 190

Zenger, John Peter, 14

Date Due

MAR 28 '67

MAR

OCT 7 1982

Demco 293-5